The International Cook

Campbell Soup Company

Contents

Illustrations

Introduction

It's a small world. Or so the expression goes. But it's still big
enough to hold a wonderful diversity of people, places and ideas.
Despite the influence of satellite TV and jumbo jets, our "global
village" offers a living kaleidoscope of countries and cultures which,
with the slightest bit of delving beneath surface clichés, excites the
imagination and brightens the spirit.

One of the most fascinating components of any culture is its food.
Like music and art, the great cuisines speak a universal language
that must be experienced to be appreciated.

To recreate a few of these masterpieces, we invite you to prepare
the recipes and menus on the following pages.

Each is a tribute to the joys of travel and good food. But beyond
that, each is eminently do-able. Here are authentic recipes culled
from the finest national dishes of more than twenty-five different
countries and presented in a marvelously practical manner. More
than anything else, it is this sensitive adaptation of traditional
recipes to today's lifestyle which sets this cookbook apart from
others of its genre.

Complicated techniques have yielded to common sense and the
resulting directions are straightforward and easy to follow. In this
context the use of condensed soup as an ingredient comes into its
own. In most dishes condensed soup bolsters flavor. Often it
enhances consistency. Always it contributes a measure of freedom
from the least creative aspects of the cooking art. The same can be
said for popular appliances like the food processor and blender.
Their use is suggested where appropriate.

Another important consideration affecting the ease with which
international dishes are prepared is the availability of recipe
ingredients. Fortunately, we Americans have the best of the world in
our supermarkets and it is from this remarkable array of food that
the ingredients in this cookbook were chosen.

Just as any cuisine is a reflection of its larger culture, so these
recipes are a response to today's adventuresome tastes and changing
time priorities. We think they are special. Certainly they are
representative of the world's rich culinary heritage. And enjoying
that heritage to the utmost is what this cookbook is all about.

China & Japan

Sukiyaki

The food of China and Japan reflects ancient and honorable cuisines. In both countries, the land available for farming as well as the fuel for cooking has always been scarce. Instead of depending on meat as the mainstay of their diets, both the Chinese and the Japanese use a wide variety of vegetables and grains. It is part of their culinary inventiveness that they do more with less.

The emphasis is on maximum preparation with a minimum of cooking. Because chopsticks are used instead of knives and forks, all cutting and chopping is done before the cooking process begins.

Part of the magic of Oriental cooking lies in the beautiful presentation at the table. It is important to Oriental cooks that their food looks, tastes and smells delicious. Textures and colors of the various foods are weighed so that they balance each other. The Japanese or Chinese cook creates a "harmony" between salty foods and sweet ones, smooth foods and crunchy ones and hot foods and cold ones. Each dish is prepared quickly over high heat to preserve the texture, flavor and color.

The major cooking fuel in both China and Japan is charcoal. Most dishes come from that all-in-one cooking utensil, the *wok*. Its curved bottom allows for maximum heat distribution whether food is being braised, steamed, stir-fried, stewed or deep-fat fried.

Stir-frying is a typical way in which the Chinese prepare food. It means that the food is cooked over high heat with a minimum amount of oil. The various ingredients are kept moving with chopsticks or a paddle-like utensil called a *chan* to prevent the food from burning or overcooking. The results are crunchy or, as the Italians would say, *"al dente."*

The most important common ingredients in both Japanese and Chinese cuisines are rice and soybeans. Rice appears in some form

at every meal and not just as a side dish. It is the base from which meals are planned.

Both the Chinese and Japanese make fine noodles from rice. The Japanese also serve rice cold and vinegared as a foundation for one of their favorite snacks, *sushi*. The rice is shaped and sometimes wrapped with a thin sheet of *nori*, a seaweed; it is then topped with a slice of raw fish or a piece of cold omelet. Rice is also the source of the potent Japanese rice wine, *sake*, as well as of rice wine vinegar.

Soybeans are an important source of protein. They appear as sprouts, fermented bean sauce, soy sauce and bean curd, which is sometimes referred to as "poor man's meat." In Japanese, bean curd is called *tofu*. It's difficult to imagine what Chinese or Japanese cooking would be like without soybeans. Other beans are also used, such as mung beans, from which the cellophane noodles so enjoyed by the Chinese are made, and red beans, which are often sweetened and mashed into a paste-like dessert.

Oriental cooking has an ancient heritage. Many of the dishes go back to the time of Confucius, who established Chinese eating patterns. He insisted that vegetables be fresh and of good quality, rice be polished and meat properly cut. The Taoists were a religious group in China who advocated eating for health as part of their philosophy, a thought that is still followed today. The influence of Buddha, who believed that all animals have a right to live, can also be felt to this very day, as many Orientals practice vegetarianism. But even apart from religious reasons, many are vegetarians of necessity because of the scarcity of meat and other animal protein foods. Perishable vegetables are often preserved by salting, drying, fermenting or pickling. Both China and Japan with their long coastlines rely also on fish and shellfish as protein sources.

There are many similarities between the two countries, but each has its own distinct cuisine. And although Japanese and Chinese

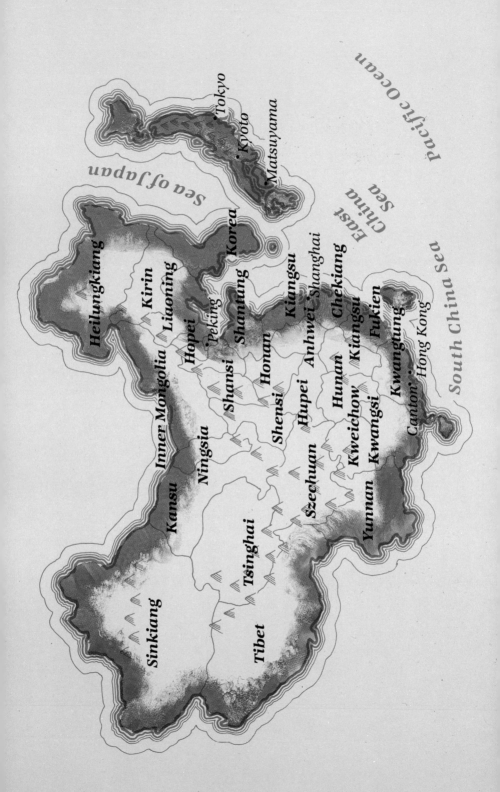

Pacific Ocean

Sea of Japan

•Tokyo

Kyoto•

Matsuyama•

East China Sea

South China Sea

Heilungkiang

Kirin

Liaoning

Inner Mongolia

Korea

Shantung

Peking•

Hopei

Kiangsu

•Shanghai

Anhwei

Chekiang

Shansi

Honan

Fukien

Shensi

Hupei

Hunan

Kiangsi

Kansu

Ningsia

Kweichow

Kwangtung

Szechuan

Kwangsi

Canton'•

Hong Kong

Tsinghai

Yunnan

Sinkiang

Tibet

share many ingredients, probably due to the fact that they were trading partners for centuries, they still maintain distinctly different eating habits. For example, the Chinese use many ingredients mixed together in one dish; the Japanese prefer to keep each ingredient distinct, so that each flavor can be savored for itself. Much of Japanese food is cooked in or over water or broth rather than in oil as the Chinese do. Except for some Japanese dishes that are deep-fat fried, most of their food is grilled, steamed or simmered. The Chinese family will eat together out of several common pots, but the Japanese enjoy small, single servings, sometimes elaborately garnished.

China is a vast country with high mountain ranges, deserts, tundra and humid tropical areas. Because of the geographical diversity, the perishability of food and poor transportation between areas at least until recently, each region of China learned to survive as well as thrive on what was available locally.

The northern region, which comprises the provinces of Shantung, Honan and Hopei, developed a light, mild style of cooking, which is less salty and less oily than that of the rest of China. Peking, the city of the Imperial Palace is situated here and it is known for its delicate and subtly seasoned dishes such as slow-cooked and crispy Peking Duck or *"jia ting peking ya."* It is usually served as part of a formal banquet. Carp with sweet and sour sauce is another favorite; the fish is first deep-fat fried and then lightly heated in a delicate sauce of wine, garlic and sugar.

It is said that the northern Chinese developed a taste for garlic and scallions from the Mongols as far back as the 13th century. Another borrowing from the Mongols is the Mongolian fire pot or *ho go.* To prepare it, small strips of meat, preferably lamb, are simmered with cellophane noodles, celery cabbage and spinach in broth right at the table in a tall metal brazier. The cooked meat is then dipped into a peppery sauce. Perhaps the best-known dish of the area is *mo shu ro*, shredded pork, eggs and seasonings, stir-fried and served with thin crepe-like pancakes known as Peking doilies or *bo bing.*

To the west lies Szechuan and Hunan, mountainous provinces with hot humid summers and icy-cold winters. Their hot and spicy cooking is related to the climate. Eating chili peppers is said to have a warming effect in the winter and a cooling effect in the summer. Here you'll find such delicacies as *kung bao gee ding*, which is chicken with peanuts in an eye-watering chili-pepper sauce, or carp in hot bean sauce or *dow ban jiong yu.*

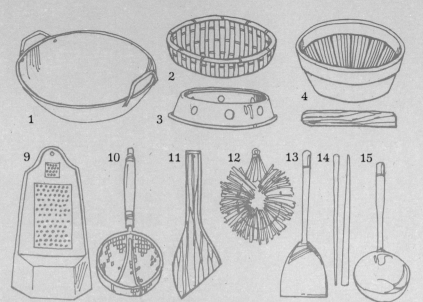

1. Wok   2. Zaru (bamboo colander)   3. Wok Support   4. Suribachi (serrated bowl) and Surikogi (pestle)   5. Sudare (bamboo mat) 6. Pressing Sack   7. Mongolian Fire Pot with Lid   8. Bamboo Steamer Trays with Lid   9. Oroshi-Gane (grater)   10. Mesh Skimmer 11. Wooden Spatula

Much of this region's cooking revolves around preserved pork and bacon products as well as the strong and hot Szechuan pepper, *fa jiu*. It's an important ingredient in the preparation of Szechuan duck, *siang sue yah*, which is heavily seasoned with the pepper and five-spice powder, then steamed to remove the excess fat and finally deep-fat fried. *Hwang gwa bong bong gee*, a cold chicken and cucumber salad with a peppery chili-sesame paste sauce, is another fiery favorite.

The eastern region of China includes the provinces of Kiangsu and Chekiang. It's an area known for its excellent soy sauce, especially around the area of Fukien. Here is the home of the red cooking of pork and chicken dishes; these are slowly cooked with soy sauce and fermented rice or bean paste to produce the distinctly red coloring.

Eastern Chinese also use both salt and sugar together to enhance the flavor of foods. A large variety of vegetables, especially bamboo shoots, are grown here and they take well to the salt-sugar method of cooking. Pork-stuffed cucumbers or *rong hwong gwa* and "lady in the cabbage," made with Chinese cabbage or *bok tsoi*, are two good examples of this method of cooking.

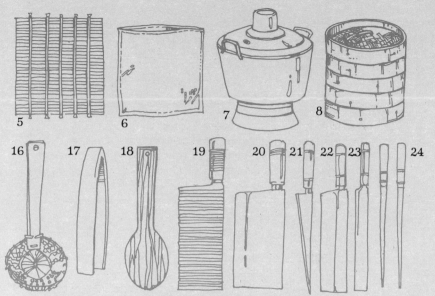

12. *Tawaski (scrub brush)*   13. *Spatula*   14. *Chopsticks*   15. *Ladle*
16. *Wire Sieve or Strainer*   17. *Bamboo Tongs*   18. *Wooden Rice Paddle*
19. *Tofu Slicing Knife*   20. *Cleaver*   21. *Sashami Knife*
22. *Hochu (vegetable knife)*   23. *Knife for Fish*   24. *Cooking Chopsticks*

Shanghai is located in the eastern region, and one of its popular snacks is *chwin guen* or spring rolls. Thin dough wrappers cover a stuffing of shredded vegetables and pork or shrimp; the rolls are then fried. They are almost always served during the Chinese New Year as a symbol of prosperity.

The Chinese foods most familiar to the Western world come to us from the southern region (Kwangsi and Kwangtung provinces, whose capital is Canton). The Cantonese were the first to emigrate in the 19th century, and as a result many restaurants around the world that offer Chinese cuisine usually feature Cantonese dishes. *Kam tsein mein bao har* or shrimp toast, is just one of their creations. Shrimp is ground with pork fat, ginger and sherry and then spread on a round of bread and fried.

Other creations include *cha shu* or Chinese roast pork (marinated strips of pork roasted by hanging in an oven; this is an ingredient in many dishes), *gu lau yoke*, sweet and sour pork, which is first batter-fried and then combined with sauce and vegetables and eggs *fu yong*, a Chinese omelet with stir-fried meat and vegetables. Stir-frying is probably this region's most popular method of cooking.

Another typical snack-food is *dim sum*, a wide assortment of steamed dumplings or buns filled with ground meat, poultry or seafoods and vegetables.

In contrast to China, Japan is a very much smaller, island country. Much of its food comes from the sea—fish, shellfish and seaweeds which are dried and salted. These seaweeds are used mainly as a base for flavoring soups or simmered meat dishes. *Dashi* is a combination of *kombu*, a large-leafed seaweed and shredded, dried bonito fish, which form a flavorful stock when boiled together.

Probably the most popular fish dish is *tempura* or batter-coated seafood and vegetables quickly cooked in hot oil. This dish was brought to Japan in the 16th century by Portugese traders or missionaries and was adapted by the Japanese to fit their own ingredients. Another favorite is *yosenabe*, which means "a gathering of everything." It's a Japanese version of *bouillabaisse* with chunks of fish, shellfish, *tofu*, noodles, scallions, carrots and *kombu* in a rich broth.

Beef is very expensive here, and specially fed cattle are raised to produce the famous Kobe steaks. Small amounts of beef are used with many vegetables as the basis for *sukiyaki*, a stir-fried dish of beef strips, spinach, onions, noodles with soy sauce and *mirin*, the sweetened rice wine, and as the basis for *shabu shabu*, thin beef slices, simmered with vegetables, *tofu* and *dashi* and served with noodles and a peppery sauce. It's very similar to Mongolian hot pot.

Chicken appears often on Japanese menus—perhaps as *yakitori*, grilled chicken strips marinated in soy sauce, *sake*, sugar and ginger or as *nabeyaki udon*, sliced chicken, dried black mushrooms and scallions simmered with *udon* noodles in *dashi*.

Eggs are frequently used in Japanese cooking. One of the more interesting ideas is *dashimaki tamago*, an omelet sweetened with *mirin* and cooked in thin layers before rolling. It is often served cold or as a topping for *sushi*.

Daikon, or giant white radishes, are often eaten raw after shredding as an accompaniment to fried foods or in a salad; it has very pungent flavor when eaten this way. When cooked in a soup, for example, *daikon* becomes sweeter.

Wheat and buckwheat noodles play a big role in Japanese foods, and they come in a variety of shapes. A favorite dish is *tempura soba* or batter-fried fish strips served with noodles, bean sprouts and lemon in a soy-scented broth.

The Chinese eat three meals a day plus *dim sum* in the afternoon with tea for the more well-to-do. They eat their meals without tea, and so a bowl of soup is served between courses or with other dishes instead of at the beginning of the meal to provide liquid. Breakfast in south and central China is usually *congee*, a rice porridge to which other ingredients may be added; in the north, noodles are the base for breakfast.

Lunch and dinner are similar in content, except that lunch is lighter. It might include vegetables, meat and fish dishes plus a soup. Dinner might consist of two vegetable or soybean recipes; a fish or shellfish plus a pork or poultry dish. There are also the inevitable rice and/or steamed buns. Desserts are generally not included.

The Japanese, on the other hand, have a fairly substantial breakfast of *miso shiru* or *dashimaki tamago*, the many-layered omelet and rice. Lunch and dinner in Japan are similar to one another. Soup comes first, followed by several dishes—one may be fried, another steamed or bar-becued. This is served with bowls of rice and pickled vegetables or *sunomono*, a Japanese salad. Sweets are served between meals rather than as part of the meals themselves.

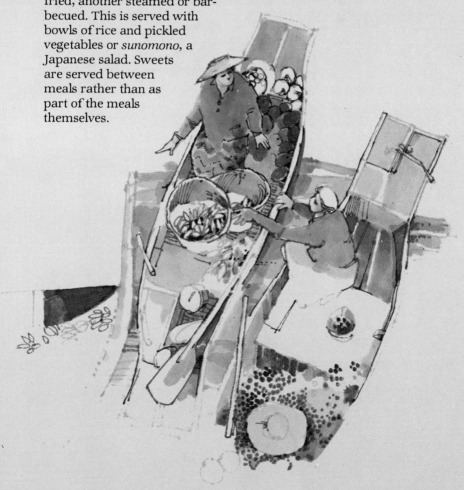

Glossary

Notes on pronunciation: *There are two things to be kept in mind when pronouncing Japanese. The first is that all the syllables in a Japanese word get about the same amount of stress and the second is that under certain circumstances (e.g., position in the word, part of Japan where the speaker is from), the vowels "i" and "u" are sometimes "whispered." These vowels are underlined below. With regard to Chinese, it has been deemed impractical to provide pronunciations because of the difficulty of notating the all-important differences in pitch and also because of the wide regional variations in pronunciation. In the glossary, therefore, a version approximating the Cantonese pronunciation, which is the standard dialect of Chinese cuisine, and a Mandarin version, which is the official dialect, are provided for the basic ingredients used all over China, whereas the names of individual dishes are rendered as they would be pronounced in their home region.*

Agemono (ah-geh-moh-no)—Japanese fried foods.

Bamboo shoots (jook sun/chu sun)—strips of the inner core of young bamboo shoots.

Chinese cabbage (bok tsoi/bai tsai)—commonly known as "bok choy"; slender vegetables with white stems and green leaves; looks a little like Swiss chard.

Celery cabbage (sheo tsoi/tientsin bai tsai)—tall crisp Chinese vegetable with whitish, tightly packed leaves; used raw as a salad or for stir-frying.

Cellophane noodles (fun see/fun si)—also called bean threads; thin, transparent Chinese noodles made from ground mung beans; they are crisp and sweet-tasting and have a glassy look.

Cha shu—a Cantonese specialty consisting of pork strips first marinated and then roasted by hanging in the oven.

Chwin guen—spring rolls; shredded vegetables and pork or shrimp wrapped in a thin dough covering and fried; a specialty of Shanghai.

Congee—essentially a Chinese soup or porridge, in which a small amount of rice has been cooked in a large amount of water; it is eaten for breakfast with eggs, etc. or as a late evening snack with bits of meat.

Daikon (dye-kawn)—the giant white Japanese radish, which can be sliced and cooked or served grated as a garnish for fried foods. It is considered an aid to the digestion.

Dashi (dah-shih)—base for Japanese soup stock made by boiling together dried shreds of bonito fish and chopped *kombu* (kelp).

Dashimaki tamago (dah-shih-mah-kee tah-mah-go)—omelet flavored with *dashi* and *shoyu* served with a variety of sauces.

Dim sum—Chinese snack food consisting of a wide variety of steamed dumplings or buns filled with ground meat, poultry or seafoods and vegetables.

Five-spice powder (<u>ng</u> hiong fun/<u>wu</u> hsiang fun)—a ground, reddish-brown spice combination used in Chinese cooking; it is made from fennel, cinnamon, cloves, Szechuan pepper and star anise.

Fu yong—a Chinese omelet with stir-fried meat and vegetables.

Gohan (go-han)—Japanese, plain cooked rice; also a general word for "meal."

Goma-abura (go-mah-ah-boo-rah)—Japanese sesame seed oil extracted from toasted sesame seeds and used for flavoring foods, not as a cooking oil. *Ma yow* in Chinese.

Gu lau yoke—Cantonese sweet-and-sour pork, batter-fried and served with sauce and vegetables.

Hoisin sauce (<u>hoy</u> sin jiong/<u>hai</u> hsien jiang)—Chinese sweet and spicy, reddish-brown sauce made from soybeans, garlic, hot pepper and spices. It is used to marinate spareribs, duck or shellfish or can be combined with other ingredients as a dip for deep-fried foods.

Jia ting peking ya—"Peking duck," a special Chinese roast duck with a crispy skin.

Kam tsein mein bao har —shrimp toast as made in Canton; shrimp ground with pork fat, ginger and sherry and then spread on rounds of bread and fried.

Kombu (kawm-boo)—the seaweed kelp, used for cooking in Japan.

Litchi (la-ee-tzee/li-tze)—a Chinese small oval red fruit with sweet white flesh and a large pit, about the size and shape of strawberries; available canned.

Lotus root (leen gnow/lien ngo)—long potato-like root with a series of round holes running lengthwise; usually cooked as a vegetable or in soups.

Mein (mein/mein)—Chinese for noodles.

Mirin (mih-rin)—Japanese sweet sake or rice wine used for cooking; sherry is a good substitute.

Miso (mih-so)—fermented soybean and wheat or rice paste used as flavoring in Japanese soups or as base for dressing or marinade for fish and vegetables.

Miso shiru (mih-so shih-roo)—*miso* soup with seafood, bean curd, and scallions.

Mushimono (moo-shih-moh-no)—Japanese steamed dishes.

Nabeyaki udon (nah-beh-yah-ki oo-dawn)—sliced meat, dried black mushrooms and scallions simmered with *udon* noodles in *dashi*.

Rice stick noodles (my fun/mi fun)—thin, brittle, white noodles made from rice flour, which need to be soaked in water before cooking. They are then stir-fried with other ingredients or served in soups.

Rong hwong gwa —cucumbers stuffed with a ground pork mixture and steamed; a Chinese specialty.

Sake (sah-keh)—Japanese rice wine.

Sashimi (sah-shih-mih)—sliced raw fish which is served as an appetizer in Japan. It is dipped in soy sauce and eaten with green horseradish.

Shabu shabu (shah-boo shah-boo)—thin beef slices simmered with vegetables, *tofu*, noodles and *dashi*, served with a variety of sauces.

Shoyu (show-you)—Japanese soy sauce made from fermented soybeans; it is less salty than the Chinese version, known as *sin tsow/shien tsou*.

Snow peas (<u>shieh dow/shieh do</u>)—pale green pea pods, eaten pod and all. Used in Chinese stir-fried dishes with meat, poultry and seafood.

Star anise (<u>ba gok/ba chio</u>)—star-shaped seed cluster with anise-like flavor; used ground to season Chinese poultry and red-simmered dishes.

Soba (so-bah)—fine Japanese buckwheat noodles.

Somen (so-men)—thin Japanese wheat-flour noodles, which resemble vermicelli. Usually eaten cold.

Sunomono (soo-no-moh-no)—a Japanese vinegared salad.

Sukiyaki (soo-kih-yah-kih)—stir-fried dish of beef strips, spinach, onions, noodles, with soy sauce and *mirin*.

Szechuan pepper (<u>fa jiu/hwa jiao</u>)—also known as anise pepper; light brown kernels with a stronger and more pungent taste than black pepper; used for dipping as well as for preparing Szechuan duck and many other dishes.

Tempura (tem-poo-rah)—a Japanese dish of fish, shellfish or vegetables, dipped in a light batter and deep-fried until golden and crisp; served with a dipping sauce, pungent green-horseradish and slices of fresh ginger.

Tempura soba (tem-poo-rah so-bah)—batter-fried fish strips and scallions served with *soba* noodles in *dashi*.

Udon (oo-dawn)—thick Japanese wheat-flour noodles which resemble spaghetti.

Water chestnuts (<u>ma tie/ma ti</u>)—roughly translates to "horse hoof" in Chinese; crisp, small white vegetable, which is commonly used in stir-frying.

Yakimono (yah-kih-moh-no)—Japanese broiled dishes.

Yakitori (yah-kih-toh-rih)—grilled chicken strips marinated in soy sauce, *sake*, sugar and ginger; a Japanese dish.

Yosenabe (yoh-seh-nah-beh)—"a gathering of everything," a Japanese version of *bouillabaisse*.

19

Szechuan Shrimp

Beef Lo Mein

Sweet and Sour Pork

Sweet and Pungent Spareribs

Rice with Peas*

Rice appears at every Japanese meal in some form. Celery and carrots add crunch to this delicious dish. Dry sherry makes a good substitute for the more traditional sake.

1 can (10¾ ounces)	condensed chicken broth
1 tablespoon	soy sauce
2 teaspoons	dry sherry
⅔ cup	raw regular rice
½ cup	thinly sliced carrot
½ cup	diagonally sliced celery
⅛ teaspoon	ground ginger
1 cup	frozen peas

In saucepan, combine all ingredients except peas. Bring to boil; reduce heat. Cover; cook over low heat 15 minutes. Add peas. Cook 10 minutes more or until done. Stir occasionally. Makes about 3 cups.

Menu:
Clear Broth with Soy Sauce
Skewered Beef Teriyaki
*Rice with Peas
Fresh Pineapple

---

* Because in many cases there is no literal translation of Oriental terms, the recipes in this chapter have been given English titles.

Hot and Sour Soup

Dried lily buds and dried cloud ears are readily available in any oriental grocery. They add an authentic taste to this savory soup. Be sure to soak them before cooking.

½ pound	boneless pork tenderloin
10	dried lily buds, soaked in cold water 30 minutes
2 tablespoons	dried cloud ears, soaked in cold water 30 minutes
6	dried mushrooms, soaked in cold water 30 minutes
1 tablespoon	sesame seed oil
1 can (10¾ ounces)	condensed chicken broth
1 can (10½ ounces)	condensed consomme
1½ soup cans	water
½ cup	bamboo shoots, cut in thin sticks
½ cup	sliced water chestnuts
¼ teaspoon	ground ginger
½ cup	bean curd cut in thin strips
1 tablespoon	soy sauce
¼ teaspoon	sugar
1	egg, well beaten
¼ cup	Chinese red vinegar
2 tablespoons	diagonally sliced green onions

Freeze meat 1 hour to firm (makes slicing easier); slice into very thin strips. Drain lily buds, cloud ears and mushrooms. Cut off tough parts of lily buds and cloud ears; cut both in half lengthwise. In large saucepan, brown pork in oil. Add broth, consomme, water, lily buds, cloud ears, mushrooms, bamboo shoots, water chestnuts and ginger. Cover; cook over low heat 10 minutes. Add bean curd, soy and sugar; bring to boil. Gradually pour egg into simmering soup, stirring gently until set. Add vinegar and green onions. Serve immediately. Makes about 7 cups.

Bean Curd Soup

Japanese bean curd or tofu is available fresh or canned. Simmer the broth and other ingredients and add cubes of tofu at the last minute. Garnish with chopped green onions.

4	dried mushrooms, soaked in cold water 30 minutes
2 cans (10¾ ounces each)	condensed chicken broth
2 soup cans	water
2 tablespoons	cornstarch
2 tablespoons	soy sauce
2 tablespoons	sweet sherry
2 thin slices	ginger root
2 cups	diced bean curd

Drain mushrooms; slice. In saucepan, combine all ingredients except bean curd. Bring to boil, stirring constantly; reduce heat. Cover; cook over low heat 15 minutes. Add bean curd; cook 5 minutes more. Stir occasionally. Remove ginger. Makes about 7 cups.

Green Beans with Chicken

The success of any stir-fried dish lies in having all the ingredients prepared ahead and then cooked quickly. Snow peas or asparagus can be used instead of beans.

2 tablespoons	peanut or salad oil
1½ cups	fresh green beans thinly sliced lengthwise (French-style)
¼ teaspoon	ground ginger
2 whole	chicken breasts, skinned, boned and cut in strips (about 1 pound boneless)
1½ cups	carrots thinly sliced diagonally
1½ cups	sliced fresh mushrooms (about ¼ pound)
1 can (10¾ ounces)	condensed cream of chicken soup
¼ cup	water
2 tablespoons	dry sherry
2 tablespoons	soy sauce

Pour oil into wok or skillet; preheat at medium heat about 2 minutes. Add beans and ginger; cook 3 minutes, stirring constantly. Add chicken and carrots; cook 5 minutes, stirring constantly. Push to one side. Add additional oil if necessary. Add mushrooms; cook 1 minute, stirring constantly. Add soup, water, sherry and soy sauce. Heat; stir occasionally. Makes about 5 cups.

Menu:
Wonton Soup
*Green Beans with Chicken
Fried Noodles
Lemon Sherbet

Szechuan Shrimp

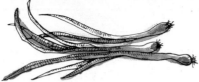

In the Szechuan Province of China, everything is served with hot peppers. This shrimp recipe is no exception. The tangy sauce just lightly coats the shrimp.

1	egg white
3 tablespoons	cornstarch
1 pound	medium shrimp (31-35/pound), shelled and deveined
1 cup	diagonally sliced green onions
½ small	red pepper, cut in squares
2 medium	cloves garlic, minced
½ teaspoon	crushed red pepper
2 tablespoons	sesame oil
1 can (10¾ ounces)	condensed chicken broth
2 tablespoons	dry sherry
2 teaspoons	soy sauce

In small bowl, beat egg white until soft peaks form, gradually adding 2 tablespoons cornstarch. Dip shrimp in egg white mixture. Fry, a few shrimp at a time, in deep fat at 350°F. until lightly browned. Drain on absorbent towels. Meanwhile, cook onions and red pepper with garlic and crushed red pepper in oil until *just* tender. Add shrimp, broth, remaining cornstarch, sherry and soy sauce. Cook, stirring until thickened. Serve with rice. Makes about 3 cups.

Chicken Corn Soup

Chinese soups are served as part of the selection of main dishes rather than as a first course. Fresh ginger adds a special something to this tasty soup.

4	dried mushrooms, soaked in cold water 30 minutes
1 can (about 17 ounces)	whole kernel golden corn, undrained
2 whole	chicken breasts, skinned, boned and cut in bite-size pieces (about 1 pound boneless)
2 thin slices	ginger root
2 tablespoons	peanut oil
1 can (10¾ ounces)	condensed cream of chicken soup

Drain mushrooms; slice. Drain corn, reserving liquid. Add water to corn liquid to measure 1¼ cups. In saucepan, cook chicken with ginger in oil about 5 minutes, stirring constantly. Add soup, mushrooms, corn and corn liquid. Cover; cook over low heat 10 minutes. Stir occasionally. Remove ginger. Makes about 5 cups.

Menu:
*Chicken Corn Soup
*Szechuan Shrimp
Steamed Rice
Chilled Canned Litchis

Sukiyaki

Sukiyaki can be easily prepared in an electric skillet at the table. Be sure to add the spinach last so it won't overcook.

2 pounds	boneless sirloin steak (1-inch thick)
1 can (10¾ ounces)	condensed chicken broth
¾ cup	soy sauce
¼ cup	sugar
3 tablespoons	dry sherry
4 medium	carrots, cut in thin sticks (about 2 cups)
2 cups	green onions diagonally sliced in 1-inch pieces
2 cups	celery diagonally sliced in ½-inch pieces
1 cup	sliced fresh mushrooms (about ¼ pound)
1 can (about 8 ounces)	bamboo shoots, drained
¼ cup	salad oil
3 cups	soaked cellophane noodles, cut in 3-inch pieces
4 cups	fresh spinach torn in bite-size pieces

Freeze meat 1 hour to firm (makes slicing easier); slice into *very* thin strips. Meanwhile, to make sauce, combine broth, soy sauce, sugar and sherry. Divide ingredients in half. In 2 skillets, cook vegetables except spinach in order listed, one at a time, in oil until *just* tender. Push vegetables to one side; add meat. Cook, stirring until color *just* changes. Stir half of sauce into each skillet; add noodles. Top with spinach. Heat 5 minutes. Serve with rice. Makes about 10 cups.

Stir-Fried Vegetables

It is important to cook the vegetables over a high heat for the shortest time possible. They will retain their color and crunch that way.

1 large	cucumber (about ½ pound), peeled
2 tablespoons	peanut oil
1 cup	sliced carrot
1 cup	quartered fresh mushrooms (about ¼ pound)
½ cup	sliced water chestnuts
2 large	cloves garlic, minced
2 cups	fresh Chinese pea pods
1 can (10¾ ounces)	condensed chicken broth
2 tablespoons	cornstarch
2 tablespoons	dry sherry
1 tablespoon	soy sauce

Slice cucumber in half lengthwise; remove seeds. Cut into strips. Pour oil into wok or skillet; preheat at medium heat about 2 minutes. Add carrots, mushrooms, water chestnuts and garlic. Cook 8 minutes; stir often. Push to one side. Add pea pods and cucumber; cook 3 minutes, stirring constantly. Stir in remaining ingredients. Cook, stirring until thickened. Makes about 4 cups.

Menu:
*Red Cooked Chicken
*Stir-Fried Vegetables
Steamed Rice
Preserved Persimmons

Hot Pot

Traditionally this meal is simmered in broth and cooked in a charcoal-fueled metal hot pot. You can easily prepare it in a wok or electric skillet right at the table.

1 whole	chicken breast, skinned and boned (about ½ pound boneless)
1 pound	medium raw shrimp (31-35/pound), shelled and deveined
1 package (10 ounces)	fresh spinach, cleaned (about 6 cups)
3 cups	asparagus sliced diagonally in 2-inch pieces
3 cups	sliced fresh mushrooms (about ½ pound)
2 cans (10½ ounces each)	condensed chicken with rice soup
1 can (10¾ ounces)	condensed chicken broth
2 soup cans	water
¼ teaspoon	ground ginger

Cut chicken into bite-size pieces. On serving platter, arrange chicken, shrimp, spinach, asparagus and mushrooms. Prepare at table in wok or electric skillet. Combine soup, broth, water and ginger; bring to boil. Add half of the chicken, shrimp, asparagus and mushrooms; simmer 3 minutes. Add half of the spinach; simmer 2 minutes more or until *just* done. Remove with slotted spoon. Repeat with remaining chicken, shrimp and vegetables. Serve with soy and duck sauce. Serve remaining soup mixture in bowls. Makes 6 servings.

Sweet and Pungent Spareribs

Precooking spareribs helps to remove the excess fat. You can also bake them in shallow trays at 350° F. for 1 hour and get the same results. Have the butcher saw spareribs in half across bones for easier handling.

4 pounds	spareribs, cut in serving-size pieces
1 can (10½ ounces)	condensed onion soup
1 can (10¾ ounces)	condensed tomato soup
2 tablespoons	vinegar
1 tablespoon	soy sauce
1 tablespoon	sugar
1 whole	star anise, crushed (about ½ teaspoon) or ½ teaspoon fennel seed
1 cup	green pepper strips
2 tablespoons	water
1 tablespoon	cornstarch

In large heavy pan, cover spareribs with water. Simmer 1 hour; drain. In wok or skillet, combine spareribs and remaining ingredients except green pepper, water and cornstarch. Bring to boil; reduce heat. Cover; simmer 15 minutes. Add green pepper; simmer 15 minutes more or until done. Stir occasionally. Push spareribs to one side. Mix water and cornstarch; slowly stir into sauce. Cook, stirring until thickened. Makes 4 servings.

Menu:
Egg Drop Soup
*Sweet and Pungent Spareribs
Stir-Fried Pea Pods
Almond Cookies

31

Egg Fu Yong

Try this dish instead of omelets for your next brunch. It's easy to prepare at the last minute and should be served piping hot. You can make the sauce ahead and keep it warm.

1 can (10¾ ounces)	condensed creamy chicken mushroom soup
6	eggs, slightly beaten
¼ teaspoon	salt
Generous dash	pepper
1½ cups	chopped cooked shrimp
1 cup	canned bean sprouts
½ cup	chopped canned water chestnuts
¼ cup	water
2 teaspoons	teriyaki sauce
1 teaspoon	sugar
1 teaspoon	vinegar

In bowl, blend ¼ cup soup, eggs, salt and pepper. Stir in shrimp, bean sprouts and water chestnuts. For each Egg Fu Yong spoon about ¼ cup egg mixture on hot, lightly greased griddle or skillet. Cook until golden brown on each side. Add additional oil if necessary. Drain on absorbent towels; keep warm. Meanwhile, in saucepan, combine remaining soup, water, teriyaki sauce, sugar and vinegar. Heat; stir occasionally. Serve with Egg Fu Yong. Makes 6 servings.

Menu:
*Egg Fu Yong
Asparagus and Tomato Stir-Fry
Steamed Rice
Candied Kumquats and Cookies

Red Cooked Chicken

The Chinese simmer meat in soy sauce, which they call "red cooking" because the soy sauce adds a red color to the meat.

2 pounds	chicken parts
2 tablespoons	peanut oil
1 can (10¾ ounces)	condensed chicken broth
2 tablespoons	soy sauce
1 tablespoon	dry sherry
1 tablespoon	sugar
2 thin slices	ginger root
2 tablespoons	water
2 tablespoons	cornstarch

In skillet, brown chicken in oil. Add broth, soy sauce, sherry, sugar and ginger. Cover; cook over low heat 45 minutes. Stir occasionally. Mix water and cornstarch until smooth; slowly stir into sauce. Cook, stirring until thickened; remove ginger. Serve with rice. Garnish with green onions if desired. Makes 4 servings.

Tempura

*This batter-coated seafood is fried in oil until crisp and golden.
Fry a few shrimp at a time and keep warm in the oven until the
rest are done. You can substitute chunks of fish for shrimp, if
you like.*

1 can (10½ ounces)	condensed beef broth
1 cup	ice water
1	egg, slightly beaten
2 teaspoons	sugar
½ teaspoon	salt
¼ teaspoon	baking soda
⅔ cup	all-purpose flour
⅓ cup	rice flour
1½ pounds	small raw shrimp (about 40-50/ pound), shelled and deveined

Using beef broth, prepare sauces listed below. To make batter,
in bowl, beat water, egg, sugar, salt and baking soda; add
flours. Mix until *just* blended. Place bowl of batter in bowl of
ice water. Dry shrimp; lightly coat with batter. Fry, a few
shrimp at a time, in deep fat at 400°F. until golden brown.
Serve with sauces. Makes 6 servings.

MUSTARD SAUCE

¼ cup	condensed beef broth
3 tablespoons	dry mustard

Combine ingredients; blend until smooth. Serve in small dish.

SOY SAUCE

¾ cup	condensed beef broth
2 tablespoons	dry sherry
2 tablespoons	soy sauce

In saucepan, combine ingredients; heat. Serve in small dish.

RADISH SAUCE

¼ cup	condensed beef broth
¾ cup	shredded radishes
¼ cup	packed brown sugar
¼ cup	wine vinegar
1 tablespoon	cornstarch
½ teaspoon	Worcestershire

In saucepan, combine ingredients. Cook, stirring until thickened. Serve in small dish.

Beef Lo Mein

*One pound of beef goes a long way when combined in the
Chinese way with a lot of vegetables. Freezing the beef slightly
helps to slice it into very thin strips.*

1 pound	boneless chuck roast (about 2-inches thick)
4 tablespoons	oyster sauce
3 tablespoons	sesame oil
4	dried mushrooms, soaked in cold water 30 minutes
1½ cups	Chinese cabbage cut in long thin shreds
1 cup	canned bean sprouts
2 tablespoons	soy sauce
1 teaspoon	brown sugar
3 cups	cooked linguini
1 cup	diagonally sliced green onions
1 cup	sliced radishes
1 can (10¾ ounces)	condensed beefy mushroom soup*
2 tablespoons	water
1 tablespoon	cornstarch

Freeze meat 1 hour to firm (makes slicing easier); slice into
very thin strips. To make marinade, in bowl, combine 3
tablespoons oyster sauce and 1 tablespoon sesame oil. Add
meat; marinate 30 minutes. Meanwhile, drain and slice
mushrooms. In skillet, brown meat in remaining oil; push to
one side. Add cabbage, bean sprouts and mushrooms; cook 2
minutes, stirring constantly. Add sugar, soy, remaining oyster
sauce, linguini, onions and radishes. Mix soup, water and
cornstarch; gradually blend into meat and vegetable mixture.
Cook, stirring until thickened. Makes about 5 cups.

*1 can (10½ ounces) condensed beef broth may be substituted
for beefy mushroom soup; increase cornstarch to 2 tablespoons.

Sweet and Sour Pork

Fried pork slices add a crisp texture to this typical sweet-and-sour dish. It's easy to eat with chopsticks.

1 pound	boneless pork tenderloin
1	egg white
4 tablespoons	cornstarch
1 cup	sliced carrot
½ small	green pepper, cut in strips
⅛ teaspoon	crushed red pepper
2 tablespoons	peanut oil
1 can (10½ ounces)	condensed consomme
1 can (about 20 ounces)	chunk pineapple in pure pineapple juice, drained
2 tablespoons	brown sugar
2 tablespoons	soy sauce
2 tablespoons	wine vinegar

Freeze pork 1 hour to firm (makes slicing easier); slice into *very* thin strips. In small bowl, beat egg white until soft peaks form, gradually adding 2 tablespoons cornstarch. Dip pork in egg white mixture. Fry, a few strips at a time, in deep fat at 350°F. until browned. Drain on absorbent towels. Meanwhile, in saucepan, cook carrot and green pepper with red pepper in oil until *just* tender. Add pork, consomme, remaining cornstarch, pineapple, brown sugar, soy and vinegar. Cook, stirring until thickened. Serve with rice. Makes about 6 cups.

Menu:
*Sweet and Sour Pork
Steamed Rice
Bean Sprout Salad
Chilled Mandarin Oranges

Chicken Kiev

Eastern Europe

Appetites in Eastern Europe come in two sizes—big and very big. As a result, the kitchens of Russia, Poland, Hungary and Czechoslovakia produce robust and filling foods. Thick soups, hefty stews and hearty meat and vegetable entrées take the edge off those appetites during the many long months of winter.

Even in the earliest times, much of the diet of this region was based on grains that could withstand the cold climate—rye, barley, millet, buckwheat and wheat. Meats, vegetables and fruits were either salted, dried or pickled to preserve them for the long winter months. Root vegetables predominate and it's amazing the variety of recipes that can be developed using beets, cabbage, potatoes and onions as a base.

Eastern Europe has historically been a buffer between the rest of Europe and Asia. Its cooking reflects the foreign invaders who came from all sides. The Scandinavians from the north brought their love of herring, crayfish and that overwhelming buffet known as the *smörgåsbord*.

The Tartars from the south and east swept over this area, bringing with them a love of grilled meats and cultured milk products. *Shashlyk*, cubes of meat skewered and grilled, became part of the Russian repetoire. Perhaps even more importantly, sour cream became a popular ingredient in many recipes. It added a tart but creamy flavor to everything from Beef Stroganoff, named for the gourmet Russian count, to *naleśniki*, Polish pancakes filled with mushrooms, dill and sour cream, to *svíčková*, a sweet-sour pot roast with sour cream from Czechoslovakia.

Sauerkraut also invaded with the Tartars and became a staple. Today it is used as a side dish as well as an ingredient in salads, soups, stews and stuffings.

Royal marriages and treaties with other European countries also influenced the cooking of this area. Beatrice d'Este of Italy and Anne of France introduced cheese, garlic and iced desserts to Hungary. Bona Sforza of Italy made a similar contribution in 1518 when she married King Sigismund I of Poland. Green vegetables are still called "Italian things" in Polish.

Ivan III of Russia threw out the Tartars and imported Italian architects and craftsmen to rebuild his country. They, in turn, brought macaroni, sherbets and pastries with them as well as their building skills.

Peter the Great of Russia imported the first of a series of French chefs, who created a new elaborate style of court food and slowly converted the Russians from serving all their food at once to serving it as separate courses. Peter also had a close association with the Prussian court. Roast duck and goose became popular foods as a result.

Catherine the Great of Russia was a Francophile. More imported chefs added creamed soups and sauces to the Russian diet and also concocted such dishes as *charlotte russe*, a molded dessert of ladyfingers and cream filling and *salade russe*, which is also known as *salade olivier*, a chicken and cold vegetable salad with a mayonnaise, sour cream and pickle dressing.

The Turks made inroads into southern Russia and Hungary. They contributed coffee, yogurt, melons, nuts and paprika. It is difficult to imagine Hungarian cooking without paprika, which adds color as well as aroma and flavor to so many of their dishes.

Religion changed the eating patterns of Eastern Europe. Vladimir the Saint of Russia converted himself and his country to Christianity about 988 A.D.—not too long after Mieszko I of Poland had converted. The ritual of many fast days gave rise to a delicious pattern of meatless meals.

In addition, traditional foods developed around each religious holiday. *Paskha* means Easter in Russian but it also means a pyramid-shaped molded cheese dessert, served with a tall cylindrical yeast cake called *kulich*. In Poland, *babka*, a nut- and raisin-flecked yeast cake, is served at Easter.

The followers of Islam made converts in southern Russia and yogurt, mint, eggplant, okra and citrus fruits were added to the diet. *Lavash*, the thin white bread of the Caucasus and *plov*; rice *pilaf* from the same area which may be served plain or with meats, vegetables, fish, fruits and nuts, are legacies of the culinary influence of the Middle East.

Eastern Europe has historically been an area of shifting boundaries and turbulent change. Many of the ingredients and dishes are similar in Poland, Hungary, Czechoslovakia and Russia, but have different names.

The Polani tribe settled in what is now Poland in the 10th century. They farmed crops that grew during the short summer season and could be stored for use during the dark, cold months. Cabbage, beets, onions and other root vegetables still play an important role in the Polish diet. *Krupnik*, a soup made from root vegetables, barley and dill, and *gołąbki*, mushroom and barley-stuffed cabbage leaves, are two delicious examples. Dark bread made from rye or wheat appears at every meal; even the crumbs are used as a thickener in sauces or as a garnish, as in vegetables *à la polonaise.*

Game and fish have always been a good source of food. *Zupa grzybowa,* dried wild mushroom soup with dill and sour cream and *bigos* or "hunter's stew" of mixed meats (often game), sausage, onions, cabbage, sauerkraut and apples, are flavorful recipes developed from the plentiful mushrooms and game of the forests. *Śledzie,* pickled herring in sour cream, is a product of the sea.

The Polish are also known for their pork and dairy products. Polish ham is famous all over the world, but much of the pork goes into some seventy kinds of sausages they produce—*kiełbasa* is one that is commonly available in the United States. *Chłodnik,* a refreshing cucumber, beet and shrimp soup served cold in the summer, is thickened with their rich sour cream.

Although Hungary was officially created as a republic only in 1949, its history is as rich and varied as its food.

Two favorite meat dishes with romantic names from the bygone days when gypsies roamed Hungary are *rablóhús* (robber's meat), skewered lamb or beef and *zsiványpecsenye* (bandit's roast), pounded and rolled meat cooked in a golden-brown onion, vinegar and sugar sauce. These are served with *metélt,* egg noodles or *csipetke,* pinched noodles.

Gulyás, or goulash, is probably the most renowned Hungarian creation. This slow-simmered combination of meat, potatoes, peppers and tomatoes with a hint of paprika can be either a stew or a soup *(gulyásleves),* depending on the amount of liquid added to it.

Transylvania, the mountainous area of Hungary, is known for *tokány,* a veal stew with mushrooms and sour cream, seasoned with black pepper instead of paprika and *kolozsvári káposzta,* a rich cabbage dish layered with a thick sauce of onions, sour cream and paprika.

Hungary is also the home of some fabulous desserts. *Dobostorta,* a chocolate-filled many-layered cake glazed with carmelized sugar and *rigójancsi,* a rich chocolate-filled and frosted cake, are two of the many creations of Hungarian bakers.

Hungarian pancakes, *palacsinta,* are like French *crêpes.* These thin pancakes are rolled, folded, breaded and fried. *Rakott palacsinta* is thin Hungarian pancakes layered to form a cake, covered with a meringue topping. One of the more unusual sweets of Hungary is cherries coated in batter and deep-fried.

Like Hungary, Czechoslovakia is a relatively new country. It was part of the Austro-Hungarian Empire of the Hapsbergs for 400 years. Czechoslovakia is made up of Bohemia, Slovakia and Moravia, regions populated by closely related Slavic peoples. When it comes to food, what ties them together is a common use of sour cream, caraway seeds, pickles and pork. *Zelí po Česku,* Bohemian cabbage with caraway seeds, sour cream and onions, is a delicious example.

If one national dish were to be proclaimed it probably would be roast pork with caraway seeds, *vepřová pečeně* and it is served with light and feathery bread dumplings, *houskové knedlíky.* The dumplings are made in a long roll and sliced with a piece of thread before cooking, because the Czechoslovakians believe dumplings should not be cut with a knife.

In this part of the world dumplings are prepared and served in a variety of imaginative and delicious ways. They can be savory or sweet; they can be an entrée, soup ingredient or dessert with a topping of butter, sugar and nuts.

Pork is a prime ingredient in *párky*, spicy sausages which look like hot dogs, except that they are sold in pairs. *Párky* are served steamed with mustard, pickles, sauerkraut, dark bread and potato salad. Veal is also a favorite meat of the Czechoslovakians. *Dusené telecí na kmíně* is a typical veal stew made with dried mushrooms, onions and caraway seeds. Another specialty is *pečená husa se zelím*, roast goose stuffed with onions, apples and sauerkraut. Both are served with buttered noodles or dumplings.

Czechoslovakia is a landlocked country, but its rivers and lakes are filled with fish. The traditional Christmas Eve favorite is fish—*kapr na černo*, carp in black sauce, really a sweet-sour sauce made with beer, gingersnaps and currant jelly.

The Czechoslovakians and Slovakians are famous for their baked goods. *Makový koláč*, poppy-seed cake, is a delicious example of their sweets. Fruit jams and jellies make up the filling for *koláčky*, fat little yeast buns.

Russia shares a basic Slavic cuisine with her neighbors to the west, but the similarities end there. The U.S.S.R. is fifteen republics which stretch from the eastern edge of Europe across the continent of Asia. It is a mosaic of cuisines, but to simplify it a bit, the major differences lie between the cold north and the warmer south. *Borshch*, the meaty beet and cabbage soup of the north is practically unknown in the southern region of the Caucasus, where they enjoy *chikhirtma*, a saffron-seasoned lamb or chicken soup thickened with egg yolks and lemon juice.

A clearer difference can be seen in the pork, cottage cheese and sour cream eaten in the north versus the lamb, olive oil and yogurt of the south.

For example, *mulgikapsad*, Estonian pork with sauerkraut and barley and *golubtsi*, Ukranian cabbage rolls stuffed with beef and onions with a tomato-sour cream sauce, hail from the colder north. *Khyar dolmasi*, cucumber stuffed with ground lamb, rice and onions topped with a cinnamon-yogurt sauce and *kaburga po-bukharskiy*, a rice-, nut- and pepper-stuffed breast of lamb, are from Azerbaijan and Uzbekistan in the south, respectively.

One phenomenon that seems to be universal in Russia, however, is *zakuski*, the hot and cold hors d'oeuvres eaten before dinner. *Bliny*, thin buckwheat pancakes served with butter, sour cream, caviar or smoked salmon, would be featured at an elegant dinner. A more down-to-earth selection might include herring, *lobio*—cold kidney

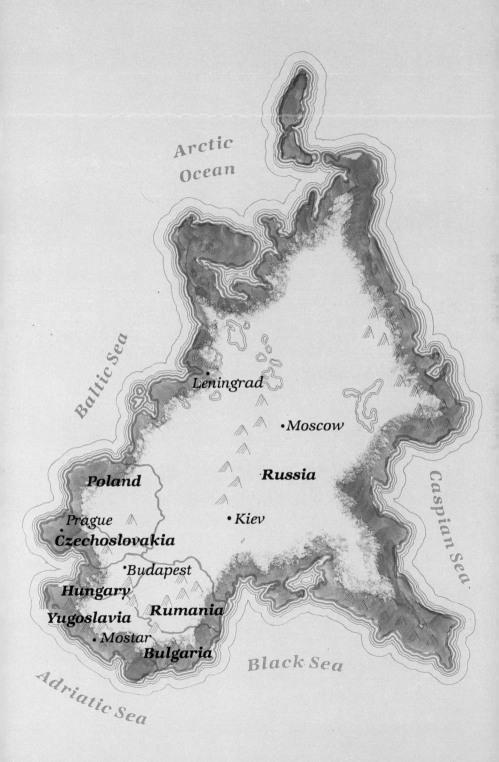

Arctic
Ocean

Baltic Sea

•Leningrad

•Moscow

Poland

Russia

Prague
•Czechoslovakia

•Kiev

•Budapest

Hungary

Yugoslavia

Rumania

•Mostar

Bulgaria

Black Sea

Adriatic Sea

Caspian Sea

45

beans, onions and garlic in a crushed walnut sauce, *beoreg*—an Armenian stuffed flaky pastry or radishes in sour cream.

Chicken is a favorite menu item all over Russia. One of the classic dishes is *kotlety po-kievskiy*, or chicken Kiev, a deep-fried chicken cutlet wrapped around seasoned butter. Another less-known chicken entrée is *tsyplyata tabaka*, a Georgian recipe for partially boned and flattened chicken served with *tkemali* sauce, a sour prune sauce.

Kasha, nutty buckwheat groats cooked with mushrooms and onions, appears on many Russian tables. It is sometimes enriched with ham, hard-cooked eggs or cottage cheese and is often eaten with soup.

Russians love pastries and turnovers. *Pirozhki*, small flaky turnovers, are served as an appetizer or as a side dish with soup; they are filled with ground meat, cabbage or even chicken livers. A larger variation, which is a main dish, is *kulebyaka*, which is folded around a hearty combination of salmon and mushrooms or cabbage, hard-cooked eggs and dill.

Pastry takes on a sweet taste with such specialties as *Alexander torte*, pastry strips filled with raspberry preserves. One of the favorite fruit desserts is *kisel'*, which is frequently made with apples, apricots, cranberries or rhubarb. The fruit is puréed, slightly sweetened and then thickened with potato starch. It's a perfect and refreshing way to end a hearty meal.

Sour cream, root vegetables and stick-to-your-ribs meats are not the only common thread in eastern Europe. These countries also share a similar pattern of eating. Breakfast starts early with dark bread and tea. Lunch, which is served around noon, is a relatively simple meal—fish and vegetables or perhaps a *pirog*, a meat or cabbage-filled turnover, with stewed fruit for dessert.

Dinner, however, is another matter. *Zakuski*, the array of hors d'oeuvres, begins the meal. Soup or *pirozhki* follow and then the main course such as a fish cutlet with sour cream and mushroom sauce, *kasha* and rice pudding, with *kisel'* for dessert. Dinner is eaten early, so a few hours later comes a snack of cold meats, cheese and bread with the ever-present tea.

Glossary

À la polonaise (ah lah puh-luh-NEZ)—French for "in the Polish style"; usually means cooked vegetables topped with buttered crumbs. *Sauce polonaise* is a bread crumb, butter and hard-cooked egg sauce.

À la russe (ah lah RYOOSS)—French for "in the Russian style"; usually refers to a cold vegetable salad with a mayonnaise-sour cream dressing, made tart with pickles and capers.

Babka (BAHP-kah)—"grandmother" in Polish, a nut- and raisin-flecked yeast cake served at Easter.

Beoreg (bay-oh-REGG)—an Armenian stuffed flaky pastry.

Bigos (BEE-gohss)—"hunter's stew"; made of leftover game, cabbage, mushrooms and a variety of vegetables plus apples. It is the national dish of Poland.

Borshch (BOHRSHCH)—a Russian or Ukranian beet soup with meat, cabbage and other vegetables.

Chłodnik (KHWUHD-neek)—Polish cold soup of cucumbers, beets and shrimp.

Chikhirtma (chee-kirt-MAH)—a saffron-seasoned lamb or chicken soup from the Caucasus.

Csárda (CHAHR-duh)—a Hungarian country inn.

Csipetke (CHEE-pett-keh)—Hungarian noodle dough that is pinched between fingers before cooking; it is served with soups and stews.

Dobostorta (DOH-bosh-torr-tuh)—a Hungarian chocolate-filled many-layered cake glazed with carmelized sugar.

Fogas (FOH-gush)—a Hungarian fish from Lake Balaton similar to a pike or perch.

Gołąbki (guh-WUMP-kee)—Polish recipe for cabbage leaves stuffed with mushrooms and barley.

Golubtsi (huh-loob-TSEE)—Ukrainian cabbage rolls stuffed with beef and onions, with a tomato-sour cream sauce.

Gulyás (GOO-yahsh)—goulash; Hungarian combination of meat, potatoes, peppers and tomatoes, with a hint of paprika.

Gulyásleves (GOO-yahsh-leh-vesh)—goulash thinned to a soup consistency.

Houskové knedlíky (HOH-skoh-vaay KNEDD-leee-kee)—Czechoslovakian bread dumplings.

Kaburga po-bukharskiy (kah-boor-GAH puh boo-KHAR-skee)—a rice-, nut- and pepper-stuffed breast of lamb from Uzbekistan.

Kapr na černo (KAH-pur NAH cher-noh)—Czechoslovakian Christmas Eve dish of carp in black sauce.

Kasha (KAH-shuh)—a Russian cooked grain often made of buckwheat groats; resembles a dry porridge and is often cooked with onions and mushrooms.

Khyar dolmasi (KHYAHR dohl-MAH-tsee)—an Azerbaijani dish consisting of cucumber stuffed with ground lamb, rice and onions, topped with a cinnamon-yogurt sauce.

Kiełbasa (kiew-BAH-sah)—Polish sausage. Sold in the United States as a highly spiced beef-and-pork sausage.

Kisel' (kee-SYELL)—a tart fruit puree thickened with potato starch, eaten in Russia.

Knedlíky (KNEDD-leee-kee)—Czechoslovakian dumplings.

Kolácky (KOH-laach-kee)—Czechoslovakian yeast buns filled with fruit jams and jellies.

Kolozsvári káposzta (KOH-loh-zhvah-ree KAH-pohs-tuh)—Hungarian recipe for cabbage layered with a thick sauce of onions, sour cream and paprika.

Kotlety (kutt-LYEH-tee)—"cutlets" or "chops"; a Russian ground meat pattie fried in the shape of cutlets.

Kotlety po-kievskiy (kutt-LYEH-tee puh KEE-yeff-skee)—chicken Kiev; deep-fried chicken cutlet wrapped around seasoned butter.

Krupnik (KROOP-neek)—a Polish soup made from root vegetables, barley and dill.

Kulebyaka (koo-lih-BYAH-kah)—Russian pastry dough folded around a combination of salmon and mushrooms or cabbage, hard-cooked eggs and dill.

Kulich (koo-LEECH)—Russian cylindrical Easter yeast cake studded with nuts and raisins.

Lavash (LAH-vahsh)—the thin white bread of the Caucasus.

Lecsó (LECH-oh)—a Hungarian dish of sweet peppers, tomatoes, bacon and onions; similar to the Italian *cacciatore*.

Leves (LEH-vesh)—Hungarian word for soup.

Liptovský sýr (LEEP-tohff-skeee SIHR)—Liptauer cheese enjoyed in Hungary and Czechoslovakia. It is a mixture of cottage cheese, butter, caraway and paprika.

Lobio (LOH-byoh)—red kidney beans in walnut sauce, a Georgian specialty.

Makový koláč (MAH-koh-veee KOH-laach)—Czechoslovakian poppy-seed cake.

Metélt (MEH-taylt)—Hungarian egg noodles.

Mulgikapsaď (mool-gee-kahp-SAHD)—Estonian pork with sauerkraut and barley.

Pączki (POHNCH-kee)—Polish jelly doughnuts.

Palacsinta (PUH-luh-cheen-tuh)—thin Hungarian pancakes that look like French *crêpes*.

Párky (PAAHR-kee)—Czechoslovakian frankfurters, usually sold in pairs.

Pečená husa se zelím (PEH-cheh-naah HOO-sah SEH zeh-leeem)—Czechoslovakian specialty consisting of roast goose stuffed with onions, apples and sauerkraut.

Pečeně (PEH-cheh-nyeh)—Czechoslovakian word for "roast."

Pel'meni (pyel-MYEH-nee)—Russian meat-filled dumplings.

Pieczeń huzarska (PYEH-chenn hoo-ZAHR-skah)—Polish for "Hussar's roast"; a sweet and sour pot roast with onions that is sliced and stuffed with onion and bread.

Pirog (pee-ROHK)—Russian meat or cabbage-filled turnover.

Plov (PLOHV)—rice *pilaf* from the Caucasus; served plain or with meats, vegetables, fruits, nuts, etc.

Pörkölt (PURR-kult)—Hungarian dish of braised meat and onions in a thick paprika gravy.

Rablóhús (RUH-bloh-hoosh)—Hungarian dish of skewered lamb or beef.

Rakott palacsinta (RUH-kott PUH-luh-cheen-tuh)—thin Hungarian pancakes layered to form a cake, covered with a meringue topping.

Rétes (RAY-tesh)—Hungarian for strudel; often filled with jam, fruit, nuts, meats, cheese and cabbage.

Rigójancsi (REE-goh-yunn-chee)—a rich Hungarian chocolate-filled and frosted cake.

Salade russe (sah-LAHD RYOOSS)—also known as *salade olivier* (sah-LAHD uh-lee-VYEH); Russian cold chicken and vegetable salad with a mayonnaise, sour cream and pickle dressing.

Satsivi (saht-SEE-vee)—a walnut sauce used with meats, poultry or fish in the Soviet Republic of Georgia.

Shashlyk (shahsh-LEEK)—Russian version of shish kebob.

Shchi (SHCHEE)—Russian cabbage soup.

Śledzie (SHLEH-dzheh)—Polish dish of pickled herring in sour cream.

Smetana (SMEH-tah-nah)—Czechoslovakian word for "sour cream."

Špekové knedlíky (SHPEKK-oh-vaay KNEDD-leee-kee)—Czechoslovakian potato dumplings made with smoked ham.

Tarhonya (TUHR-hoh-nyuh)—Hungarian egg barley; cooked in lard with onions. It is served as an accompaniment to stews and other meats.

Tkemali (tkeh-MAH-lee)—a tart sauce made with wild plums or sour prunes and served with meat or fish in the Soviet Republic of Georgia.

Tokány (TOH-kaah-nyih)—Hungarian veal stew with mushrooms and sour cream; seasoned with black pepper rather than paprika.

Töltött (TULL-tutt)—Hungarian word for "stuffed."

Vecherniy chay (vyeh-CHER-nee CHAI)—"evening tea"; a light meal of tea and cheese or cold cuts served a few hours after dinner in many Russian homes.

Vepřová pečeně (VEPP-zhoh-vaah PEH-cheh-nyeh)—Czechoslovakian roast pork with caraway seeds.

Zakuski (zah-KOOSS-kee)—Russian version of hors d'oeuvres.

Zelí po česku (ZEH-leee POH chess-koo)—Bohemian cabbage with caraway seeds, sour cream and onions.

Zsiványpecsenye (ZHEE-vah-nee-peh-cheh-nyeh)—Hungarian recipe for pounded and rolled meat cooked in an onion, vinegar and sugar sauce.

Zupa grzybowa (ZOO-pah gzhih-BOH-vah)—Polish dried wild mushroom soup with dill and sour cream.

Ryba Nacierana i Pieczona

Shashlyk

Kulebyaka

Salade Olivier

Čorba od Pasulja

Beans are a nutritious and low cost addition to the Eastern European diet. The flavor of this delicious soup will long be remembered after the last bean has been eaten. It's great for cold weather eating!

1½ cups	dried white beans
½ pound	smoked pork shoulder roll, cut in 1-inch cubes
2 tablespoons	salad oil
2 cans (10¾ ounces each)	condensed cream of potato soup
1 can (10¾ ounces)	condensed chicken broth
3 soup cans	water
1 cup	chopped onion
1 teaspoon	paprika
2 medium	cloves garlic, minced
2 tablespoons	chopped parsley

Wash and drain beans. In large heavy pan, brown meat in oil; pour off fat. Add remaining ingredients except parsley. Cover; cook over low heat 2 hours 30 minutes or until done. Stir occasionally. Add parsley. Makes about 8½ cups.

Menu:
*Čorba od Pasulja
Baked Fish and Potatoes
Mashed Rutabaga or Yellow Turnips
Thin Pancakes with Jam and Sugar

Chikhirtma

Lamb shanks are one of the most inexpensive cuts of lamb you can buy. They have a lot of fat on them so it is best to prepare this soup ahead and let it cool. Fat will be easier to skim and the flavor of the soup will become richer.

3 slices	bacon, coarsely chopped
4 medium	lamb shanks (about ¾ pound each)
2 tablespoons	flour
2 cans (10¾ ounces each)	condensed chicken broth
2 soup cans	water
½ cup	chopped onion
½ teaspoon	tarragon leaves, crushed
¼ teaspoon	pepper
1 cup	sliced carrot
1 cup	sliced celery
1 cup	sliced parsnip
1 tablespoon	lemon juice

In large heavy pan, cook bacon until crisp; remove. Brown lamb shanks in drippings. Add flour; cook a few minutes, stirring constantly. Remove from heat. Add broth and water, a little at a time, stirring after each addition until smooth. Cook, stirring until thickened. Add onion, tarragon and pepper. Cover; cook over low heat 1 hour 30 minutes. Add carrots, celery and parsnips; cook 30 minutes more or until done. Stir occasionally. Spoon off fat; add lemon juice. Garnish with bacon. Makes about 7 cups.

Eszterházy Rostélyos

This beef dish is gently braised in a subtly-flavored vegetable sauce. Be sure not to add the sour cream until the end of the cooking time; otherwise, it will curdle.

2 pounds	round steak (about ½-inch thick)
3 slices	bacon
1 can (10¾ ounces)	condensed cream of mushroom soup
¼ cup	water
¼ cup	chopped carrot
¼ cup	chopped celery
2 tablespoons	chopped parsley
1 medium	bay leaf
¼ cup	sour cream
2 tablespoons	capers

Cut steak into serving-size pieces. In skillet, cook bacon until crisp; remove and crumble. Brown steak in drippings. Add soup, water, carrot, celery, parsley and bay leaf. Cover; cook over low heat 1 hour 30 minutes or until done. Stir occasionally. Remove bay leaf. Remove steak to serving platter. Pour gravy into electric blender; blend until smooth. Return to skillet; add sour cream and capers. Heat; stir occasionally. Serve with steak and noodles; garnish with bacon. Makes 6 servings.

Menu:
*Eszterházy Rostélyos
Paprika Potatoes
Green Pepper Salad
Batter-fried Cherries

Ryba
Nacierana i Pieczona

The two most common ways of handling fish in Eastern Europe are either poaching or baking. This recipe is very typical with its sweet-sour sauce. Apple and lemon juice contrast with sugar.

1 cup	sliced fresh mushrooms
1 cup	chopped onions
1 teaspoon	thyme leaves, crushed
¼ cup	butter or margarine
1 can (10¾ ounces)	condensed cream of celery soup
4 cups	bread cubes
1 cup	chopped apple
1 teaspoon	sugar
¼ teaspoon	pepper
3-pound	dressed sea trout
1 tablespoon	lemon juice
2 tablespoons	chopped parsley

To make stuffing, in saucepan, brown mushrooms and cook onion with thyme in butter until tender. Add ¼ cup soup, bread cubes, apple, sugar and pepper. Stuff fish. Place in shallow baking pan (18 × 12 × 2″). Brush with melted butter; bake at 350°F. for 1 hour or until done. Meanwhile, in saucepan, combine remaining soup, lemon juice and parsley. Heat; stir occasionally. Makes 6 servings.

Salade Olivier

Czar Nicholas II had a French chef who created this salad. Outside of Russia, it is called Salade Russe, which is often served as mixed vegetables in mayonnaise. This is a more imaginative and authentic version.

1 can (10¾ ounces)	condensed cream of chicken soup
½ cup	sour cream
2 cups	cooked chicken cut in strips
3 cups	sliced cooked potatoes
½ cup	coarsely chopped dill pickle
3	hard-cooked eggs, chopped
¼ teaspoon	salt
¼ teaspoon	pepper
2 tablespoons	capers
1 tablespoon	chopped fresh dill weed

To make dressing, in large bowl, combine soup and sour cream. To make salad, in large bowl combine chicken, potatoes, pickles, eggs, salt and pepper. Toss chicken mixture with 1 cup dressing; chill. Shape salad into a pyramid on bed of salad greens. Spread salad with remaining dressing; sprinkle with capers and dill. Garnish with olives, tomatoes and additional hard-cooked eggs cut in wedges if desired. Makes about 5½ cups.

Menu:
*Chikhirtma
*Salade Olivier
Cucumber Pickles
Apricot Pie

Bef Stroganov

The secret of making successful stroganoff is to partially freeze the steak so it can be easily sliced very thin. Then the strips of meat cook quickly and evenly. Do be careful not to overcook.

1 pound	boneless round steak (¾-inch thick)
2 cups	thinly sliced onions
2 tablespoons	salad oil
1 can (10¾ ounces)	condensed beefy mushroom soup*
½ cup	sour cream
1 teaspoon	sugar
½ teaspoon	dry mustard
⅛ teaspoon	pepper

Freeze meat 1 hour to firm (makes slicing easier); slice into *very* thin strips. In skillet, cook onions in oil until *just* tender; push to one side. Add meat; cook until color *just* changes. Add remaining ingredients. Heat; stir occasionally. Serve over noodles. Makes about 4 cups.

*1 can (10¾ ounces) condensed cream of mushroom soup may be substituted for beefy mushroom soup.

Menu:
*Bef Stroganov
Buttered Noodles
Wilted Lettuce with Hot Dressing
Raspberry Pudding

Shashlyk

Combining pork and chicken livers is an Eastern European tradition. Be careful not to overcook the chicken livers and vegetables.

3 slices	bacon
1 pound	well-trimmed boneless pork loin, cut in 1-inch cubes
1 can (10¾ ounces)	condensed beefy mushroom soup*
2 tablespoons	Madeira wine
2 tablespoons	tomato paste
1 teaspoon	Worcestershire
1 medium	bay leaf
12 small	whole white onions (about ¾ pound)
1 package (8 ounces)	frozen chicken livers, thawed
1 small	green pepper, cut in squares
1 small	red pepper, cut in squares

In skillet, cook bacon until crisp; remove and crumble. Pour off all but 2 tablespoons drippings; brown pork in drippings. Add remaining ingredients except livers and peppers. Cover; cook over low heat 45 minutes. Add livers and peppers; cook 15 minutes or until done. Stir occasionally. Remove bay leaf. Serve with rice. Garnish with bacon. Makes about 5½ cups.

*1 can (10¾ ounces) condensed golden mushroom soup may be substituted for beefy mushroom soup.

Menu:
Eggplant Caviar
*Shashlyk
Rice Pilaf
Raw Onion, Tomato Wedges, Lemon
Strawberry Frozen Yogurt

Wątroba z Ryźem

In most liver recipes, the liver cooks by itself, but in this one, the liver flavors the rice as they simmer together. A hint of onion and ground red pepper add additional seasoning to the pilaf.

½ cup	chopped onion
2 tablespoons	butter or margarine
1 can (10¾ ounces)	condensed beef broth
⅓ cup	water
1 cup	raw regular rice
⅛ teaspoon	cayenne pepper
½ pound	calf's liver, chopped
¼ cup	chopped parsley

In saucepan, cook onion in butter until tender. Add broth, water, rice and cayenne pepper. Bring to boil; reduce heat. Cover; simmer 15 minutes. Add liver. Cook 10 minutes more or until done. Stir occasionally; add parsley. Makes about 4 cups.

Menu:
*Wątroba z Ryźem
Green Beans and Eggs
Cold Beet Salad
Yogurt Cake

Kulebyaka

There are as many different variations to Kulebyaka as there are different spellings. Sometimes white fish and bulgar are substituted for salmon and rice. Make it up ahead and let it sit before baking. It's a showy dish if you are planning a party.

1 cup	finely chopped onion
½ cup	shredded carrot
½ cup	finely chopped celery
1¼ teaspoons	dried dill weed, crushed
2 tablespoons	butter or margarine
2 cans (10¾ ounces each)	condensed cream of mushroom soup
2 cans (16 ounces each)	salmon, drained and flaked
1½ cups	cooked rice
3	hard-cooked eggs, finely chopped
2 tablespoons	Chablis or other dry white wine
Pastry	for 2-crust pie
1	egg yolk
1 tablespoon	milk
½ cup	sour cream
¼ cup	water

To make filling, in large saucepan, cook onion, carrot and celery with 1 teaspoon dill in butter until tender. Stir in ½ cup soup, salmon, rice, hard-cooked eggs and wine. Meanwhile, roll half of pastry into rectangle (14 × 7″). Arrange pastry on buttered cookie sheet. Spoon filling on pastry to within 1-inch of edges. Combine egg yolk and milk; brush on edges of pastry. Roll remaining pastry into rectangle (16 × 9″); arrange over filling. Seal edges; garnish with additional pastry if desired. Brush pastry with remaining egg mixture. Bake at 400°F. for 1 hour or until golden brown. Meanwhile, in saucepan, combine remaining soup and dill, sour cream and water. Serve with salmon loaf. Makes 8 servings.

Füszeres Hal

Fish is a favorite menu item throughout Eastern Europe. Even in the landlocked countries of Hungary and Czechoslovakia, rivers and lakes provide many tasty fish. The most popular ways to prepare fresh fish are either grill it over charcoal or stew it over vegetables, as we do here.

1 tablespoon	paprika
½ teaspoon	pepper
¼ teaspoon	salt
2 pounds	fillets of sole
¼ cup	chopped onion
2 tablespoons	olive oil
1 can (11 ounces)	condensed tomato bisque soup
¼ cup	water
2 teaspoons	vinegar
1 large	bay leaf
1 medium	clove garlic, minced

Combine paprika, pepper and salt; rub into each fillet. In skillet, brown fillets and cook onion in oil; add soup, water, vinegar, bay leaf and garlic. Cover; cook over low heat 10 minutes or until done. Stir gently now and then. Remove bay leaf. Makes 8 servings.

Menu:
*Füszeres Hal
Noodles and Mushrooms
Squash with Sour Cream
Blueberry Strudel

Guritcha Tris Pirog

Round or oval pastries made from pie crust or yeast-raised dough. Small individual ones are served as appetizers or with soup—this delectable chicken and rice filled pastry is a main dish, which can be easily made ahead.

½ cup	sliced onion
½ cup	sliced celery
1 medium	clove garlic, minced
2 tablespoons	butter or margarine
1 can (10¾ ounces)	condensed cream of mushroom soup
⅓ cup	heavy cream
1½ cups	diced cooked chicken
¼ cup	chopped parsley
1 tablespoon	lemon juice
⅛ teaspoon	ground nutmeg
⅛ teaspoon	pepper
1½ cups	cooked rice
4	hard-cooked eggs, sliced
Pastry	for 2-crust pie
1	egg, slightly beaten

In saucepan, cook onion and celery with garlic in butter until tender. Add soup, cream, chicken, parsley, lemon juice, nutmeg and pepper. Spread alternate layers of rice, hard-cooked eggs and chicken mixture in 10″ pastry-lined pie plate. Top with remaining pastry; seal and trim edges. Cut slits in pastry; brush with beaten egg. Bake at 375°F. for 1 hour or until done. Makes 8 servings.

Menu:
Cold Beet Soup
*Guritcha Tris Pirog
Braised Carrots and Onions
Cheesecake

Székely Gulyás

Goulash is a favorite dish of the Hungarians; it's a rich, thick stew with cubes of beef, onions and paprika. In Transylvania, pork is substituted for the beef and sauerkraut and sour cream are added.

3 slices	bacon
1½ pounds	pork loin cubes (1½ inch)
½ cup	chopped onion
½ teaspoon	caraway seed
1 tablespoon	paprika
1 can (10¾ ounces)	condensed cream of chicken soup
¼ cup	water
3 cups	sauerkraut, rinsed and drained
½ cup	green pepper squares
½ cup	chopped tomato
½ cup	sour cream
2 tablespoons	flour

In large heavy pan, cook bacon until crisp; remove and crumble. In drippings, brown pork and cook onion with seasonings until tender. Stir in soup, water and sauerkraut. Cover; cook over low heat 1 hour. Add green pepper and tomato; cook 30 minutes more or until done. Stir occasionally. Combine sour cream and flour; stir into pork mixture. Cook, stirring until thickened. Garnish with bacon and parsley. Makes about 7 cups.

Menu:
*Székely Gulyás
Boiled Potatoes
Marinated Cucumbers
Plum Dumpling

Chicken Kiev

The butter-stuffed boned chicken breast from Kiev (the capital of the Ukraine) is one of Russia's most famous creations. Beware of spurting butter when you cut into it.

½ cup	butter or margarine, softened
2 tablespoons	chopped parsley
1 medium	clove garlic, minced
¼ teaspoon	thyme leaves, crushed
Dash	pepper
3	chicken breasts, split, skinned and boned (about 1½ pounds boneless)
1	egg, slightly beaten
½ cup	fine dry bread crumbs
2 tablespoons	chopped onion
2 tablespoons	butter or margarine
1 can (10¾ ounces)	condensed creamy chicken mushroom soup
⅓ cup	milk
2 tablespoons	dry sherry or cognac

Blend ½ cup softened butter, 1 tablespoon parsley, garlic, thyme and pepper. On waxed paper, form butter mixture into patty ¾-inch thick; freeze until firm. Meanwhile, flatten chicken breasts with flat side of knife to ¼-inch thickness. Cut butter into 6 equal pieces; place one piece in center of each breast. Tuck in ends; roll up tightly. Secure with toothpicks. Dip in egg, then in bread crumbs; chill. Fry in deep fat at 350°F. for 10 to 12 minutes or until well browned. Drain on absorbent towels. Meanwhile, to make sauce, in saucepan, cook onion with remaining parsley in 2 tablespoons butter until tender. Blend in soup, milk and sherry. Heat; stir occasionally. Serve with roll-ups. Serve on rice. Makes 6 servings.

Kiełbasa ż Jażynami

Polish sausage and ham are known all over the world. Kiełbasa is a spicy and garlicky sausage that should be steamed before eating. If you prick the skin with a fork before cooking, it will not burst.

1½ pounds	garlic-flavored ring sausage
1½ cups	sliced onions
2 tablespoons	butter or margarine
1 can (10¾ ounces)	condensed beef broth
1 cup	beer
1 tablespoon	vinegar
¼ teaspoon	pepper
4 medium	potatoes (about 1 pound), cut in half
3 medium	carrots (about ½ pound), cut in 2-inch pieces
2 tablespoons	chopped parsley

Prick sausage with fork. In large saucepan, cook onions in butter until tender. Stir in broth, beer, vinegar and pepper. Add sausage, potatoes and carrots. Cover; cook over low heat 35 minutes or until done. Stir occasionally. Add parsley. Thicken to desired consistency. Makes 6 servings.

Menu:
*Kiełbasa ż Jażynami
Mushrooms in Sour Cream
Sweet-Sour Cabbage
Honey Cake

France

Potage Garbure

Cooking the French way is cooking with love and with style. The French chef insists on only the freshest, best-quality ingredients and these are combined with tender, loving care.

French cuisine is imaginative and rich in flavor, but not necessarily high in calories. The fabulous, elaborate dishes prepared by chefs, which are called *haute cuisine*, are served in much smaller portions than we are accustomed to. Recently, a group of younger chefs have broken with tradition to develop *nouvelle cuisine*, an inventive, simpler style of cooking that doesn't rely on butter or heavy cream. Puréed vegetables are often used to thicken and flavor sauces. The presentation of the new or *nouvelle cuisine* is, however, just as elaborate as the older *haute cuisine*.

There is a third type of food preparation which comes out of ordinary French home kitchens. It's called *cuisine bourgeoise* and is prepared with fewer frills. It is equally flavorful. The French housewife relies heavily on fresh ingredients. Nothing is ever wasted. She even recycles yesterday's bread into a thickening for a soup, crumbs for breading, *croutons* for garnish or into French toast.

What differentiates French food from other foods of the Western

World is the ingenious use of stocks and sauces. The French really think of a sauce as a liquid seasoning, which demands a light touch. It should be something to bring out the flavor, not smother the taste.

The second most outstanding feature of French cooking is the imaginative use of vegetables. They are not just an accompaniment to the main course but frequently stand on their own—in the form of a *quiche* or *soufflé* or lightly dressed in a *vinaigrette* sauce. The great variety of colors, flavors and textures add a special touch to French food.

Vegetable salads are, indeed, an area in which the French excel. The simplest concoction is fresh, raw greens tossed delicately with *vinaigrette* sauce, which we call French dressing. A more complicated salad is called a composed salad. Here, the skill the French have with vegetables becomes quickly apparent. Mixtures of raw and cooked vegetables, all neatly cut, are combined with each other, meat, fish or even fruit. The real secret behind these vegetable masterpieces is cooking them just until tender.

A review of some highlights from the history of what is known today as France gives insight into how its cuisine evolved.

English Channel

Bay of Biscay

Mediterranean Sea

Artois
Flanders
Picardy
Ile de France
Normandy
• Mont St. Michel
• Paris
Alsace-Lorraine
Brittany
Champagne
Maine
Orléanais
Anjou
Touraine
Dijon
• Tours
•
Franche Comté
Poitou
Berry
Nivernais
Bourbonnais
Aunis
Marche
Burgundy
Angoumois
Lyonais
Saintonge
Limousin
Périgord
Auvergne
Bordeaux •
Dauphine
Guyenne
Comtat
Gascony
Provence
Languedoc
• Marseille
Bearn
Foix
Roussillon

During the Middle Ages, a large variety of vegetables were already in evidence, from watercress and cucumbers to parsnips and lentils. The Crusades in the 12th and 13th centuries enriched the larder with exotic spices from the East, such as anise, cinnamon and nutmeg. Prunes, shallots and sugar also made an appearance at this time. During the reign of Charles VIII, the cheeses and butter for which France is famous became more prominent.

Henry II married Catherine de Medici, and this union was the beginning of the concept *gourmet*. Catherine came armed with her own Italian chefs, who intrigued the French court with artichokes, truffles and iced desserts. Abundant courses began to appear on the table. Catherine's cousin Marie de Medici married Henry IV, who is famous for wishing a chicken in every pot. During his reign a novelty item, the fork, was introduced.

Puff pastry was created during Louis XIII's reign. In 1765, a parisien, Monsieur Boulanger, founded the first restaurant by serving soups in his tavern as "restoratives."

In the early 1800's, Antonin Carême brought a refinement of taste and order to the great number of dishes being served. He added many cold dishes as well as meatless ones to the repertoire. Elaborate pastry was his forte and Carême's legacy is still enjoyed today.

Escoffier, the second prophet of *haute cuisine*, reorganized the kitchen and simplified techniques. He invented Melba toast and *pêche Melba* (both named for the Australian soprano, Nellie Melba), as well as *poularde Derby*, which is roast chicken with a rice, *pâté*, and *truffe* stuffing.

Although what is usually served in most French restaurants would give the impression that there is a nationwide style of cooking, there are numerous regional variations.

À *la provençale* means that a dish will be flavored with tomatoes, onions, garlic and herbs. À *la bordelaise* indicates that a dish is prepared in the style of Bordeaux, that is, with red wine, shallots and thyme. À *la bourguignonne* tells the taster that the dish will be simmered in red Burgundy wine, mushrooms and white onions. The list is almost endless, because each town or area has its own variation—based primarily on what is available locally.

For a fast culinary tour of France, let's begin on the western coast in Brittany, where seafood, particularly oysters, are a way of life. Here *cotriade*, a spicy fish soup made with onions, potatoes, vinegar, pepper and herbs could be sampled. Brittany's mild climate and its salt marshes are ideal for raising cattle and pigs. *Pâté de campagne*, country-style *pâté*, is found on Breton menus, as are *rillettes*, a seasoned, shredded pork spread. Brittany is also the home of the *crêpe*, the thin French version of the pancake and a dry, fruity wine called *Muscadet*.

Further up the coast lies Normandy, another province that is influenced by the sea. Inland, it is all rich green meadows dotted with apple orchards for making their famous apple tarts, cider and *Calvados*, applejack brandy. Here also are the dairylands of France. *Camembert*, *Port l'évêque* and *Livarot*, rich-flavored cheeses, are products of this dairyland, which also provides the main ingredient for Norman cooking—cream.

The northernmost region of Champagne, Artois and Picardy is very flat land with a soil and climate suited for carrots, potatoes and other root vegetables, as well as for growing the grapes that make Champagne.

The heartland of France is the Touraine, and it is also the wine country of the Loire Valley with its magnificent *châteaux*. *Coq au vin* (chicken in wine sauce) tastes very special in this region.

This is also marvelous fruit country. Prunes, apples, pears and peaches almost fall from the trees. *Pêche de touraine à la royale* (peaches in a creamy sauce) makes a superb ending to a meal of *noisette de porc aux pruneaux* (roast pork with prunes). Another not-to-be missed specialty is *champignons avec beurre d'escargots* (mushrooms stuffed with the garlic, shallot and parsley butter usually used for snails). What a way to start a meal!

Paris lies in the Ile de France and is surrounded by what is fondly known as the garden of France. In season come truckloads of cauliflower, artichokes, asparagus, peas and mushrooms. *Potage Saint-Germain* (fresh pea soup) and *potage parisienne* (a vegetable soup containing potatoes, leeks and carrots) are hearty contributions of this region, which is equally famous for its strawberries and *Brie* cheese.

Bakery products are especially unique—chocolate *éclairs*, golden *brioche* dripping with butter and Parisian *baguette* (French bread) originated in this area. The most famous creation is *crêpes suzette*, paper-thin pancakes served flaming with orange-flavored liqueur.

To the east, along the German border sits Alsace-Lorraine. The German influence is felt heavily here, but with subtle French touches. The pig and the goose are favored animals in this region.

The specially fat-
tened goose of Stras-
bourg is the highlight of
Alsatian gastronomy. From it
comes *pâté de foie gras* and *oie à l'alsacienne*
(goose cooked with sauerkraut).

Choucroute, or sauerkraut, which we think of as very German, has
a special place on tables here. *Choucroute garnie*, a dish of
sauerkraut cooked in wine and broth and garnished with sausages
and pork, is a local favorite. Pigs play a starring role in *potée
alsacienne*, a cabbage soup with pork and vegetables. *Quiche lorraine*
is another typical menu item of the area; the bacon and cheese
filling makes it a tasty luncheon dish.

Alsace is also the third largest wine area after Burgundy and
Bordeaux and its wine is light and fresh-tasting.

Burgundy is directly south of Alsace-Lorraine and is famous not
only for its excellent wines but also for its equally superb foods.
Boeuf bourguignon is a well-known favorite of beef cooked in red
wine sauce with mushrooms, onions and bacon. *Escargots à la
bourguignonne* (snails in shallot and garlic butter) are probably just

as popular. *Gougère*, a local savory cheese pastry, can be eaten hot or cold as an *hors d'oeuvre*.

Dijon is the mustard capital of France. The Romans may have brought the mustard seed to France but it took the creative French to mix it with grape vinegar to make the epicurean delight—Dijon mustard. From the nearby hillsides come black currants that go into *crème de cassis*, a delightful liqueur sipped by itself or mixed with white wine for an *apéritif* called *kir*.

Bordeaux in the southwest of France is also a very special wine region. Familiar wine names such as *Médoc, Graves, Saint-Emilion* and *Pomerol* are typical of this area.

Roquefort cheese is also made in the province but next to its wines, the most famous export to other regions of France and the world is *truffe* (truffles) from Périgord. In fact the phrase, *à la périgordienne* means that truffles are included somewhere in the sauce or stuffing.

The mountainous regions of France bordering the Swiss and Italian Alps are known as Franche-Comté, Savoie and Dauphiné. Fig and nut trees flourish here. Cheese is an important man-made product. *Comté* (like Swiss cheese without the holes), *Gruyère* and *Emmental* are examples of this area's products.

Potatoes also play a prominent role in the food here. *Omelette à la savoyarde* is an omelet cooked with sliced potatoes fried in butter and grated cheese. *Pommes de terre dauphinoises* are potatoes with milk and egg sauce seasoned with nutmeg and grated cheese. *Quenelles de brochet*, those fat little dumplings of creamed pike, are another specialty.

Along the Spanish border and the Mediterranean are found the combined provinces of Languedoc, Foix and Roussillon. The warm climate and proximity to Spain have influenced the eating habits here.

The most incredible dish of the area is *cassoulet*, which is a white bean-based stew. This hearty dish is usually made with beans, pork, ham and sausage plus additions of mutton and/or preserved goose or duck, depending on which recipe is followed.

Another example of the strong Spanish influence on the food of this region is *oeufs à la catalane*, which is simply fried eggs served on a bed of tomatoes, eggplant, hot peppers, garlic and parsley.

The last stop for our tour is Provence, where cooking is brilliantly colored and spicy. Olive oil, tomatoes, onions, garlic and herbs are found in almost every dish. *Ratatouille*, a marvelous vegetable stew or relish includes all of these ingredients plus eggplant and squash. *Pissaladière*, the Provençal version of pizza, is a flat tart of onions, peppers, tomatoes and anchovies. Probably the most renowned dish of the region is *bouillabaisse*, a zesty fish and shellfish soup-stew which is spiced at the end with *rouille*, a hot pepper sauce with garlic and oil.

Despite the great diversity of available ingredients, most of France dines in a similar pattern. Breakfast *(petit déjeuner)* is simply a cup of coffee or tea with a *brioche* or *croissant* plus butter and jam. The main meal comes at noon and may consist of soup or *hors d'oeuvre*, a meat and vegetable dish, cheese and dessert. In the north lunch is eaten quickly; but in the Midi, in southern France, lunch is leisurely and there might be a little nap afterwards. Dinner is a simple version of lunch, except that the meat course might be replaced by a fish or egg dish, with a salad and dessert.

Glossary*

À la bordelaise (ah lah bor-dih-LEZZ)—"in the style of Bordeaux." Sauce bordelaise is a brown sauce made with red wine, shallots, pepper and thyme.

À la bourguignonne (ah lah boor-gee-NYUNN)—"in the style of Burgundy." The dish will be simmered in red Burgundy wine, mushrooms and white onions.

À la périgordienne (ah lah pay-ree-gohr-DYENN)—"in the style of Périgord." Means that truffles are included somewhere in the sauce or stuffing.

À la provençale (ah lah pruh-vahn-SAHL)—"in the style of Province." Means that a dish will be flavored with tomatoes, onions, garlic and herbs.

Au gratin (oh grah-TAN)—food topped with grated cheese, butter or bread crumbs, and then browned quickly under the broiler.

Baguette (bah-GETT)—long narrow loaf of French bread.

Boeuf bourguignon (BUHF boor-gee-NYOHN)—beef cooked in red wine sauce with mushrooms, onions and bacon.

Bonne femme (bunn FAHM)—home style. A simple dish with several vegetables.

Bouillabaisse (bwee-ah-BESS)—fish and shellfish soup-stew.

Brioche (bree-YUSH)—rich, buttery yeast dough, made into rolls for breakfast or mid-afternoon or baked around chicken, meat, fish or sausage.

Cassoulet (kah-soo-LAY)—white bean-based stew.

Champignons avec beurre d'escargots (shahm-pee-NYOHN ah-vehk BURR deh-skahr-GOH)—mushrooms stuffed with the garlic, shallot and parsley butter usually used for snails.

Charcuterie (shahr-kyoo-teh-REE)—butcher shop that originally sold only pork products, but now includes all kinds of sausages, pâtés and cured meats.

Choucroute (shoo-KROOT)—sauerkraut.

Cocotte (kuh-KUHT)—heavy covered casserole that can be used on top of the stove as well as in the oven.

Consommé (kohn-suh-MAY)—meat or poultry stock that has been strained and clarified with an egg white.

Coquille (kuh-KEE)—"shell"; dish into which food is served.

Court bouillon (koor bwee-YAHN)—a seasoned broth used for poaching fish.

Crêpe (KREPP)—thin pancakes of egg and flour wrapped around a filling and frequently served with a sauce. Can be either an *hors d'oeuvre*, main dish or dessert.

Crêpes suzette (krepp syoo-ZETT)—paper-thin pancakes served flaming with orange-flavored liqueur.

Croissant (krwah-SAHN)—buttery, flaky pastry rolled into a crescent shape; usually served with butter and jam at breakfast.

Cuisine bourgeoise (kwee-zeenn boor-ZHWAHZ)—ordinary home-style French cooking.

Déglacer (day-glah-SAY)—to remove the fat from a cooked dish and make a sauce with wine or broth from browned bits remaining in the pan.

d'Uxelles (dyoo-SELL)—a cooked combination of chopped mushrooms, onions or shallots used in stuffings or sauces.

Escargots à la bourguignonne (eh-skahr-GOH ah lah boor-gee-NYUNN)—snails in shallot and garlic butter.

Farci (fahr-SEE)—stuffed.

Fermière (fehr-MYEHR)—"farmer's wife." Usually a braised meat with vegetables; a pot roast.

Foie (FWAH)—liver; *foie gras* (fwah GRAH) is liver of fattened goose.

Garbure (gahr-BYOOR)—a hearty cabbage soup-stew seasoned with goose fat.

Gougère (goo-ZHEHR)—a savory cheese pastry.

Haute cuisine (oht kwee-ZEENN)—elaborate dishes prepared in the tradition of professional chefs.

Hors d'oeuvre (or DUH-vrih)—"outside the work"; an appetizer served before the meal or the first course.

Julienne (zhyoo-LYENN)—thin strips of meat or vegetables.

Kir (KEER)—an *apéritif* made from *crème de cassis* (black currant liqueur) mixed with white wine.

Macédoine (mah-say-DWAHNN)—combination of cut-up cooked or raw fruits or vegetables; usually served cold.

Maison (may-ZOHN)—"house." Means specialty of the house or restaurant.

Marmite (mahr-MEET)—kettle for soup or stock.

Noisette de porc aux pruneaux (nwah-zett dih POHRK oh pryoo-NOH)—roast pork with prunes.

Nouvelle cuisine (noo-vell kwee-ZEENN)—a newer and simpler style of cooking developed by chefs.

Oeufs à la catalane (uh ah lah kah-tah-LAHNN)—fried eggs served on a bed of tomatoes, eggplant, hot peppers, garlic and parsley.

Oie à l'alsacienne (WAH ah lahl-zah-SYENN)—goose cooked with sauerkraut.

Omelette à la savoyarde (uhm-LETT ah lah sah-vwah-YAHRD)—an omelet cooked with sliced potatoes fried in butter and grated cheese.

Pâté (pah-TAY)—mixture of ground meat, fish or poultry with seasonings, baked in a crust or wrapped in strips of fat; usually served cold.

Pâte brisée (paht bree-ZAY)—pastry for a pie.

Pâte à choux (paht ah SHOO)—puffed pastry dough.

Pêche de touraine à la royale (pesh dih too-RENN ah lah rah-YAHL)—peaches in a creamy sauce.

Pêche Melba (pesh MELL-bah)—a cream-filled peach half set on a bed of vanilla ice cream and covered with raspberry sauce.

Petit déjeuner (pih-tee day-zhuh-NAY)—breakfast.

Pissaladière (pee-sah-lah-DYEHR)—a flat pizza-like tart of onions, peppers, tomatoes and anchovies.

Pistou (pee-STOO)—a vegetable soup which is much like the Italian *minestrone*.

Pommes de terre dauphinoises (pumm dih TEHR doh-fee-NWAHZ)—potatoes with milk and egg sauce seasoned with nutmeg and grated cheese.

Potage (poh-TAHZH)—strained cream soup or puréed vegetable soup.

Potage parisienne (poh-TAHZH pah-ree-ZYENN)—a vegetable soup containing potatoes, leeks and carrots.

Potage Saint-Germain (poh-TAHZH sahṅ-zher-MAИ)—fresh pea soup.

Potée alsacienne (poh-TAY ahl-zah-SYENN)—a cabbage soup with pork and vegetables.

Poularde Derby (poo-lahrd DER-bee)—roast chicken with a rice, *pâté* and truffle stuffing.

Quenelles de brochet (keh-NELL dih bruh-SHAY)—dumplings of creamed pike.

Quiche (KEESH)—a single-crust pie with a baked cheese and custard filling which may also contain cut-up vegetables, pieces of meat or fish, etc.

Quiche lorraine (keesh loh-RENN)—a *quiche* with a bacon, cheese, and custard filling.

Rafraîchir (rah-freh-SHEER)—"to refresh"; chilling vegetables or fruits to stop cooking by plunging into cold water, icing or refrigerating.

Ragoût (rah-GOO)—a stew.

Ratatouille (rah-tah-too-yih)—a vegetable stew or relish made from tomatoes, onions, garlic, eggplant, squash and herbs.

Rillettes (ree-YETT)—a seasoned, shredded pork spread.

Rouille (ROO-yih)—a hot pepper sauce with garlic and oil.

Roux (ROO)—combination of melted butter and flour used to thicken sauce.

Soupe (SOOP)—broth with vegetables and bits of meat.

Tarte (TAHRT)—open-faced pie made with fruit.

Truffe (TRYOOF)—"truffle"; mushroom-like product that is used as a garnish or for flavoring a sauce or stuffing.

Vinaigrette (vee-neh-GRETT)—the vinegar and oil-based sauce which we call French dressing.

*[И] or [ŋ] indicates that the preceding vowel is very nasal; the "n" is not really pronounced.

Bouillabaisse

Navarin Printanier

Beignets aux Pommes

Carbonades de Boeuf

Côtes de Porc

Potage Garbure

French vegetable soup is hefty and hearty. This time-saving variation uses canned beans which are added at the end; just heat and serve.

1 cup	coarsely chopped cabbage
1 cup	diced carrot
1 cup	coarsely chopped green onions
¼ cup	diced celery
1 large	clove garlic, minced
½ teaspoon	marjoram leaves, crushed
2 tablespoons	butter or margarine
2 cans (10¾ ounces each)	condensed beefy mushroom soup*
2 soup cans	water
1 pound	garlic-flavored sausage, cut in ½-inch slices
2 cups	cubed potatoes
1 cup	canned white beans or chick peas

In large saucepan, cook cabbage, carrot, green onions and celery with garlic and marjoram in butter until tender. Add remaining ingredients except beans. Bring to boil; reduce heat. Simmer 20 minutes or until done; stir occasionally. Add white beans; heat. Makes about 9½ cups.

*2 cans (10¾ ounces each) condensed golden mushroom soup may be substituted for beefy mushroom soup.

Boeuf Bourguignon

Cubes of beef, onions and carrots are braised in red Burgundy in this classic French recipe. Prepare it ahead; the flavor improves on standing.

4 slices	bacon
1½ pounds	beef cubes (1½ inch)
1 can (10¾ ounces)	condensed beefy mushroom soup*
1 cup	Burgundy or other dry red wine
2 tablespoons	tomato paste
¼ teaspoon	thyme leaves, crushed
1 medium	bay leaf
2 medium	cloves garlic, minced
8 small	whole white onions (about ½ pound)
2 medium	carrots, cut in 2-inch sticks

In large saucepan, cook bacon until crisp; remove and crumble. Brown beef in drippings. Add soup, wine, tomato paste, crumbled bacon and seasonings. Cover; cook over low heat 1 hour. Add onions and carrots; cook 1 hour more or until done. Stir occasionally. Remove bay leaf. Serve over noodles. Makes about 5 cups.

*1 can (10¾ ounces) condensed golden mushroom soup and ⅓ cup water may be substituted for beefy mushroom soup.

Menu:
*Boeuf Bourguignon
Herb-Buttered Noodles
Hot Garlic Bread
Pears and Roquefort Cheese

Beignets aux Pommes

Deep fried apple fritters are cooked until they are just golden brown. Serve them hot with a topping of creamy vanilla sauce.

1⅔ cups	flour
2 teaspoons	baking powder
1 can (10¾ ounces)	condensed chicken broth
1 tablespoon	salad oil
5 large	cooking apples
2 tablespoons	kirschwasser
1 cup	sugar
1 tablespoon	cornstarch
1	egg, separated
1¾ cups	milk
1 teaspoon	vanilla
2 teaspoons	ground cinnamon

To make batter, in small bowl, combine flour and baking powder; add broth and 1 tablespoon oil, stirring until *just* moistened. Cover with towel; let stand 30 minutes. In shallow dish, arrange apples; sprinkle with kirschwasser and 2 tablespoons sugar. Set aside; turn apples occasionally. To make vanilla sauce, in saucepan, combine ⅓ cup sugar, cornstarch and egg yolk; gradually add milk. Cook, stirring until thickened; add vanilla. In small bowl, combine remaining sugar and cinnamon. To make fritters, beat egg white until soft peaks form; fold in batter. Drain apples well; dip into batter. Fry, a few at a time, in deep fat at 375°F. until golden brown; drain on absorbent towels. Coat with cinnamon and sugar mixture. Serve with vanilla sauce. Makes 6 servings.

Mousse de Volaille

This is a delightful way to serve cold chicken or even leftover turkey. The mousse is made easily with the help of a blender or food processor.

2 envelopes	unflavored gelatine
½ cup	cold water
2 teaspoons	lemon juice
1 can (10¾ ounces)	condensed creamy chicken mushroom soup
2 cups	finely chopped cooked chicken
¼ cup	chopped celery
¼ cup	chopped onion
¼ teaspoon	ground nutmeg
Generous dash	pepper
¾ cup	heavy cream, whipped

Sprinkle gelatine over water and lemon juice to soften; place over low heat, stirring until gelatine is dissolved. In electric blender or food processor, combine soup, chicken, celery, onion, nutmeg and pepper. Blend until smooth. Fold in dissolved gelatine mixture and whipped cream. Pour into 5-cup mold. Chill until firm. Unmold on salad greens; garnish with pimiento. Makes about 4½ cups.

Menu:
*Mousse de Volaille
French Potato Salad
Beet and Endive Salad
Lemon Bavarian Cream

Pistou

An elegant side dish of eggplant, peppers and tomatoes that has its origins in the Provence area of southern France. The touch of vinegar adds a piquant taste.

6 cups	cubed eggplant
½ cup	diced green pepper
½ cup	sliced onion
1 medium	clove garlic, minced
1 tablespoon	chopped parsley
1 teaspoon	basil leaves, crushed
¼ cup	salad oil
1 can (10¾ ounces)	condensed tomato bisque soup
1 teaspoon	vinegar

In skillet, brown eggplant and cook green pepper and onion with garlic, parsley and basil in oil until tender. Add remaining ingredients. Cover; cook over low heat 10 minutes or until done. Stir occasionally. Makes about 3 cups.

Menu:
Sautéed Chicken Breast with Lemon
*Pistou
Cucumber and Dill Salad
Almond Cookies

Quiche à l'Oignon

A quiche is not just made with ham and bacon plus cheese. The French often use onions for a delicious variation. You'll enjoy this for lunch or dinner.

3 cups	chopped onion
¼ cup	butter or margarine
1 can (10¾ ounces)	condensed cream of chicken soup
4	eggs, slightly beaten
½ cup	heavy cream
½ cup	shredded Swiss cheese
9-inch	unbaked pie shell

In skillet, cook onion in butter until tender; stir in remaining ingredients except pie shell. Pour into pie shell. Bake at 350°F. for 45 minutes or until knife inserted in center comes out clean. Makes 4 to 6 servings.

Menu:
*Potage Garbure
*Quiche à l' Oignon
Grilled Tomatoes with Basil Bread Crumbs
Raspberry Sherbet

Côtes de Porc

Wine and tomatoes make a perfect base for these braised pork chops. The pickle and caper are added at the end for a unique piquant flavor.

6	pork chops (about 2 pounds)
1 can (10¾ ounces)	condensed tomato soup
½ cup	Chablis or other dry white wine
½ cup	chopped onion
1 medium	clove garlic, minced
¼ teaspoon	thyme leaves, crushed
¼ cup	sliced dill pickle
2 tablespoons	chopped parsley
1 tablespoon	chopped capers

In skillet, brown chops (use shortening if necessary); pour off fat. Add soup, wine, onion, garlic and thyme. Cover; cook over low heat 30 minutes or until done. Stir occasionally. Uncover; add remaining ingredients. Cook to desired consistency. Makes 4 servings.

Menu:
*Côtes de Porc
Shoestring Potatoes
Broccoli with Hollandaise Sauce
Orange Slices and Toasted Almonds

Navarin Printanier

Lamb stew takes on a French name and a French taste when cooked with rosemary and thyme with a splash of consomme.

2 pounds	lamb cubes (about 1½ inch), well trimmed
2 tablespoons	flour
2 tablespoons	salad oil
1 can (10½ ounces)	condensed consomme
1 can (about 16 ounces)	tomatoes, cut up
1 large	clove garlic, minced
1 medium	bay leaf
¼ teaspoon	rosemary leaves, crushed
¼ teaspoon	thyme leaves, crushed
4 medium	carrots (about ½ pound), cut in 2-inch pieces
8 small	whole white onions (about ½ pound)
2 medium	potatoes, quartered
2 medium	purple top turnips, quartered
1 package (10 ounces)	frozen peas

Dust lamb with flour. In large saucepan, brown lamb in oil; pour off fat. Add consomme, tomatoes, garlic and seasonings. Cover; cook over low heat 45 minutes. Add remaining ingredients except peas; cook 45 minutes. Add peas, cook 5 minutes more or until done. Stir occasionally. Makes about 10 cups.

Pain d' Epinards

Spinach takes on a French flavor when prepared in this creamy loaf form. The dish makes a delicious change of pace for any fish or veal recipe.

2 tablespoons	finely chopped onion
¼ teaspoon	ground nutmeg
2 tablespoons	butter or margarine
1 can (10¾ ounces)	condensed cream of chicken soup
2 packages (10 ounces each)	frozen chopped spinach, cooked and *well drained*
1 cup	soft bread crumbs
3	eggs, separated

In saucepan, cook onion with nutmeg in butter until tender. Add soup, spinach, bread crumbs and egg yolks. In bowl, beat egg whites until soft peaks form; fold into spinach mixture. Pour into buttered and floured loaf pan (8½ × 4½ × 2½''). Bake at 375°F. for 1 hour or until knife inserted in center comes out clean. Let stand 10 minutes; invert on serving platter. Garnish with croutons. Serve with cream. Makes 8 servings.

Menu:
Fillet of Sole in Almond Butter
*Pain d' Epinards
Buttered New Potatoes
Mocha Cake

Fricassée de Veau

Only the French could have created this flavorful veal dish with its delicate, creamy sauce flavored with mushrooms and wine. It's perfect for family or friends.

2 pounds	veal cubes (1½ inch)
2 tablespoons	salad oil
1 can (10¾ ounces)	condensed cream of mushroom soup
⅓ cup	Chablis or other dry white wine
3 cups	sliced onions
¼ teaspoon	thyme leaves, crushed
¼ cup	heavy cream

In large saucepan, lightly brown meat in oil; add soup, wine, onions and thyme. Cover; cook over low heat 1 hour 30 minutes or until done. Stir occasionally. Stir in cream. Serve over noodles. Garnish with parsley. Makes about 5 cups.

Menu:
*Fricassée de Veau
Fried Noodles
Braised Carrots and Celery
Peach Melba

Carbonades de Boeuf

Beer gives a rich taste to this savory beef dish. You'll be surprised how well the flavors blend when you sample the recipe.

3 to 4-pound	boneless rump roast
¼ cup	salad oil
1 can (10¾ ounces)	condensed cream of mushroom soup
1 cup	beer
3 cups	sliced onions
1 large	clove garlic, minced
½ teaspoon	thyme leaves, crushed
⅛ teaspoon	pepper

Trim fat from meat; slice ½-inch thick. In large heavy pan, brown meat in oil; pour off fat. Add remaining ingredients. Cover; cook over low heat 1 hour 30 minutes or until done. Stir occasionally. Uncover; cook to desired consistency. Makes 6 to 8 servings.

Menu:
*Carbonades de Boeuf
Scalloped Potatoes
Sautéed Mushrooms
Individual Cherry Tarts

Bouillabaisse

*In southern France, especially Marseilles, bouillabaisse is made
with an assortment of the freshest local seafood. You can make
this fish stew by substituting any local fish or shellfish.*

1 cup	sliced onion
1 can (about 16 ounces)	tomatoes, cut up and drained
4 medium	cloves garlic, minced
2 tablespoons	chopped parsley
1 medium	bay leaf
⅛ teaspoon	pepper
2 tablespoons	olive oil
2 cans (10¾ ounces each)	condensed chicken broth
2 soup cans	water
2 medium	potatoes, sliced
Generous dash	ground saffron or turmeric
1½ pounds	fillets of white fish, cut in 2-inch pieces
¾ pound	fillets of red snapper, cut in 2-inch pieces
12 small	fresh clams
½ pound	medium shrimp (31-35/pound), shelled and deveined

In large saucepan, cook onion and tomatoes with garlic,
parsley, bay leaf and pepper in oil until tender. Add broth,
water, potatoes and saffron. Bring to boil; reduce heat.
Simmer 5 minutes. Add remaining ingredients except shrimp;
simmer 5 minutes. Add shrimp; simmer 5 minutes more or
until done. Stir gently now and then. Remove bay leaf. Makes
about 16 cups.

Cassoulet

There are many ways to prepare cassoulet. You can use lamb or even pieces of duck or goose, as they do in southeastern France.

1 pound	pork cubes (½ inch)
½ pound	pork sausage links, cut in half
½ cup	chopped onion
2 medium	cloves garlic, minced
2 cans (11½ ounces each)	condensed bean with bacon soup
½ soup can	water
1 cup	chopped tomato
¼ cup	Chablis or other dry white wine
1 medium	bay leaf

In skillet, brown pork and sausage and cook onion with garlic until tender; pour off fat. Add remaining ingredients. Pour into 2-quart casserole; bake at 375°F. for 1 hour or until done. Remove bay leaf. Makes about 7 cups.

Menu:
Mushroom Consomme
*Cassoulet
Tomato and Cucumber Salad
Chocolate Mousse

Fricassée de Poulet à l'Estragon

Chicken is simmered gently until it is just done in this light and creamy sauce. The crumbled tarragon gives a delicate but memorable flavor.

2 pounds	chicken parts
¼ cup	butter or margarine
1 can (10¾ ounces)	condensed cream of chicken soup
¼ cup	Chablis or other dry white wine
8 small	whole white onions (about ½ pound)
2 tablespoons	chopped parsley
1 teaspoon	lemon juice
½ teaspoon	tarragon leaves, crushed
¼ teaspoon	rosemary leaves, crushed
¼ cup	heavy cream

In skillet, brown chicken in butter. Add remaining ingredients except cream. Cover; cook over low heat 45 minutes or until done. Stir occasionally. Arrange chicken on platter. Stir cream into sauce; serve with chicken. Makes 4 servings.

Menu:
*Fricasée de Poulet à l'Estragon
Parslied Rice
Braised Peas and Lettuce
*Beignets aux Pommes

Germany

Stollen

1. *Schlachtwurst*   2. *Frische Leberwurst*   3. *Speck Blutwurst*
4. *Kalbsleberwurst*   5. *Fleishwurst*   6. *Bierwurst*   7. *Braunschweiger
Leberwurst*

Eating well is a way of life in Germany and the Germans do just that with their hale and hearty foods. This is the land of meat and potatoes; a meal simply isn't a meal without a substantial proportion of both! And Germans take their food seriously—no delicate sauces or simple desserts for them.

Sauerkraut and sausage figure heavily in meal planning for the German *hausfrau.* The idea of preserving cabbage by pickling it is a technique originated by the Chinese. The Mongols or Tartars who swept over northern Europe in the 13th century passed the recipe for "sour cabbage" on to the natives of Germany, who eagerly adapted it. They saw its natural affinity to such staples as apples, wine, beer, caraway seeds and that indispensable menu item, pork.

To realize how indispensable pork really is, all you need to do is walk past a fabulous display of sausages in the window of any butcher shop. There are over 300 different kinds of sausages sold in Germany from the pale *weisswurst* of Munich to the bright-red and smoky *mettwurst.*

The Romans were the first foreigners to discover the delights of German food. They recorded tales of gargantuan feasts featuring wild boar, an equally ancient ancestor of today's succulent pig. If the

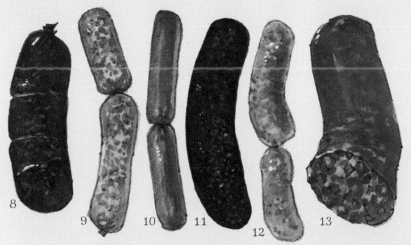

8. *Thuringer Blutwurst*   9. *Holsteiner Kochwurst*   10. *Hildesheimer Streichleberwurst*   11. *Touristenwurst*   12. *Koch-bratwurst*   13. *Sulze (headcheese)*

Romans took back with them the beginnings of culinary delicacies such as *wurst* (sausage) and *bier* (beer), which they called "barley wine," they also left a legacy of vineyards behind—a tradition maintained today.

After a brief exposure to the country's view of cooking the Romans realized that the Germans did not live by beer and pork alone. Wild game, nuts, sour milk products and fruits, both fresh and dried, were equally important staples. This has not really changed in almost 2,000 years. Fruits, for example, figure in every meal—used in soups, with potatoes, in place of a vegetable in a meat stew, or when not cooked with the meat, served as a tangy relish to accompany the main dish.

Potatoes found their way into German meal patterns through King Frederick the Great in the late 18th century. He distributed free seed potatoes with instructions on how to grow them. It's hard to imagine today the Teutonic diet without *kartoffeln* (potatoes) on the menu in some form, but up to that point they were considered a curiosity.

In the last century, contact with foreigners has influenced what's found on the table from Hamburg to Heidelberg. Pineapples, curry, bananas and even *pasta*—a gift from the Italian laborers found in heavy concentrations in Germany—are good examples of foods now integrated as ingredients or by themselves in German cooking. Modern kitchen equipment wrought a more important change; now, oven roasting and broiling are used with the same frequency as frying and pot-roasting, the more traditional methods of cooking.

Like Italy, Germany has spent most of its existence as a series of loosely bound city-states or small duchies. Bismarck was largely responsible for unifying it as one nation in the 1870's. Because of this division, there are many regional favorites which have slowly become national dishes.

To understand the diversity of the names as well as the dishes, let's take a quick cook's tour.

The cold and damp northern region is influenced by its proximity to the sea, Germany's only coastline and the fruits of the sea— halibut, sole, herring and eel—are featured on menus prominently in the two main cities of the north—Hamburg and Berlin. *Aalsuppe*, eel soup, is a hefty meal-in-one dish or *eintopf* enjoyed in this region and is like *bouillabaisse* is to the French. Soups of cabbage, bacon or dried beans or lentils are also popular. *Labskaus*, "sailor's hash," is the Hamburg version of New England corned beef hash; it features pickled pork, potatoes, beets and anchovies topped with a fried egg.

Just south of Hamburg is the Vierlande, an area famous for its chickens and ducks. *Stubenküken*, chicken browned in butter, is a local specialty. Buckwheat and rye are used in breads and also as hot cooked cereal topped with cream and stewed fruit. You could not leave this area without sampling *birnen, bohnen und speck,* an unusual combination of pears, green beans and bacon, or that Berlin creation called *eisbein mit erbsenpüree,* a pickled shin of pork with yellow split pea purée served with ubiquitous potatoes and sauerkraut.

The central part of Germany is a land of rolling hills and fertile valleys—formerly known as Saxony, Westphalia and Silesia. Near Holland, Westphalia is the land of nutty pumpernickel bread, white asparagus and Westphalian ham, a pungent smoked ham served thin-sliced like *prosciutto. Pfefferpotthast,* a heavily peppered short rib dish, is a delicious example of the hearty casseroles enjoyed in this area.

To the east lies Frankfurt, whose *Wüstchen* was the father to our frankfurter. *Handkäs mit musik* is not a song but a favorite appetizer of soft cheese with marinated onion topping. Onions also transform into *zwiebelkuchen*, a German version of *quiche.* Silesia is influenced by its Polish neighbors and uses sour cream and poppy seeds in its

North Sea

Baltic Sea

Schleswig Holstein

Hamburg

Lower Saxony

Berlin

East Germany

Westphalia

Hesse

Rhineland Palatinate

Frankfurt

Saarland

Heidelberg

Rothenburg

Bavaria

Baden-Wurttemberg

Black Forest

Munich

cooking. *Schwärtelbraten*, a pot-roasted leg of pork cooked with sauerkraut, is at home here.

The Germans have a marvelous sense of humor when it comes to naming recipes. *Schlesisches Himmelreich* which translates to Silesian Heaven, is a heavenly combination of pork and dried fruits; this is usually served with potato dumplings instead of bread dumplings.

Try *Himmel und Erde* (Heaven and Earth), a southern German favorite of puréed potatoes and apples topped with fried onions or crisp bacon. The south is an area of rugged mountains. Close to France and Switzerland, Swabia lies in the Black Forest. *Kirschwasser*, clear cherry brandy and *Schwarzwälder kirschtorte*, Black Forest cherry torte, are two of its more famous culinary contributions. *Spätzle*, tiny flour dumplings, replace the heavier bread and potato dumplings of the north.

One of the most interesting dishes found in this region is *maultaschen* ("pouts"), which are small meat and spinach pastries, not unlike *ravioli*. Bavaria, which borders on Austria, is the home of Munich and *weisswürste*, small sausage links of veal or pork and veal, which are eaten with rolls, white radishes and a special sweet mustard as a snack food. *Nürnberger lebkuchen* is a spicy cookie that appears in southern German kitchens at Christmas. Veal as *schnitzel* is found on menus in a dozen forms here.

Wherever you are in Germany you can be assured of good eating. Food is the national pastime of this country. A typical day in the life of a German includes five stick-to-your-ribs meals.

Frühstück, breakfast, begins in the traditional continental style of coffee, crisp rolls, rye and dark breads with butter and jam. In northern Germany, this early morning meal includes cheese and cold cuts also. *Zweites frühstück* is a second breakfast that is nibbled around 9:00 or 10:00 a.m. at work or in school. For children, it might include *belegtes brot*, "covered bread," which is a sandwich of meat

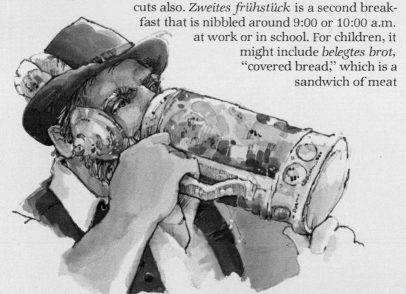

or cheese plus an apple. If the adults have been imbibing too much beer or wine from the night before, they might have *katerfrühstück*, a hangover breakfast of herring, sausage or goulash soup. Otherwise, this meal might include food from a delicatessen—salads of meat, vegetables or fish or whatever little leftovers the frugal German housewife is recycling that day.

The main meal of the day is called the *mittagessen*; it is usually eaten in the early afternoon and includes at least four or five courses. Soup is the starter and to most Germans, there is something wrong with the meal that does not start with a *suppe. Fleischbrühe*, a clear soup, one with dumplings or *brotsuppe*, a bread soup flavored with apples, cream or a bit of gravy, might be featured. The fish course, *fisch*, is served next. *Zanderschnitte mit senfbutter*, fillet of pike in mustard butter or *rollmops*, rolled herring fillets, are possible choices for this course.

The main course is usually a combination of meat, vegetable or fruit and a salad. If game is "in season," then *hasenpfeffer*, rabbit in pepper sauce or pheasant might be a choice. Pork, veal or beef are other alternatives. Perhaps *königsberger klopse*, a delicate meatball dish in a cream and caper sauce, might be on the menu. Königsberg, once the capital of East Prussia, is now part of Russia. The dish, however, remains as a favorite.

Cabbage, served as sauerkraut or stuffed and sauced, might be the vegetable. Other root vegetables are frequently featured such as kohlrabi, turnips, parsnips and celeriac. Mustard and horseradish sauce are used as condiments or as a sauce, much like mayonnaise is used in the United States.

Desserts are usually fruit-based. *Rumtopf* ("rum pot") is a favorite. Here the fresh fruit is marinated in rum. *Armer ritter* ("poor knight") is a German version of French toast frequently served with almonds and a fruit sauce topping. Cheese and crackers follow and then perhaps another dessert—a *bon-bon* or elaborate cookie platter. Coffee comes next—topped with whipped cream, blended with chocolate or with cream and sugar.

In the late afternoon, when everyone has recovered from the main meal, it's time for *kaffee*, a snack with a cup of coffee. But this is no simple snack. A visit to a *konditorei*, a pastry shop, would break down the resistance of the most ardent dieter. An elaborate display of cookies, cakes, pastries and coffeecakes are offered and who could resist? This is accompanied with a strong cup of coffee. Then later in the evening comes *abendbrot*, a light supper. This translates to "bread of the evening." Usually it means an open-faced sandwich of cheese, sausage or cold cuts, which is eaten with a knife and fork.

Glossary

Abendbrot (AH-bent-broht)—"bread of the evening"; a light supper.

Armer ritter (AHR-mehr RITT-ehr)—a German version of French toast frequently served with almonds and a fruit sauce topping.

Belegtes brot (beh-LAYK-tehz BROHT)—"covered bread"; a sandwich.

Bier (BEER)—a malted and hopped somewhat alcoholic beverage.

Birnen, bohnen und speck (BEER-nen BOH-nen oont SHPECK)—a combination of pears, green beans and bacon.

Braten (BRAH-ten)—a pot roast cooked with little liquid in a covered saucepan on top of the stove.

Bratwurst (BRAHT-voorrst)—a type of sausage that is sold raw and then pan-fried.

Brotsuppe (BROHT-zoo-peh)—bread soup flavored with apples, cream, or a bit of gravy.

Brühwurst (BREE-voorrst)—a type of sausage that is smoked and blanched; can be eaten as is or heated by simmering.

Delikate kleinigkeit (deh-lee-KAH-teh KLINE-ik-kite)—"a delicate little something"; a snack that might be eaten after the theatre.

Dunkles (DOONNG-kless)—a dark-colored beer.

Eintopf (INE-tawppf)—a one-dish meal.

Eisbein mit erbsenpüree (ICE-bine mitt EHRP-sen-pyoo-ray)—pickled shin of pork with yellow split pea purée.

Fleischbrühe (FLYSH-bree-eh)—meat broth or consommé, served with dumplings.

Gemütlichkeit (geh-MYOOT-likh-kite)—warm and congenial atmosphere.

Handkäs mit musik (HANNT-cayss mitt moo-ZEEK)—an appetizer of soft cheese with marinated onion topping.

Hasenpfeffer (HAH-zen-PFEFF-ehr)—rabbit in pepper sauce.

Helles (HELL-ehz)—a light-colored beer.

Himmel und Erde (HIMM-mel oont AIR-deh)—puréed potatoes and apples topped with fried onions or crisp bacon.

Kaffee (KAHFF-ay)—afternoon coffee which might include cookies or sandwiches and cakes.

Kirschwasser (KEERSH-vahss-ehr)—clear cherry brandy.

Klopse (KLAWPP-seh)—meatballs.

Knödel (KNAY-dull)—dumplings.

Kochwurst (KOKH-voorrst)—a type of sausage that is often smoked but always cooked before purchase; similar to our cold cuts.

Konditorei (kawn-DIT-oh-RYE)—a pastry shop.

Kuchen (KOO-khen)—a cake made of yeast dough or a concoction made of potatoes.

Mittagessen (MIT-tahk-ess-sen)—main meal of the day taken at midday.

Nachtisch (NAHKH-tish)—final dessert course of main midday meal, which may include *bon-bons* or elaborate cookies.

Nürnberger lebkuchen (NEERN-behrg-ehr LAYP-koo-khen)— a type of spicy Christmas cookie.

Pfefferpotthast (PFEFF-ehr-pawt-hahst)—heavily peppered short rib stew.

Ratskeller (RAHTS-kell-ehr)—an informal restaurant.

Reibekuchen (RYE-beh-koo-khen)—Rhineland-style potato pancakes.

Rohwurst (ROH-voorrst)—a type of sausage that is cured and smoked; eaten as is.

Rollmops (RAWL-mawps)—herring fillets rolled up with chopped gherkins, onions, capers and mustard.

Rotwein (ROHT-vine)—red wine.

Rumtopf (ROOM-tawpf)—fresh fruit marinated in rum.

Salat (zah-LAHT)—salad.

Schnaps (SHNAHPS)—clear brandy.

Schnitzel (SHNIT-zell)—very thin slices of meat, usually prepared by sautéing; usually veal but could also be pork or beef.

Stollen (SHTAWL-len)—fruit cake-bread, popular at Christmas.

Stubenküken (Shtoo-ben-KYOO-ken)—chicken browned in butter.

Vorspeisen (FOR-shpyze-en)—appetizers.

Weinstube (VINE-shtoo-beh)—a restaurant that specializes in serving wine.

Würstchen (VEERST-khen)—any kind of small sausages.

Zanderschnitte (ZAHN-dehr-SHNITT-teh)—fillet of pike.

Geräuchertes mit Kraut

Kartoffelsalat

Rinderrouladen

Hasenpfeffer and Spätzle

Gefüllte Kalbsbrust

Breast of veal is a most economical buy and it is not difficult to bone. Be sure to carefully tie veal roll-up well because sausage mixture will escape.

½ pound	pork sausage
¼ cup	chopped onion
1 can (10¾ ounces)	condensed golden mushroom soup
3 slices	fresh rye bread, crumbled
2 tablespoons	chopped parsley
1	egg, slightly beaten
Dash	ground nutmeg
Dash	pepper
2-pound	boneless breast of veal, trimmed
2 tablespoons	shortening
⅓ cup	water

In saucepan, brown sausage and cook onion until tender; stir to separate meat. Pour off fat. Stir in ¼ cup soup, bread, parsley, egg, nutmeg and pepper. To make roll-up, pound veal. Spread sausage mixture across long end of veal. Roll up; tuck in ends. Tie with string or fasten with skewers. In large heavy oven-proof pan, brown veal in shortening; pour off fat. Stir in remaining soup and water. Cover; bake at 350°F. for 1 hour. Turn; bake 1 hour more. Uncover; bake 30 minutes more or until done, spooning sauce over roll-up. Remove roll-up to serving platter. Let stand 10 minutes before slicing. Serve with sauce. Makes 8 servings.

Spätzle

They are called noodles but really spätzles are like tiny dumplings. They can be made with spinach or ham also. Sometimes they are served with sautéed mushrooms or shredded Swiss cheese.

4 cups	sifted all-purpose flour
1 teaspoon	salt
¼ teaspoon	pepper
1 can (10¾ ounces)	condensed chicken broth
4	eggs, slightly beaten
¼ cup	milk

To make dough, in large bowl, combine flour, salt and pepper. Blend broth, eggs and milk; add to flour mixture, beating until bubbles form (about 2 minutes). To make spätzles, force dough through large holed colander or place small amounts of dough on edged plate. Tilt plate cutting off strands of dough into boiling salted water.* Cook gently 5 minutes or until spätzles float. Rinse in cold water; drain. In skillet, brown spätzles in butter. Sprinkle with bread crumbs. Makes about 9 cups.

*Add a small amount of oil to water to prevent spätzles from sticking together.

Selleriesalat

Celery is a favorite winter vegetable. The apples, beets and pickles add crunch as well as color.

1 can (10¾ ounces)	condensed cream of chicken soup
1 tablespoon	lemon juice
2 medium	sweet gherkin pickles, chopped
½ teaspoon	dried dill weed, crushed
2 cups	thickly sliced celery
1 small	apple, diced (about 1 cup)
1 cup	sliced cooked beets
1 cup	diced cooked potatoes

In bowl, blend soup, lemon juice, pickles and dill. Toss with celery, apple, beets and potatoes. Chill 4 hours or more. Serve on salad greens. Makes about 4 cups.

Menu:
*Gefüllte Kalbsbrust
Buttered Noodles
*Selleriesalat
Mocha Cake

Kartoffelsalat

If you marinate the potatoes while they are still warm, they will pick up more flavor. Using sour cream instead of the usual mayonnaise gives this salad a different taste.

1 can (10¾ ounces)	condensed chicken broth
½ cup	finely chopped onion
¼ cup	wine vinegar
3 tablespoons	olive oil
1 tablespoon	lemon juice
1 teaspoon	Dijon mustard
¼ teaspoon	salt
⅛ teaspoon	pepper
5 cups	cubed potatoes (about 2½ pounds)
1 cup	sour cream
2 tablespoons	chopped parsley

In skillet, combine all ingredients except potatoes, sour cream and parsley; add potatoes. Bring to boil; reduce heat. Simmer 25 minutes or until done. Let stand 30 minutes. In bowl, blend sour cream and parsley; toss with potato mixture. Serve with grilled knockwurst. Makes about 4 cups.

Bohnensuppe mit Tomaten

We think of lima beans only as a vegetable but the Germans love lima beans as an ingredient in a soup, too. Mash half of the beans to act as a thickener for the soup.

2 packages (10 ounces each)	frozen baby lima beans, well cooked and drained
2 tablespoons	finely chopped onion
⅛ teaspoon	thyme leaves, crushed
1 medium	clove garlic, minced
2 tablespoons	butter or margarine
1 can (10¾ ounces)	condensed chicken broth
1 can (10½ ounces)	condensed beef broth
1½ soup cans	water
1 cup	diced tomatoes

Mash 2 cups lima beans with fork; set aside. In saucepan, cook onion with thyme and garlic in butter until tender. Blend in remaining lima beans, mashed limas, broths, water and tomatoes. Simmer a few minutes to blend flavors; stir occasionally. Makes about 7 cups.

Menu:
*Bohnensuppe mit Tomaten
Pork Sausage Links in Beer
*Kartoffelsalat
Sauerkraut
Spice Cookies

Kartoffelsuppe

Potato soup is enjoyed all over Germany. This soup takes no more than 10 minutes to prepare from start to finish. Garnish with croutons made from leftover pumpernickel bread.

2	knockwurst, sliced
½ cup	chopped celery
¼ cup	finely chopped onion
½ teaspoon	caraway seed
2 tablespoons	butter or margarine
2 cans (10¾ ounces each)	condensed cream of potato soup
1½ soup cans	milk
¼ cup	chopped parsley

In large saucepan, brown knockwurst and cook celery and onion with caraway seed in butter until tender. Blend in soup, milk and parsley. Heat; stir occasionally. Makes about 5½ cups.

Menu:
*Kartoffelsuppe
Braised Liver and Onions
Green Beans and Bacon
Cucumber Salad
Poppyseed Cake

Apfelkuchen

A "kuchen" is usually made with fruit or jam baked in a dough not unlike a richer version of our pie crust. It can also be made with a sweet yeast dough, as this apple cake is.

Dough:	**1 can (10¾ ounces)**	condensed chicken broth
	½ cup	butter or margarine
	4½ cups	all-purpose flour
	2 packages	active dry yeast
	½ cup	sugar
	2	eggs
Topping:	**3 medium**	apples, peeled and thinly sliced
	1 tablespoon	lemon juice
	1 cup	sugar
	2 teaspoons	ground cinnamon
	¼ cup	flour
	2 tablespoons	butter or margarine

To make dough: In saucepan, combine broth and butter. Heat to lukewarm (110°F.). Meanwhile, in large bowl of electric mixer, combine 3 cups of flour, yeast and sugar. Add broth mixture and eggs to dry ingredients. Beat at high speed 2 minutes, scraping bottom and sides of bowl often. Stir in remaining flour to make a soft dough (but not sticky). On lightly floured board, knead dough until smooth (about 10 minutes). Place in greased bowl, turning once. Cover; let rise in a warm place 1 hour or until doubled in bulk. Punch down on lightly floured board, roll out dough to fit greased jelly-roll pan (15 × 10 × 1″); press into corners of pan. *To make topping:* Toss apples with lemon juice, ½ cup sugar and 1 teaspoon cinnamon. Arrange apples in single layer on dough. In bowl, combine remaining sugar, flour and cinnamon. Cut in butter until mixture resembles coarse cornmeal. Sprinkle over apples. Cover; let rise until doubled (about 1 hour). Bake at 375°F. for 35 minutes or until done. Makes 25 servings (3 × 2″).

Käsekuchen

No one loves a rich wedge of cheese cake more than the Germans. It's one of their all-time favorite desserts. This particular recipe combines three different cheeses with raisins.

Pastry:	**1 cup**	all-purpose flour
	3 tablespoons	sugar
	½ teaspoon	baking powder
	¼ cup	butter or margarine
	1	egg
	1 tablespoon	water
Filling:	**1 pound**	large curd creamed cottage cheese
	2 packages (8 ounces each)	farmer or pot cheese
	4	eggs, separated
	⅔ cup	sugar
	¼ cup	milk
	1 teaspoon	grated lemon rind
	1 teaspoon	vanilla extract
	¼ teaspoon	almond extract
	1 can (11 ounces)	condensed Cheddar cheese soup
	¼ cup	cornstarch
	½ cup	raisins

To make pastry: In bowl, sift together flour, sugar and baking powder. Cut in butter until mixture resembles coarse cornmeal. Beat egg and water. Mix into flour mixture to form a stiff dough. On lightly floured board, roll pastry into 10-inch circle. Line bottom of 9-inch spring-form pan, pressing dough around sides. Roll out remaining dough into 2½-inch wide strips. Press around sides; chill 2 hours or more. *To make filling:* In electric blender, combine cottage cheese, farmer cheese, egg yolks, sugar, milk, lemon rind and extracts. Blend until smooth. Meanwhile, in large bowl, blend soup and cornstarch until smooth; stir in cheese mixture and raisins. Beat egg whites until soft peaks form. Gradually fold into cheese mixture. Pour into pastry-lined pan. Bake at 325°F. for 2 hours or until knife inserted within 1 inch from edge comes out clean. Cool on rack 10 minutes; remove outer rim. Chill.

Rinderrouladen

This recipe is sometimes known as beef birds. Boned, rolled and stuffed beef rolls are cooked slowly to tenderize the less expensive cut of meat. Prepare ahead and just quickly reheat.

3 slices	bacon
1½ pounds	thinly sliced round steak (¼-inch thick)
2 tablespoons	Dijon mustard
3 medium	dill pickles, cut in quarters lengthwise
6 medium	carrots (about 1 pound), cut in quarters lengthwise
¼ cup	finely chopped onion
1 can (10¾ ounces)	condensed beefy mushroom soup*
½ cup	chopped celery
½ cup	chopped parsnips
2 tablespoons	chopped parsley

In skillet, cook bacon until crisp; remove and crumble. Cut meat into 6 pieces (6×4″); pound. Spread each with 1 teaspoon mustard. Place 2 pieces of pickle and 4 pieces of carrot across the narrow end; sprinkle with 2 teaspoons onion. Starting at narrow end, roll up. Tuck in ends; fasten with toothpicks or skewers. Brown roll-ups in drippings; pour off fat. Stir in soup, celery, parsnips, parsley and bacon. Cover; cook over low heat 1 hour 15 minutes. Stir occasionally. Serve with mashed potatoes. Makes 6 servings.

*1 can (10¾ ounces) condensed golden mushroom soup and ⅓ cup water may be substituted for beefy mushroom soup.

Geräuchertes mit Kraut

Sauerkraut is not just meant as an accompaniment to frankfurters. It's used in everything from soups to salads to stews. Caraway seed is often used to flavor it.

4	smoked pork hocks (about ¾ pound each)
2 cups	diced cooking apples
½ cup	sliced onion
1 can (about 16 ounces)	sauerkraut, rinsed and drained
½ teaspoon	caraway seed
2 tablespoons	butter or margarine
1 can (10¾ ounces)	condensed cream of celery soup
3 medium	potatoes (about 1 pound), peeled and quartered
4 medium	carrots (about ½ pound), cut in 3-inch pieces
4	peppercorns

In large heavy pan, cover pork hocks with water. Cover; simmer 2 hours 30 minutes. Drain, reserving 1 cup liquid. Remove hocks. In same pan, cook apples and onion with sauerkraut and caraway in butter until tender. Stir in soup, reserved liquid, potatoes, carrots and peppercorns; add hocks. Cover; simmer 30 minutes or until done. Makes 4 servings.

Menu:
*Geräuchertes mit Kraut
Yellow Split Pea Purée
Lettuce with Buttermilk Dressing
Warm Jelly Doughnuts

No Christmas would be complete without the candied fruited and nutted yeast bread called Stollen. Don't leave baking until the last moment; stollens freeze beautifully if wrapped tightly.

1 cup	candied citrus peel
1 cup	raisins
½ cup	candied cherries
½ cup	light rum
1 can (11 ounces)	condensed Cheddar cheese soup
1 cup	milk
1 cup	butter or margarine
8½ cups	all-purpose flour
1 cup	sugar
2 packages	active dry yeast
2	eggs, slightly beaten
½ teaspoon	grated lemon rind
½ teaspoon	almond extract
½ cup	sliced almonds

In bowl, combine fruits and rum; let stand 1 hour. Drain fruit, reserving rum. Meanwhile, in saucepan, heat soup, milk, butter and reserved rum to lukewarm (110°F.). Meanwhile, in large bowl of electric mixer, combine 3 cups flour, sugar and yeast. Add eggs, lemon rind, extract and milk mixture. Beat at low speed 30 seconds, scraping bottom and sides of bowl often. Beat at high speed for 3 minutes. Stir in fruit, nuts and remaining flour to make a stiff dough. On lightly floured board, knead dough until smooth (about 10 minutes), adding flour as needed. Place in greased bowl, turning once. Cover;

let rise in warm place 1 hour or until doubled in bulk. Punch down. To make loaves, divide dough in half. Divide each half into 2 parts, one about ⅔ of dough and the other about ⅓ of dough. Divide larger part into 3 equal pieces for bottom braid. Roll each piece into a 12-inch long rope. Press ends together; braid ropes. Place on greased baking sheet. Divide smaller part into 3 equal pieces. Roll each piece into a 10-inch rope. Pinch ends together; braid ropes. Place on top of larger braid. Seal braids together at ends. Repeat with remaining dough to form second loaf. Brush each loaf with melted butter. Cover; let rise until doubled (about 1 hour). Bake at 375°F. for 30 minutes or until done; cool on rack. Sprinkle with confectioners' sugar. Makes 2 loaves.

Hasenpfeffer

Rabbit is often served in stews in Germany. The most famous dish for rabbit is Hasenpfeffer. The peppery sauce adds good contrast to the sweet rabbit meat, which tastes a little like dark meated chicken.

1 can (10½ ounces)	condensed onion soup
½ cup	wine vinegar
3	whole cloves
1 large	bay leaf
6	peppercorns
1 tablespoon	lemon juice
1 package (about 2½ pounds)	frozen rabbit, thawed
4 slices	bacon
2 tablespoons	water
1 tablespoon	flour

To make marinade, in saucepan, combine soup, vinegar, cloves, bay leaf, peppercorns and lemon juice. Cover; simmer 5 minutes. Meanwhile, arrange rabbit in shallow dish; pour marinade over rabbit. Marinate overnight, turning once. Remove rabbit from marinade, reserving marinade. Drain on absorbent towels. In skillet, cook bacon until crisp; remove and crumble. Brown rabbit in drippings. Stir in reserved marinade. Cover; cook over low heat 1 hour 30 minutes. Spoon off fat; remove bay leaf. Remove rabbit to serving platter; keep warm. Blend water into flour until smooth; slowly stir into sauce. Cook, stirring until thickened. Serve with rabbit and spätzles. Makes 4 servings.

Menu:
*Hasenpfeffer
*Spätzle
Glazed Turnips
Lemon Cream Pudding

Konigsberger Klopse

Meatballs of many sizes and shapes are favorite menu items in Germany. This dish which originated in Konigsberg is simmered in broth rather than fried.

2 slices	white bread, crumbled
2 tablespoons	heavy cream
1 pound	ground meat loaf mix (beef, pork and veal)
⅓ cup	finely chopped onion
2	anchovy fillets, chopped
1	egg, slightly beaten
2 tablespoons	chopped parsley
⅛ teaspoon	grated lemon rind
¼ teaspoon	salt
⅛ teaspoon	pepper
1 can (10¾ ounces)	condensed cream of chicken soup
¼ cup	sour cream
1 tablespoon	chopped capers
1 tablespoon	lemon juice

In bowl, soak bread in cream. Mix *thoroughly* bread mixture, meat loaf mix, onion, anchovies, egg, parsley, lemon rind, salt and pepper. Shape into 16 meatballs; roll in flour. Simmer meatballs in boiling water 10 minutes; drain, reserving ⅓ cup liquid. In skillet, blend soup, sour cream, reserved liquid, capers and lemon juice. Add meatballs. Cover; cook over low heat 10 minutes or until done. Stir occasionally. Garnish with additional chopped parsley. Makes about 4 cups.

Menu:
*Konigsberger Klopse
Parsley-Buttered Potatoes
Green Bean Salad
*Käsekuchen

Westphalian Pfefferpotthast

Sweet and sour flavor is one that the Germans love. This beef stew has the tart flavor of lemon and capers which contrasts with sweetish flavor of cloves. Pumpernickel bread crumbs thicken the stew instead of flour.

3 pounds	short ribs, cut in serving-size pieces
2 tablespoons	shortening
1 can (10½ ounces)	condensed onion soup
1 tablespoon	lemon juice
1 teaspoon	capers
1 medium	bay leaf
¼ teaspoon	pepper
⅛ teaspoon	ground cloves
Generous dash	grated lemon rind
2 tablespoons	fresh pumpernickel bread crumbs

In large saucepan, brown ribs in shortening; pour off fat. Add remaining ingredients except bread crumbs. Bring to boil; reduce heat. Cover; cook over low heat 2 hours 45 minutes. Stir occasionally. Spoon off fat; add bread crumbs. Cook, stirring until thickened. Remove bay leaf. Serve with mashed potatoes. Makes 4 servings.

Menu:
*Westphalian Pfefferpotthast
Mashed Potatoes
Pickled Beets, Dill Pickles
*Apfelkuchen

Nudelpudding mit Käse

This simple-to-make casserole is delicious with any cold roast meat. The creamy cheese mixture gets golden brown on top as it bakes with the noodles.

1 can (11 ounces)	condensed Cheddar cheese soup
1 soup can	heavy cream
½ cup	sugar
4	eggs, separated
⅓ cup	raisins
½ teaspoon	grated lemon rind
¼ teaspoon	rum extract
5 cups	cooked medium noodles (about ½ pound)
¼ cup	chopped toasted almonds

In bowl, blend soup, cream, sugar, egg yolks, raisins, lemon rind and rum extract. Stir in noodles and nuts. Meanwhile, beat egg whites until soft peaks form. Gently fold into noodle mixture. Pour into buttered 2-quart shallow baking dish ($12 \times 8 \times 2''$). Bake at 350°F. for 40 minutes or until knife inserted in center comes out clean. Makes 8 servings.

Menu:
Cold Roast Pork or Ham
*Nudelpudding mit Käse
Buttered Brussels Sprouts
Cherry Tarts

Antipasto

Italy

If there is one thing that can be said about Italians and their attitudes toward food, it is that Italians know how to eat well. The same zest they have for life applies to their cooking. And unlike their nearby neighbors, the French, whose best known cuisine is found in their restaurants, the Italians go home for simple, flavorful meals *alla casalinga.*

Indeed, the hallmarks of Italian cooking are simple, uncomplicated recipes handed down from grandmother to mother to daughter and fresh-looking as well as fresh-tasting ingredients. Italian housewives shop daily for the freshest produce and foods readily available: olive oil, tomatoes, wine and cheese, to name a few.

Most of us, unless we are fortunate to have some Italian ancestors or friends, associate Italian cooking with pizza, spaghetti and meatballs and veal scaloppine. But these dishes represent only a very small part of eating the Italian way. Italians have influenced our way of cooking, but America has also influenced Italian cooking. The New World gave Italy its tomato for sauces, beans for *minestrone* and salads and corn for *polenta.*

To understand Italian food, it is necessary to look at its culinary history. Much has been written about the ancient Romans and their gastronomic extravaganzas. Marcus Apicius, one of the first cookbook writers, recorded details of elaborate feasts staged by emperors and nobles that amounted to food orgies. Ordinary citizens dined on simpler fare than peacocks' brains and flamingo tongues. Bread, vegetables, fruits, olive oil, honey and a wheat porridge (a forerunner of *polenta,* cornmeal mush) were important ingredients in Roman meals, much as they are today. Meat, primarily lamb or pork, was reserved for special occasions.

Italy's long coastline has frequently been the target of foreign invaders. The Phoenicians and Greeks colonized before the Romans gained control of the peninsula. After the fall of the Roman Empire, Italy was repeatedly invaded by foreigners, each of whom left their culinary mark on Italian cooking. The Spanish brought rice from the New World; the French left behind cream and butter; and the Moslems in Sicily grew oranges and lemons and created a sweet tooth in southern Italy which still persists today. *Torrone,* almond nougat, and candied citrus peel, a favorite ingredient in many Italian desserts, were gifts of the Moslems.

But the Italians gave as well as received. Catherine de Medici of Florence brought her own chef with her when she became the bride of Henri II of France in 1533, and that was the beginning of the flowering of "gourmet" French cooking. Artichokes, asparagus, broccoli, melons, macaroons and even ice cream came into the French cuisine.

The most well known Italian gift is probably *pasta*. There is a legend that Marco Polo, the famous Italian merchant and adventurer, brought the art of noodle-making back with him from China. There is evidence from tomb-paintings, however, that the Etruscans, an ancient Italian people, actually ate a form of *pasta*. Whatever the truth is, it is probably lost in history; but we do know that the Italians are responsible for making *pasta* famous.

Italians usually include *pasta* at their main meal of the day. It is served as a separate course and in small quantities. There are hundreds of shapes and sizes of *pasta*. There are the tiny ones which appear in soups, such as *anelli* (rings) and *stelle* (stars). There's *pasta* that's cooked and sauced like spaghetti but called *fusilli* ("twists"—they look like spaghetti twisted like a corkscrew) or *vermicelli* ("little worms"—a very thin spaghetti).

Some *pasta* is cooked, sauced and then baked. *Lasagne* is the most common of this type. *Ziti* ("bridegrooms"), a fat tubular macaroni, is another example. Still other *pasta* is stuffed, then cooked and sauced. *Agnolotti*, meat-filled, round *ravioli* and *tortellini*, small twisted meat-filled *pasta* usually served in cream, fall into this category.

Then there's also *pasta* that is cooked, stuffed, sauced and baked. *Cannelloni*, large squares of pasta which are cooked and then stuffed with cheese or meat filling, rolled and sauced before baking is the Italian equivalent of a French crêpe.

The list of *pasta* types goes on and on. There are probably several hundred different types of sauces to dress up the several hundred *pasta* shapes. Many of the regions in Italy have developed their own special blend of sauces, based on what is available locally.

The reason behind the richness and diversity of *pasta* sauces and other products of regional Italian cuisine is that until the second half of the 19th century, Italy was divided into independent rival city-states.

Most of the immigrants from Italy to the U.S. came from Naples or Sicily, so most of the Italian food served in America reflects the heavy, earthy foods of these areas.

The difference between the North and South of Italy as well as the difference between the provinces is as varied as our own regional cuisine. Order veal in Milan, and it will be coated with crumbs and cheese before sautéing; in Naples, you'll find veal seasoned with a tomato-onion sauce and mozzarella cheese. In the South, where wheat grows best, *pasta* in many different shapes and sizes are staple menu items, but in the North, in the fertile plain of the Po

River Valley, rice and corn flourish, which forms the basis for *risotto* and *polenta*. Olive trees thrive in the poor, rocky soil of southern Italy, and their oil is the basic fat of the region, while the plentiful cows in the North are responsible for the butter used in the cooking of that area.

Let's take a quick cook's tour of the Italian peninsula. The alpine province of Valle d'Aosta in northwestern Italy is the home of mild and buttery-soft fontina cheese. Borrowing from their Swiss neighbors, local cooks turn this cheese into a *fonduta*, on which sliced white truffles are sprinkled in season.

Truffles come from the nearby Piedmont province and find their way into many dishes of the region, from *risotto* to game recipes. Turin, the Detroit of Italy, is famous for its *grissini* (bread sticks), chocolates and caramels. *Bagna Caldo* ("hot bath") is a traditional sauce of oil, butter, garlic, anchovies and sometimes cream, into which raw vegetables are dipped. Among the famous wines of Italy, Barolo and Barbaresco as well as the bubbly Asti Spumante are natives to this region.

The temperate climate and beautiful coastline of Liguria are the

*1. Manicotti   2. Conchiglie   3. Farfalle   4. Gnocchi   5. Fettucine
6. Rote   7. Agnolotti   8. Ravioli   9. Penne   10. Rigatoni
11. Tortiglione*

reason it is known as the Italian Riviera. The sea provides the fish for the local stew, *burrida*. Genoa, capital of this province, is renowned for the invention of *ravioli* and *cima alla genovese*, which is breast of veal stuffed with ground veal, peas and cheese. Genoa's greatest contribution to Italian cuisine is *pesto*, the basil and cheese sauce which is pounded smooth in a mortar with a pestle before tossing with hot *pasta* or *gnocchi*.

A little further east is Lombardy, which is highly industrialized. Milan, one of the principal cities in that province, has a unique cuisine. Some of their favorite dishes include *osso buco*, veal shanks served with saffron rice, *costolette alla milanese*, golden-brown veal cutlets and *risotto alla milanese*, rice cooked in broth and flavored with butter, saffron and grated cheese. *Panettone*, the rounded cake with raisins and candied fruit, is the Christmas gift of the Milanese. Two of the region's popular cheeses are gorgonzola, the blue-veined cheese, and bel paese, a creamy and mild cheese.

Venezia is the name of the province of which Venice is the major city. Fish of all types and varieties are enjoyed in this historic island setting. Venice is also known for *risi e bisi*, rice with peas and *fegato*

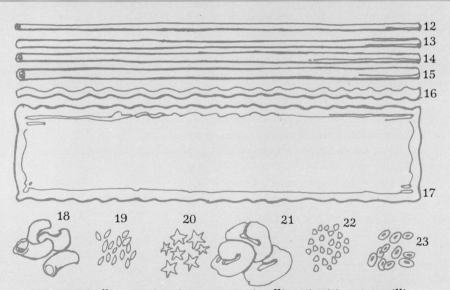

12. *Vermicelli*   13. *Linguine*   14. *Perciatelli*   15. *Ziti*   16. *Fusilli*
17. *Lasagne*   18. *Ditalini*   19. *Orzo*   20. *Stelline*   21. *Tortellini*
22. *Acini*   23. *Anellini*

alla veneziana, thinly sliced calf's liver with onions. Nearby Verona is reputed to contain the oldest food market in Italy. From the vineyards in this region come Bardolino, Soave and Valpolicella.

Trentino-Alto Adige, another mountainous area in the North is influenced in its cooking by its closeness to Austria; this can be sampled in its sauerkraut and dumplings. *Polenta,* the cornmeal mush, is frequently served with tiny game birds. Over 30 varieties of wild mushrooms are found here and are usually served broiled.

Emilia-Romagna is the birthplace of Parmesan cheese, *prosciutto,* the famous ham of Parma and *mortadella,* a fat-flecked bologna. *Tortellini,* tiny filled pasta served with cream and grated cheese, *tagliatelle,* long egg noodles and *lasagne verdi al forno,* baked green lasagne, are favorite dishes of this fertile area. But perhaps the tastiest invention is *ragú alla bolognese,* a sauce for *pasta* made of minced meats and chopped vegetables plus a few tablespoons of cream and tomato paste.

Tuscany, just to the south, is the region of Chianti wine, beefsteak and spinach. The latter appears in everything from soups to *pasta,* and the term, *"alla fiorentina"* usually means the dish contains spinach. Livorno on the Tyrrhenian Sea is the home for many delicious fish dishes including *cacciucco,* a spicy fish stew seasoned with wine and red peppers. *Panforte,* the Christmas fruitcake of Siena, which is flat and round, is said to have been developed during the Middle Ages.

Umbria, home for Perugia, Orvieto and Assisi, and the Marches, along the Adriatic Sea, are mountainous regions halfway down the leg of Italy. *Porchetta,* whole roast suckling pig, is a local favorite. Spit-roasting is a common cooking method for the hearty fare of these provinces. *Brodetto,* the Italian equivalent of the French bouillabaisse, is created in the seaside towns of the Marches, each of which has a slightly different variation. Two marvelous white wines come from this area—Orvieto and Verdicchio.

Rome is the center of Italy and another great area for dining and enjoying superb food. *Fettuccine Alfredo,* egg noodles tossed with butter and grated cheese and *carciofi alla romana,* fried baby artichokes with garlic, are creations of the region of Latium. *Saltimbocca alla romana,* which translates as "jump into your mouth," is a sinfully delicious combination of veal *scaloppine,* ham and cheese from Rome. The nearby Alban Hills, where Romans love to picnic is the home of Frascati wine.

Abruzzi e Molise has a reputation for serving gigantic meals. One of the dishes sure to be enjoyed is *maccheroni alla chitarra,* noodles cut

Valle d'Aosta

Trentino-Alto-Adige

Lombardy

Turin

Milan

Piedmont

Veneto

Friuli-Venezia Giulia

Verona

Venice

Liguria

Genoa

Emilia Romagna

Ligurian
Sea

Pisa

Livorno

Tuscany

Perugia

Assisi

Adriatic Sea

Orvieto

The Marches

Umbria

Abruzzi

Latium

Rome

Molise

Sardinia

Campania

Naples

Basilicata

Tyrrhenian
Sea

Apulia

Mediterranean Sea

Calabria

Sicily

Ionian Sea

in a frame with wires strung like a guitar. This is usually served with a peppery tomato sauce and grated pecorino cheese. The rocky landscape makes this area perfect for grazing sheep, which provide the milk for the cheese. Lamb is served in many ways: roasted, fried or cooked as a fricassee with an egg-lemon sauce.

Pizza and spaghetti are the mainstays of the diet of Naples, which lies in the province of Campania. *Calzone*, a turnover of pizza dough, cheese and ham or salami, is another local variation of pizza which found its way to America, as well as *melanzane alla parmigiana*, that we know as eggplant parmigiana. Campania is the land of mozzarella and provolone cheeses, which were originally made from the milk of the white water buffalo. *Zeppole* are one of Naple's many contributions to Italian desserts; these orange-flavored doughnuts are often served with *spumone*, molded ice cream with rum-flavored whipped cream and nuts.

The heel, instep and toe of the Italian "boot" are known to Italians as Apulia, Basilicata and Calabria, respectively. It is a poor area where the sun beats down on the land unmercifully. Residents are addicted to spicy dishes and sweet ones. Favorites include *caponata*, a pepper, tomato and eggplant relish and *triglie alla calabrese*, baked mullet with black olives and capers.

Just south of the toe of Italy lies Sicily, the largest island in the Mediterranean. Tuna and sardines, often in combination with *pasta*, are staples of the Sicilian diet. *Falsomagro* is a variation of *braciole*, beef which is stuffed with salami, hard-cooked eggs, cheese and crumbs and rolled before baking. *Cannoli*, ricotta-filled tubes of fried pastry and *cassata alla siciliana*, a sponge cake with ricotta,

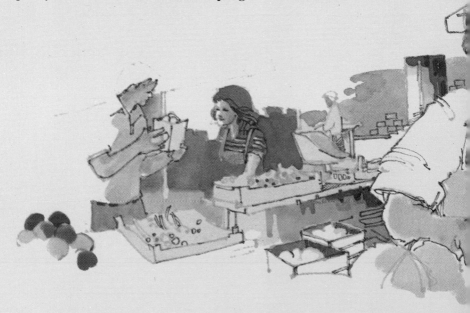

chocolate, candied fruits and nuts, are two of the most famous Sicilian desserts.

Last but not least, is Sardinia, a mountainous island several hundred miles west of Italy. The sheep which abound give milk for their famous cheese, pecorino sardo; this is grated and served over *malloreddus*, flour *gnocchi* topped with tomato sauce.

Whether one lives in the Piedmont or Apulia, Italians do have the love of eating in common. Their breakfast begins with a simple meal of coffee and a roll or a chunk of bread. Lunch, however, is a big event; two hours are devoted to it. People rush home or to their favorite *trattoria* for several courses accompanied by bread and the ever-present carafe of wine. It often includes an *antipasto*, a choice of marinated vegetables, seafoods, eggs, olives, cheese or sausage, or a *minestrone*, a soup. This is followed by an *asciutta*, a course of *risotto*, *gnocchi* or *pasta*. A modest portion of fish, meat or chicken is next with a vegetable of the season and a green salad. The meal ends with a choice of cheese or fruit. Sweet desserts *(dolci)* are served only at special occasion meals. Dinner is eaten late and is usually an abbreviated version of lunch. But before dinner, it is common to serve an aperitif instead of a cocktail. Vermouth, a fortified wine flavored with herbs, might be the choice. And a main meal is not a complete meal without *caffè espresso*, that rich, strong black coffee, or one of its variations, such as *cappuccino*.

Glossary

Agnolotti (ah-nyoh-LOHT-tee)—round, meat-filled *ravioli*.

Al dente (ahl DENN-teh)—"[firm] to the tooth"; term used to describe the doneness of *pasta*—firm-textured but not overcooked.

Anelli (ah-NELL-lee)—*pasta* shaped in rings.

Antipasto (ahn-tee-PAH-stoh)—"before the meal"; hors d'oeuvres or first course.

Asciutta (ah-SHOOT-tah)—a course of *risotto, gnocchi* or *pasta.*

Bagno caldo (BAH-nyoh KAHL-doh)—literally, "hot bath," a traditional sauce of oil, butter, garlic, anchovies and sometimes cream, into which raw vegetables are dipped.

Bel paese (bell pah-EH-zeh)—a mild and creamy cheese.

Bollito (bohl-LEE-toh)—"boiled"; boiled meat.

Braciola (brah-CHOH-lah)—cutlet or steak for braising.

Brodetto (broh-DETT-toh)—fish soup with oil, garlic, parsley and tomatoes.

Buon appetito (bwohn ahp-peh-TEE-toh)—"Good eating."

Burrida (boor-REE-dah)—local stew of Liguria.

Alla cacciatora (ahl-lah kaht-chah-TOH-rah)—"hunter's style"; meat or fish cooked in a tomato sauce with onions, mushrooms and red or white wine.

Cacciucco (kaht-CHOOK-koh)—a spicy fish stew seasoned with wine and red peppers.

Caffè espresso (kahf-FEH eh-SPRESS-soh)—very strong black coffee made by forcing steam through finely ground coffee.

Calzone (kahl-TSOH-neh)—turnover made from pizza dough.

Cannelloni (kahn-nell-LOH-nee)—large rolled-up tubes of *pasta* served stuffed with cheese or meat filling and baked.

Cannoli (kahn-NOH-lee)—crisp tubes of flaky pastry filled with *ricotta* cheese or chocolate or vanilla cream filling and candied fruit.

Caponata (kah-poh-NAH-tah)—a pepper, tomato and eggplant relish.

Cappuccino (kaph-poot-CHEE-noh)—very strong coffee mixed with hot beaten milk and sometimes spiced.

Carciofi alla romana (kahr-CHOH-fee ahl-lah roh-MAH-nah)—fried baby artichokes with garlic.

Alla casalinga (ahl-lah kah-sah-LEENG-gah)—homemade.

Cassata (kahss-SAH-tah)—an ice cream dish made with chocolate or cream enclosing ice cream; Sicilian dish made with cake.

Cima alla genovese (CHEE-mah ahl-lah jeh-noh-VEH-zeh)—breast of veal stuffed with ground veal, peas and cheese.

Contorni (kohn-TOHR-nee)—vegetables accompanying the meat course.

Costoletta (koh-stoh-LETT-tah)—chop or cutlet.

Dolci (DOHL-chee)—sweets, desserts.

Falsomagro (fahl-soh-MAH-groh)—variation of *braciole*; beef which is stuffed with salami, hard-cooked eggs, cheese and crumbs, and rolled before baking.

Fegato alla veneziana (FEH-gah-toh ahl-lah veh-neh-ZYAH-nah)—thinly sliced calf's liver with onions.

Fettuccine Alfredo (fett-toot-CHEE-neh ahl-FREH-doh)—egg noodles tossed with butter and grated cheese.

Alla fiorentina (ahl-lah fyoh-renn-TEE-nah)—"in the Florentine way": means the dish contains spinach.

Fonduta (fohn-DOO-tah)—fondue.

Formaggio (fohr-MAHD-joh)—cheese.

Frittata (freet-TAH-tah)—flat omelet browned on both sides.

Frutti di mare (FROOT-tee dee MAH-reh)—"fruit of the sea": an assortment of fish and shellfish.

Fusilli (foo-ZEEL-lee)—*pasta* shaped in twists.

Gelato (jeh-LAH-toh)—ice cream.

Gnocchi (NYOHK-kee)—small dumplings made from semolina, potatoes or *ricotta*.

Gorgonzola (gohr-gohn-ZOH-lah)—a strong, blue-veined cheese.

Granite (grah-NEE-teh)—Italian flavored ices.

Grissini (greess-SEE-nee)—very thin breadsticks.

Lasagne verdi al forno (lah-ZAH-nyeh VEHR-dee ahl FOHR-noh)—baked green *lasagne* made with spinach.

Maccheroni alla chitarra (mahk-keh-ROH-nee ahl-lah kee-TAHR-rah)— noodles cut in a frame with wires strung like a guitar.

Malloreddus (mahl-loh-REDD-dooss)—a flour *gnocchi* topped with tomato sauce.

Alla marinara (ahl-lah mah-ree-NAH-rah)—"sailor's style"; sauce using tomatoes, garlic, onion and oregano.

Melanzane alla parmigiana (meh-lahn-ZAH-neh ahl-lah pahr-mee-JAH-nah)—eggplant parmigiana.

Minestrone (mee-neh-STROH-neh)—thick vegetable soup with rice or small *pasta* shapes.

Mortadella (mohr-tah-DELL-lah)—fat-flecked bologna.

Osso buco (OHSS-soh BOO-koh)—veal shanks served with saffron rice.

Panettone (pah-nett-TOH-neh)—rounded cake with raisins and candied fruit.

Panforte (pahn-FOHR-teh)—the Christmas fruitcake of Siena.

Alla parmigiana (ahl-lah pahr-mee-JAH-nah)—with Parmesan cheese.

Pasta (PAH-stah)—a shaped dough, usually made from flour, water and possibly egg or oil.

Pecorino sardo (peh-koh-REE-noh SAHR-doh)—cheese which is grated and served over *malloreddus*.

Pesto (PEH-stoh)—sauce or crushed fresh basil or other herbs, garlic, Parmesan cheese and oil, served with *pasta* or in soups.

Pizza (PEET-tsah)—a large open pie usually consisting of a crust of flat rolled bread dough topped with cheese or spiced meat and usually a spicy tomato sauce.

Alla pizzaiola (ahl-lah peet-tsah-YOH-lah)—tomato sauce flavored with garlic and oregano.

Polenta (poh-LENN-tah)—cornmeal mush.

Porchetta (pohr-KETT-tah)—whole roast suckling pig.

Prezzemolo (prett-TSEMM-oh-loh)—Italian parsley, with leaves which are not as curly and a flavor which is not as strong as in regular parsley.

Prosciutto (proh-SHOOT-toh)—dry-cured spiced ham.

Ragù (rah-GOO)—meat sauce, stew.

Ragù alla bolognese (rah-GOO ahl-lah boh-loh-NYEH-zeh)—a sauce for *pasta* made of minced meats and chopped vegetables.

Ravioli (rah-VYOH-lee)—small pillows of *pasta* stuffed with meat, cheese, spinach or other fillings.

Risi e bisi (REE-zee eh BEE-zee)—rice with peas.

Risotto (ree-SOHT-toh)—rice dish made with broth or wine and cheese.

Saltimbocca alla romana (sahl-teem-BOHK-kah ahl-lah roh-MAH-nah)—combination of veal *scaloppine*, ham and cheese from Rome.

Scaloppine (skah-lohp-PEE-neh)—thin, small slices of veal sautéed in a sauce.

Spaghetti (spah-GETT-tee)—*pasta* shaped in long strings, thicker than *vermicelli*.

Spumone (spoo-MOH-neh)—light and airy ice cream made with egg whites or whipped cream.

Stelle (STELL-leh)—*pasta* shaped in stars.

Stufato (stoo-FAH-toh)—stew, cooked on top of the stove.

Tagliatelle (tah-lyah-TELL-leh)—long egg noodles.

Torrone (tohr-ROH-neh)—almond nougat.

Tortellini (tohr-tell-LEE-nee)—small twisted meat-filled *pasta*.

Trattoria (traht-toh-REE-yah)—restaurant.

Triglie alla calabrese (TREE-lyeh ahl-lah kah-lah-BREH-zeh)—baked mullet with black olives and capers.

Vermicelli (vehr-mee-CHELL-lee)—literally, "little worms," a very thin spaghetti.

Vitello (vee-TELL-loh)—milk-fed veal.

Zeppole (ZEPP-poh-leh)—sweet fried doughnut or fritter, a favorite on St. Joseph's day in June.

Ziti (ZEE-tee)—literally, "bridegrooms"; a fat tubular macaroni.

Pollo alla Cacciatora

Cannelloni

Lasagne Verdi

Minestrone

Saltimbocca

This quick and easy recipe translates into English as "jump in your mouth", and it is so delicious that it will do just that. Traditionally it is made of veal, but boneless chicken breasts make a tasty, less expensive substitute. To save even more money, bone your own chicken breasts.

3 whole	chicken breasts, split, skinned and boned (1½ pounds boneless)
¼ teaspoon	rubbed sage
6 thin slices	prosciutto (Italian ham) or boiled ham (about 4 ounces)
¼ cup	flour
¼ cup	butter or margarine
½ cup	Marsala wine
1 can (10¾ ounces)	condensed chicken broth

Flatten chicken breasts with flat side of knife; rub with sage. Top each with slice prosciutto; secure with toothpicks. Dust with flour. In skillet, brown in butter. Add wine; bring to boil, stirring to loosen browned bits. Add chicken broth; bring to boil. Reduce heat; simmer 5 minutes or until sauce is slightly thickened. Makes 6 servings.

Menu:
*Saltimbocca
Spaghetti with Pesto Sauce
Orange and Red Onion Salad
Zabaglione (soft custard with Marsala)

Caponata

This thick vegetable relish is an antipasto or first course. It should be served chilled on lettuce leaves or with crusty bread.

2 pounds	eggplant (2 small)
2 cups	chopped onion
2 cups	diced peeled tomatoes (about 3 medium)
1 cup	chopped celery
¼ cup	olive oil
1 can (11 ounces)	condensed tomato bisque soup
¼ cup	wine vinegar
¼ cup	water
½ cup	sliced pitted ripe olives
2 tablespoons	chopped pine nuts
2 tablespoons	sugar
1 small	clove garlic, minced

Peel eggplant; cut in ½-inch cubes. In large saucepan, cook eggplant in boiling salted water 10 minutes; drain *well*. Meanwhile, in skillet, cook onion, tomatoes and celery in olive oil until tender. Add eggplant and remaining ingredients. Cook over low heat 10 minutes; stir occasionally. Chill 6 hours or more. Makes about 7½ cups.

Brodetto

This tasty fish stew comes from the eastern coast of Italy where fish is plentiful. The fish is adjusted to what is available in the United States, but the flavor is pure Italian.

½ cup	chopped green pepper
⅓ cup	chopped onion
1 large	clove garlic, minced
1 small	bay leaf
1 teaspoon	basil leaves, crushed
½ teaspoon	oregano leaves, crushed
½ teaspoon	thyme leaves, crushed
2 tablespoons	olive oil
½ cup	Burgundy or other dry red wine
1 can (10¾ ounces)	condensed chicken broth
1 can (11 ounces)	condensed tomato bisque soup
1 soup can	water
¼ cup	chopped parsley
1 pound	fillets of white fish, cut in 2-inch pieces
½ pound	medium shrimp (31 to 35/pound), shelled and deveined

In large saucepan, cook green pepper and onion with seasonings in oil until tender. Add wine; simmer 2 minutes. Add remaining ingredients. Bring to boil; reduce heat. Cover; simmer 10 minutes or until done. Stir gently now and then. Remove bay leaf. Makes about 6½ cups.

Menu:
*Brodetto
Chick Pea and Onion Salad
Crusty Italian Bread
Pears and Bel Paese Cheese

Polenta

Polenta is a dish commonly found in the area near Venice and Florence. The cornmeal mush is flavored with butter and cheese and makes a good substitute for rice when serving veal or chicken dishes.

1 can (10¾ ounces)	condensed chicken broth
1¾ cups	water
1 cup	cornmeal
1 tablespoon	butter or margarine

In saucepan, bring broth and ¾ cup water to a boil. Blend remaining water into cornmeal until smooth. Pour into simmering broth, stirring constantly. Cover; cook over low heat 15 minutes (mixture will be very thick); stir often. Stir in butter. Spoon into buttered bowl; let stand 10 minutes. Unmold onto flat plate. Cut into thick slices. Serve with additional melted butter and freshly grated Parmesan cheese. Makes 10 servings.

Fried Polenta: Prepare as above; spoon into buttered loaf pan (9 × 5 × 3″). Chill. Cut into slices. In skillet, brown slices in butter.

Pollo alla Cacciatora

This is a good dish to prepare ahead. It's a simple but oh-so satisfying main dish. A mellow red wine complements this meal.

2 pounds	chicken parts
3 tablespoons	flour
2 tablespoons	olive oil
1 can (11 ounces)	condensed tomato bisque soup
⅓ cup	Chianti or other dry red wine
½ cup	sliced onion
1 cup	sliced fresh mushrooms (about ¼ pound)
½ teaspoon	basil leaves, crushed
½ teaspoon	oregano leaves, crushed
2 large	cloves garlic, minced
1 small	bay leaf
1 small	green pepper, cut in strips

Dust chicken with flour. In skillet, brown chicken in oil; add soup, wine, onion, mushrooms and seasonings. Cover; cook over low heat 30 minutes. Add green pepper; cook 15 minutes more or until done. Stir occasionally. Remove bay leaf. Makes 4 servings.

Menu:
Melon Wedges with Prosciutto
*Pollo alla Cacciatora
Zucchini Fritters
Orange and Cucumber Salad
Almond Macaroons

Salsa di Pomodori

This basic tomato sauce is delicious on almost every kind of pasta from spaghettini, a very thin spaghetti, to lasagne. The sauce makes enough to cover one half pound of cooked pasta. Double the recipe and then freeze half of it so you have an almost instant meal on hand.

1 pound	hot Italian sausage, cut in 3-inch pieces
½ cup	finely chopped onion
½ teaspoon	oregano leaves, crushed
1 large	clove garlic, minced
1 tablespoon	olive oil
1 can (10¾ ounces)	condensed tomato soup
1 soup can	water
1 can (about 6 ounces)	tomato paste
2 tablespoons	grated Parmesan cheese
1 small	bay leaf

In saucepan, cook sausage; pour off fat. Add onion, oregano, garlic and olive oil. Cook until onion is tender. Blend in remaining ingredients. Bring to boil; reduce heat. Simmer 30 minutes; stir occasionally. Remove bay leaf. Serve over spaghetti. Makes about 4 cups.

Involtini di Bistecche

This delicious beef is wrapped around a hearty filling of salami, cheese and eggs. For easy serving, let the meat stand, covered, for ten minutes before slicing.

1½-pound	thinly sliced round steak (about ¼-inch thick)
¼ pound	ground veal
1	egg, slightly beaten
¼ cup	small bread cubes
2 tablespoons	grated Parmesan cheese
2 slices (about 2 ounces)	salami, cut in strips
2 slices (about 2 ounces)	Provolone cheese, cut in strips
2 hard-cooked	eggs, sliced
2 tablespoons	shortening
1 can (10¾ ounces)	condensed tomato soup
¼ cup	water
¼ cup	Burgundy or other dry red wine
½ cup	chopped onion
1 medium	clove garlic, minced
1 small	bay leaf

Pound steak. Combine veal, egg, bread cubes and Parmesan cheese. Spread mixture evenly on steak to within 1 inch of edges. Press salami, Provolone cheese and sliced egg into meat mixture. Starting at narrow end, roll up; tuck in ends. Tie with string or fasten with skewers. In skillet, brown roll in shortening; pour off fat. Add remaining ingredients. Cover; cook over low heat 1 hour. Turn; cook 1 hour more or until done. Stir occasionally. Remove bay leaf. Makes 6 servings.

Menu:
Escarole Salad with Garlic Dressing
*Involtini di Bistecche
Buttered Italian Green Beans
Spumone

Risotto

Italians serve risotto as a separate course, much like they do pasta. This is an elegant way to dress up a simple meal of meat or fish. The rice is cooked slowly to a fluffy texture. Sprinkle in the cheese at the last minute and then toss gently.

1 cup	raw regular rice
½ cup	chopped onion
2 tablespoons	butter or margarine
1 can (10½ ounces)	condensed beef broth
1 cup	water
3 tablespoons	grated Parmesan cheese

In saucepan, brown rice and cook onion in butter until tender; add broth and water. Bring to boil; reduce heat. Cover; simmer 25 minutes or until done. Stir occasionally. Stir in Parmesan cheese. Makes about 3 cups.

Risotto e Bisi: Brown ¼ cup finely chopped prosciutto (Italian ham) or boiled ham with rice. Add 1 cup frozen peas the last 10 minutes. Makes about 3½ cups.

Risotto Alla Milanese: Add ⅛ teaspoon crushed saffron or ground turmeric with broth.

Risotto Verde: Substitute ½ cup sliced green onions for chopped onion; cook ¼ cup chopped celery with onion. Add 2 cups chopped fresh spinach with broth. Makes about 3½ cups.

Pallottoline in Brodo

What makes this soup unusual is that the meatballs are actually poached in the tasty soup base. It's a different way to begin a meal. And the flavor is sure to produce raves from your guests.

2 cans (10½ ounces each)	condensed chicken with rice soup
1½ soup cans	water
⅓ cup	chopped onion
¼ cup	chopped carrot
¼ cup	chopped celery
1 large	clove garlic, minced
2 tablespoons	chopped parsley
½ teaspoon	salt
½ pound	lean ground beef (twice ground)
3 tablespoons	grated Parmesan cheese
2 tablespoons	fine dry bread crumbs
1	egg, slightly beaten
⅛ teaspoon	pepper
2 to 3 tablespoons	flour
1 cup	chopped fresh tomatoes

In large saucepan, combine soup, water, onion, carrot, celery, garlic, parsley and salt. Bring to boil; reduce heat. Simmer 10 minutes; stir occasionally. Meanwhile, in bowl, combine beef, Parmesan cheese, bread crumbs, egg and pepper. Shape into 48 small meatballs. Dust meatballs with flour. Add meatballs and tomatoes to simmering soup. Simmer 10 minutes more or until done. Makes about 6½ cups.

Menu:
*Pallottoline in Brodo
Stuffed Zucchini
Asparagus Vinaigrette
Strawberries in Wine

Antipasto

A tangy salad dressing made in minutes is a delicious way to spotlight this crunchy vegetable salad. Almost any fresh vegetable will take on a new taste when tossed with this dressing.

1 can (10¾ ounces)	condensed tomato soup
½ cup	salad oil
½ cup	wine vinegar
1 package (0.6 ounce)	mild Italian salad dressing mix
2 cups	diagonally sliced carrots
2 cups	small cauliflowerets
2 cups	cubed zucchini squash
1 cup	small fresh mushroom caps
½ cup	pimiento-stuffed olives
1 medium	green pepper, cut in strips
½ cup	sliced pepperoni

To make marinade, in saucepan, combine soup, oil, vinegar and salad dressing mix; bring to boil. Reduce heat; simmer 5 minutes. Stir occasionally. In shallow dish, arrange vegetables and pepperoni. Pour marinade over vegetable mixture. Chill 6 hours or more; stir occasionally. Serve with slotted spoon. Makes about 8 cups.

Lasagna Verdi

Don't just think of lasagne as noodles with meat sauce and cheese. The Italians have many inventive ways with these large flat noodles. The spinach filling adds richness to this dish and if you make it ahead, it will taste even better the next day.

½ cup	chopped onion
2 tablespoons	butter or margarine
⅓ cup	Chablis or other dry white wine
1 can (10½ ounces)	condensed cream of chicken soup
2 packages (10 ounces each)	frozen chopped spinach, cooked and well drained
1 cup	grated Parmesan cheese
1	egg, slightly beaten
1 large	clove garlic, minced
¼ teaspoon	Italian seasoning, crushed
2 tablespoons	salad oil
1 can (10¾ ounces)	condensed tomato soup
½ cup	water
12	lasagna noodles, cooked and drained

To make filling, in saucepan, cook onion in butter until tender. Add wine; simmer a few minutes. Blend in chicken soup, spinach, Parmesan cheese and egg. To make sauce, in saucepan, cook garlic and Italian seasoning in oil. Add remaining ingredients except noodles. Simmer 30 minutes. In 2-quart shallow baking dish (12 × 8 × 2″), pour ½ sauce; top with 4 noodles. Spread with ½ of filling; top with 4 more noodles. Spread with remaining filling; top with remaining noodles and sauce. Bake at 350°F. for 45 minutes or until hot. Let stand 15 minutes before serving. Makes 6 servings.

Gnocchi

The word gnocchi means lumps in Italian, but that says nothing about the delicate flavor of these tender, little dumplings. They should be cooked soon after preparing. They may be served as is or with your favorite tomato sauce.

1 can (10¾ ounces)	condensed chicken broth
¾ cup	milk
⅛ teaspoon	ground nutmeg
⅔ cup	cream of wheat
1 cup	freshly grated Romano cheese
2	eggs, slightly beaten
4	tablespoons butter or margarine

To make gnocchi, in saucepan, combine broth, milk and nutmeg; bring to boil. Gradually add cereal, stirring constantly; reduce heat. Cook mixture over low heat 10 minutes or until *very* thick; stir often. Add ½ cup cheese, eggs and 1 tablespoon butter, stirring vigorously until well blended. Spread in buttered 2-quart shallow baking dish (12 × 8 × 2″) or spread ½-inch thick on buttered cookie sheet; chill 1 hour or more. Cut into 2 -inch circles, dipping cutter into cold water. In buttered 10″ pie plate, arrange circles, overlapping slightly. Melt remaining butter; pour over gnocchi. Sprinkle with remaining cheese. Broil 4 inches from heat 5 minutes or until lightly browned. Makes 6 servings.

Osso Buco

*Slow-simmered veal shanks make an incredible stew. The
creamy sauce has just the slightest hint of garlic and lemon,
which is typical of the way Osso Buco is prepared in the vicinity
of Milan.*

2 tablespoons	flour
¼ teaspoon	pepper
4	veal shank cross cuts (about ¾ pound each)
¼ cup	butter or margarine
1 can (10¾ ounces)	condensed creamy chicken mushroom soup
1 cup	Chablis or other dry white wine
1 medium	clove garlic, minced
1 tablespoon	chopped parsley
½ teaspoon	grated lemon rind

Combine flour and pepper; dust shanks with flour mixture (if
skin is broken tie string around shanks before flouring). In
skillet, brown shanks in butter; add soup, wine and garlic.
Cover; cook over low heat 2 hours 30 minutes or until done.
Stir occasionally. Add parsley and lemon; cook 5 minutes
more. Serve on cooked rice. Makes 4 servings.

Menu:
*Osso Buco
*Risotto Alla Milanese
Spinach Salad with Toasted Almonds
Ricotta Cheesecake

Minestrone

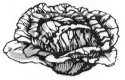

Plan a simple meal around this hot and hearty soup. It is perfect for a cold, wintery day when stick-to-your ribs food is needed. Serve in large bowls or mugs with additional Parmesan cheese.

3 slices	bacon, finely chopped
1 cup	chopped onion
½ cup	chopped celery
2 large	cloves garlic, minced
1 teaspoon	basil leaves, crushed
1 can (10½ ounces)	condensed beef broth
1 can (11½ ounces)	condensed bean with bacon soup
1½ soup cans	water
1 can (about 16 ounces)	tomatoes, undrained
½ cup	uncooked ditalini (small tube macaroni)
½ teaspoon	salt
1 cup	cabbage cut in long thin shreds
1 cup	cubed zucchini squash

In large saucepan, brown bacon and cook onion and celery with garlic and basil until tender. Stir in soups, water, tomatoes, ditalini and salt. Bring to boil; reduce heat. Cover; simmer 15 minutes. Add cabbage and zucchini; cook 10 minutes more or until done. Stir occasionally. Makes about 8 cups.

Menu:

*Minestrone
Garlic Bread
Romaine Salad with Mushrooms
Assorted Italian Ices

Cannelloni

It takes a bit of effort to make this dish, but the flavor is more than worth it. Half the fun is being able to say that you did it yourself. Cannelloni can be made ahead and frozen if covered properly up to 3 months. Thaw in refrigerator before baking.

1½ cups	flour
1½ teaspoons	salt
5	eggs, slightly beaten
1 tablespoon	salad oil
½ cup	chopped onion
1 medium	clove garlic, minced
½ teaspoon	basil leaves, crushed
2 tablespoons	butter or margarine
2 cans	tomatoes, chopped
(about 16 ounces each)	
1 can (11 ounces)	condensed Cheddar cheese soup
½ cup	milk
½ cup	grated Parmesan cheese
1½ cups	Ricotta cheese
¼ cup	chopped prosciutto (Italian ham) or boiled ham
¼ cup	chopped hard salami

To make pasta, in bowl, combine flour and salt; add 3 eggs and oil. Mix with fork to form a firm dough. On lightly floured board, knead until smooth (about 5 minutes). Cover; let rest 5 minutes. Roll dough into rectangle (12 × 18″). Cut into 18 rectangles (4 × 3″). Cover; let rest 1 hour. In large heavy pan of boiling salted water, cook, a few at a time, 5 minutes or until tender. Rinse in cold water; drain on damp towel. Meanwhile, to make sauce, in saucepan, cook onion with garlic and basil in butter until tender; add tomatoes. Bring to boil; reduce heat. Simmer 30 minutes; stir occasionally. In bottom of 3-quart shallow baking dish (13 × 9 × 2″), pour 1 cup sauce. To make filling, in bowl, combine soup, milk and Parmesan cheese. In saucepan, combine ½ cup soup mixture and remaining ingredients. Cook, stirring until thickened. To make cannelloni, spoon about 2 tablespoons filling on narrow end of each piece of pasta; roll up. Place seam-side down in baking dish. Spoon remaining soup mixture and sauce over cannelloni. Bake at 350°F. for 30 to 35 minutes or until hot. Serve with additional Parmesan cheese. Makes 6 servings.

Menu:
*Cannelloni
Mixed Green Salad with Garlic-Cheese Dressing
Bread Sticks
Bisque Tortoni

Mexico

Arroz con Pollo

Mexican food is bursting with color, flavor and excitement. Toss away any notions you might now have that it's all *tortillas* and *chiles*, because it is so much more than that.

Mexican cooking is an ancient but very much alive cuisine, deeply rooted in the time-honored traditions of the Mayan and Aztec civilizations, which flourished as far back as 900 A.D. No one is quite sure when Quetzalcoatl, the great corn god, brought his staff of life to the Indians, but his gift played an important part in the development of the rich and varied cooking that Mexicans do today.

Quetzalcoatl's dried corn is still softened in slaked lime and water and then ground into a pliable dough or *masa*, in the same way the earliest Mexicans did. Small lumps of this *masa* are patted into flat, thin pancakes and cooked quickly on a cast-iron griddle, called a *comal*—the results are *tortillas*, the "bread" of Mexico. They are used at just about every meal and appear in a variety of ways—plain, buttered, rolled, folded, soft-fried or crisp-fried. *Tortillas*, when shaped and cooked according to tradition, become the basis for the Mexican equivalent of a sandwich—*tacos*, *enchiladas*, *tostadas*, *flautas* and *quesadillas*.

The diet of the Aztecs and Mayans was interesting because of the abundance of a variety of foods to which they had access from the forests and waters that surrounded them. Their menus included wild game and turkey, fish of all types, wild pig, a myriad of luscious tropical vegetables and fruits, beans, and, of course, *chiles*.

In the 16th century, Hernando Cortés and a band of soldiers changed all that by marching into what is now Mexico City. For their part, the Spanish contributed sugar, onions, garlic, wheat flour, peaches, apricots, cinnamon, cloves, chicken and livestock to the Indians' diet. Before the arrival of the Spanish, everything was grilled or boiled over an open fire. From then on, most foods were fried, as they are today, due to Spanish use of lard and oil.

The nuns who later followed the Conquistadores in an effort to bring religion to the "natives" brought with them favorite recipes from their homeland, such as *paella, arroz con pollo* (seasoned chicken and rice) and *flan* (a light caramel custard)—today considered national dishes of Mexico!

Three centuries later, during the short reign of Maximillan in the 1860's when Napoleon tried to establish himself as ruler of Mexico, local cooks were introduced to many French and Austrian dishes. They were adapted according to what was available in the country, but Mexican cooking still remained very much the earthy vibrant cuisine that the Indians enjoyed.

Mexican cuisine is good fresh food with a spicy twist. Tomatoes, sweet and red, or tangy and green (known as *tomatillos*)—provide much of the color of the dishes. *Chiles*, ranging from mild to eyewatering, come in some 60 varieties and provide the zip for many dishes. Together, tomatoes and *chiles* make another Mexican specialty—*salsa* or sauce.

Salsa is basically uncooked piquant condiment sauces that are used on the table, as salt and pepper are in the United States. There's hardly a Mexican dish that doesn't require *salsa* in some form to enliven its taste.

Avocadoes are also an important addition to recipes, either sliced as a garnish or seasoned and crushed as *guacamole*.

One cannot forget the long list of exotic fruits and vegetables that play a large role in Mexican cuisine. Many are old favorites, such as pineapples, coconuts, mangos, pomegranates and papayas.

Beans or *frijoles* are a familiar item on Mexican shopping lists. In colors that range from pale pink (pinto) to black (turtle), they are considered indispensable by Mexican cooks. Beans are either cooked and served as a separate menu item, or are mashed and fried and become *frijoles refritos*, or refried beans.

And where would the Mexicans be without chocolate? In Montezuma's day, cocoa beans were used as currency, and the beverage made from these beans was thought to be fit for royalty or those of noble birth. It is, of course, the basis for a favorite beverage—hot *chocolate con leche*. Chocolate is found in many desserts, in *atole*, the thick cornmeal drink, and in a very special recipe—*mole poblano*, a national feast dish.

Mexico is a vast country with almost 5,000 miles of coastline. A series of rugged mountain ranges run down the middle of the country like a spine. The topography ranges from dry arid land near the Texas border, to grasslands along the coastline, to tropical rain forests in the Yucatán Peninsula.

The regional differences in cooking reflect the differences in climate and geography. The arid northern states are not corn country, but wheat and cattle country, so beef is used here frequently in many dishes. *Tortillas* are made with wheat rather than corn flour or *harina de maíz*. *Burritos*, flour *tortillas* with a beef and/or bean filling, is a popular menu item. Sonora and Chihuahua are also cheese-making areas. Here, too, *caldo de queso* (cheese soup) and *queso flameado*, the Mexican version of cheese fondue, are served with flour *tortillas* and *salsa cruda*, an uncooked, piquant sauce.

Along the coastline of the Gulf of Mexico and in Veracruz, fish *(pescado)* and shellfish *(mariscos)* are staple items. Veracruz is known for its *jaibas rellenas* (stuffed crabs) and *huachinango a la veracruzana* (a tasty red snapper served with a potent tomato, olive and chile *salsa*).

On the Pacific coast lies Jalisco, where one of the largest lakes is located. *Caldo miche* (a freshwater fish and vegetable soup) is a local favorite. Jalisco is the home of the city of Guadalajara and the world-famous *tequila* made from the fermented liquid of the agave plant. Throughout Mexico it is enjoyed straight, with a piece of lime and some salt, as a *cóctel*.

Further south is the state of Oaxaca, where *guisado*, a meat soup-stew is popular. Here *tamales*, a *masa*-covered meat, vegetable or sweet dish, are wrapped in banana leaves instead of the more traditional dried corn husks. Another dish of the area is *quesadillas*, turnovers made by stuffing unbaked *tortillas* with a filling, pinching the edges together and frying until golden. The favorite stuffing in Oaxaca is a delicious mixture of squash blossoms, grated cheese and the indispensable *chiles*.

To the southeast is the humid Yucatán Peninsula, another seafood area. *Pescado en Tikin Xik* is a Campeche specialty; it's fish (usually grouper or red snapper) seasoned with *achiote* paste and charcoaled. *Panuchos*, small puffed *tortillas* stuffed with mashed beans or chopped meat, are delicious snacks from this area. *Sierra en escabeche* (pickled fish), a typical dish of Mexico, is a favorite of the Yucatán; it's marinated or "cooked" in lime juice and then crushed spices are added.

One thing all Mexicans share in common is a pattern of eating, which is quite different from ours. The timing is undoubtedly derived from Spanish customs as well as the timetable in a basically agricultural economy.

162

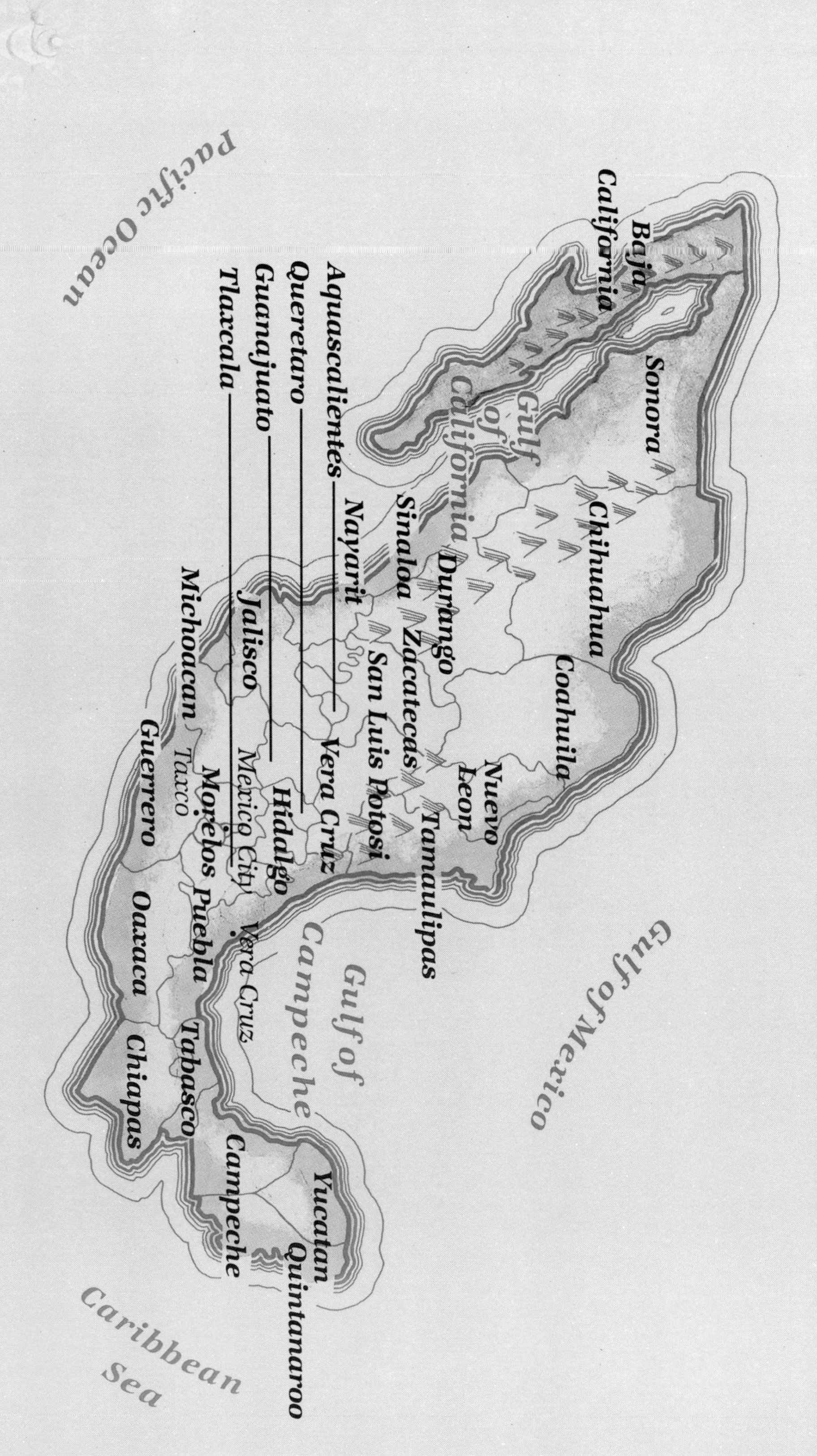

Pacific Ocean

Baja California

Sonora

Gulf of California

Chihuahua

Coahuila

Nuevo Leon

Aguascalientes

Queretaro

Guanajuato

Tlaxcala

Nayarit

Sinaloa

Durango

Zacatecas

San Luis Potosi

Tamaulipas

Michoacan

Jalisco

Vera Cruz

Hidalgo

Mexico City

Taxco

Morelos

Puebla

Vera Cruz

Guerrero

Oaxaca

Tabasco

Campeche

Gulf of Campeche

Yucatan

Quintanaroo

Gulf of Mexico

Caribbean Sea

Desayuno, or breakfast, begins very early at about 6:00 a.m. and is served continental style with *café con leche* (coffee with milk) and a sweet roll. *Almuerzo,* a second heartier breakfast of fruit or juice, an egg dish such as *huevos rancheros* (fried eggs served on *tortillas* with *salsa cruda*) or a *tortilla española,* may be served with *tortillas* or *bolillos* (hard rolls) and another cup of *café con leche.* In the city, this is often reserved for weekends since urban Mexicans work on a business schedule that is different from farm or rural living.

The main meal, however—the *comida*—is still eaten in the middle of the day at around 2:00 p.m. and may continue for several hours. It includes two soup courses—a wet soup followed by a dry soup or *sopa seca.* This is actually not a soup course at all, but a separate course of rice, noodles, *tortillas* or even pasta served as the Italians do in a fairly small quantity. Then comes the main course, which might be a meat, fish or chicken dish with beans, a green salad (almost always in the shredded lettuce form rather than in leaves) or a vegetable. There is not a great emphasis on serving vegetables as a side dish because they play such an important role as ingredients throughout the meal.

Tortillas and *bolillos* as well as some sort of *salsa* are mandatory accompaniments. Fresh fruit would cap off the meal; the fancier desserts such as *flan* would be saved for Sunday or some special occasion. Coffee is served after the meal and not with dessert. After all that food, it's time for a *siesta.*

The next meal is scheduled in the early evening and is called *merienda.* It's a light meal—almost a high tea—which might include sweet breads such as *sopaipillas* (fried biscuit puffs) or *buñuelos* (fried sweet *tortillas*) and *chocolate con leche* or *atole.*

The custom in the past has been to have dinner or *cena* later at around 10:00 p.m., which is the traditional Spanish hour of dining. This pattern, however, is slowly changing, and *cena* and *merienda* are merging into one meal.

Glossary*

Achiote (ah-CHYOH-teh)—dried seed from a tropical tree, crushed and used for seasoning and coloring; also known as annato seed.

Almuerzo (ahl-MWEHR-soh)—late breakfast or brunch.

Antojitos (ahn-toh-HEE-tohss)—appetizers or snacks.

Arroz con pollo (ah-RROHSS kohn POH-yoh)—seasoned chicken and rice.

Atole (ah-TOH-leh)—a thick cornmeal drink flavored with chocolate or fruit.

Bolillos (boh-LEE-yohss)—hard rolls.

Buñuelos (boo-NWEH-lohss)—fried sweet *tortillas*.

Burrito (boo-RREE-toh)—wheat flour *tortilla* wrapped around a filling.

Café con leche (kah-FEH kohn LEH-cheh)—coffee with milk.

Caldo (KAHL-doh)—broth or clear liquid soup.

Cena (SEH-nah)—late supper.

Chayote (cha-YOH-teh)—pale green, papaya-shaped vegetable belonging to the gourd family.

Chiles (CHEE-lehss)—chili peppers.

Chocolate con leche (choh-koh-LAH-teh kohn LEH-cheh)—hot chocolate with milk.

Chocolate mexicano (choh-koh-LAH-teh meh-hee-KAH-noh)—granular bars of sweet chocolate flavored with almonds and cinnamon.

Cilantro (see-LAHN-troh)—fresh coriander leaves; popular spice.

Cóctel (KOHK-tehl)—cocktail.

Comida (koh-MEE-thah)—main meal of the day, usually eaten at around 2:00 p.m.

Desayuno (deh-sah-YOO-noh)—light breakfast, eaten early in the morning.

Empanaditas (ehm-pah-nah-THEE-tahss)—little turnovers.

Enchilada (ehn-chee-LAH-thah)—corn *tortilla* dipped in sauce, fried and then wrapped around a filling and baked with *chile* sauce.

Epazote (eh-pah-SOH-teh)—strong-flavored herb used in bean and *tortilla* dishes.

Flan (FLAHN)—a light caramel custard.

Flautas (FLAHOO-tahss)—two or more overlapping corn *tortillas* stuffed and rolled to form a long tube.

Gorditas (gohr-THEE-tahss)—little fried *masa* snacks.

Guisado (ghee-SAH-thoh)—stew.

Huevos rancheros (WEH-vohss rrahn-CHEH-rohss)—fried eggs served on *tortillas* with *salsa cruda*.

Jaibas rellenas (HAH-ee-vahss rreh-YEH-nahss)—stuffed crabs.

Mariscos (mah-REE-skohss)—shellfish.

Masa (MAH-sah)—dough from ground corn used to make *tortillas* and *tamales*.

Merienda (meh-RYEHN-dah)—snack or light supper eaten in the early evening.

Metate (meh-TAH-teh)—oblong pitted stone mortar used to grind corn to make *masa*.

Mole (MOH-leh)—sauce cooked with chili peppers, spices and sometimes chocolate.

Nachos (NAH-chohss)—appetizer made of *tortilla* chips, *chiles* and melted cheese.

Nopal (noh-PAHL)—edible pad of the prickly-pear cactus; used in soups, salads and vegetables.

Paella (pah-EH-yah)—a saffron-flavored stew of chicken, seafood, various vegetables and rice.

Panuchos (pah-NOO-chohss)—small puffed *tortillas* stuffed with mashed beans or chopped meat.

Pepitas (peh-PEE-tahss)—seeds; pumpkin seeds, usually toasted in oil and salted or ground and used as thickening as well as flavoring.

Pescado (pehss-KAH-thoh)—fish.

Pescado en Tikin Xik (pehss-KAH-thoh ehn tee-keen HEEK)—fish (usually grouper or snapper) seasoned with *achiote* paste and charcoaled.

Picadillo (pee-kah-THEE-yoh)—a tangy Mexican hash.

Piloncillo (pee-lohn-SEE-yoh)—brown, unrefined sugar shaped into little flat-topped cones.

Postre (POHSS-treh)—dessert.

Postre de virrey (POHSS-treh deh bee-RREH)—a Mexican version of trifle.

Quesadilla (keh-sah-THEE-yah)—*tortilla* turnover filled with cheese and *chiles* and usually fried.

Ranchero (rrahn-CHEH-roh)—"of the ranch"; means country-style.

Relleno (rreh-YEH-noh)—a filling.

Salsa cruda (SAHL-sah KROO-thah)—an uncooked, piquant sauce.

Sierra en escabeche (SYEH-rrah ehn ehss-kah-VEH-cheh)—pickled fish.

Sopas (SOH-pahss)—dish consisting of pieces of bread soaked in liquid.

Sopa de fideos (SOH-pah deh fee-THEH-ohss)—thin spaghetti soup.

Sopaipillas (soh-pah-ee-PEE-yahss)—fried biscuit puffs.

Sopa seca (SOH-pah SEH-kah)—"dry soup"; a casserole of rice, noodles, *tortillas* or even pasta served as a separate course at *comida*.

Taco (TAH-koh)—corn *tortilla* wrapped or folded around filling of meat, chicken or refried beans; may be crisp-fried or soft.

Tamale (tah-MAH-leh)—*masa* dough rolled around a chili-flavored meat, vegetable or sweet filling, then wrapped in dried corn husks and steamed.

Tomatillos (toh-mah-TEE-yohss)—sweet green tomatoes about the size of small plums with thin, papery skins which are easily peeled; very different flavor from regular red tomatoes.

Tortilla (tohr-TEE-yah)—thin pancake made of *masa* or wheat flour; also an omelet.

Tortilla española (tohr-TEE-yah ehss-pah-NYOH-lah)—a flat omelet made with potatoes and onions.

Tostada (tohss-TAH-thah)—flat crisp-fried *tortilla* topped with meat, cheese and other fillings; like an open-faced sandwich on a fried *tortilla*.

*The Latin American pronunciations have been given here.

Ensalada de Carnes

Estofado de Res

Seviche

Garbanzos con Pimientos

Tacos de Carne Picada

Enchiladas de Pollo

These enchiladas can be made in three easy steps. While the sauce is simmering, prepare the filling. Leftover turkey is a good substitute if you don't have chicken on hand.

½ cup	chopped onion
¼ cup	chopped green pepper
2 tablespoons	butter or margarine
1 can (11 ounces)	condensed tomato bisque soup
¼ cup	water
1 package (1.1 ounces)	taco seasoning mix
¼ cup	sliced pitted ripe olives
2 tablespoons	chopped green chilies
2 teaspoons	vinegar
2 cups	diced cooked chicken
10	tortillas
Garnishes:	Shredded Cheddar cheese, shredded lettuce, chopped tomato and chopped onion

To make sauce, in saucepan, cook onion and green pepper in butter until tender; add soup, water, taco seasoning, olives, chilies and vinegar. To make filling, in bowl, combine ½ cup sauce and chicken. Meanwhile, in skillet, cook one tortilla at a time in hot oil for an instant until pliable; remove. To make enchiladas, place about 2 tablespoons filling near center of each tortilla; roll up. In 1½-quart shallow baking dish (10×6×2″), arrange enchiladas seam-side down; pour remaining sauce over all. Cover; bake at 400°F. for 20 minutes or until hot. Garnish with remaining ingredients. Makes 5 servings.

Ensalada de Carnes

Leftover meats take on a new taste and look in this imaginative salad. Cut meat into thin strips and then marinate until serving time. It is a delicious alternative to chef's salad.

1 can (10¾ ounces)	condensed chicken broth
½ cup	salad oil
⅓ cup	vinegar
½ teaspoon	sugar
1 teaspoon	marjoram leaves, crushed
½ teaspoon	oregano leaves, crushed
½ teaspoon	thyme leaves, crushed
Generous dash	cayenne pepper
1½ cups	cooked beef cut in strips
1 cup	cooked chicken cut in strips
1 cup	cooked ham cut in strips
1 medium	green pepper, cut in strips
1 medium	red pepper, cut in strips
1 cup	thinly sliced onion
¼ cup	thinly sliced pimiento-stuffed olives

To make marinade, in saucepan, combine broth, oil, vinegar, sugar and seasonings. Heat; stir occasionally. Meanwhile, arrange remaining ingredients in shallow dish; pour marinade over all. Cover; chill 6 hours or more. Stir occasionally. Serve with slotted spoon on salad greens. Makes about 7 cups.

Menu:
Black Bean Soup
*Ensalada de Carnes
Green Onions, Radishes, Pickled Mild Chilies
Crusty Hard Rolls
Baked Pineapple with Sherry

Arroz con Pollo

This colorful chicken dish is a combination of tomatoes, rice, peas and pimientos. After browning the meat, all the ingredients simmer until the chicken is tender.

2 pounds	chicken parts
2 tablespoons	salad oil
1 can (10¾ ounces)	condensed tomato soup
1 cup	water
½ cup	chopped onion
½ teaspoon	vinegar
2 medium	cloves garlic, minced
1 teaspoon	salt
¼ teaspoon	pepper
¼ teaspoon	ground cumin seed
¼ teaspoon	crushed saffron or ground turmeric
1 cup	raw regular rice
1 cup	frozen peas
¼ cup	diced pimiento

In skillet, brown chicken in oil; pour off fat. Add soup, water, onion, vinegar, garlic and seasonings. Cover; cook over low heat 15 minutes. Add rice; cook 20 minutes. Add peas and pimiento; cook 10 minutes more or until done. Stir occasionally. Makes 4 servings.

Garbanzos con Pimientos

Garbanzos or chick peas are a favorite bean of the Mexicans. This dish is easy-to-prepare and is a flavorful idea that was borrowed from the early Spanish colonists.

1 pound	hot Italian sausage, cut in 1-inch pieces
½ cup	chopped onion
1 large	clove garlic, minced
¼ teaspoon	oregano leaves, crushed
2 tablespoons	salad oil
1 can (10¾ ounces)	condensed bean with bacon soup
1 cup	water
1 can (about 20 ounces)	chick peas, drained
¼ cup	pimiento strips
Generous dash	pepper
2 tablespoons	chopped parsley

In skillet, brown sausage and cook onion with garlic and oregano in oil until tender. Add soup, water, chick peas, pimiento and pepper. Cover; cook over low heat 20 minutes or until done. Stir occasionally; add parsley. Makes about 5 cups.

Chile con Carne

In Mexico, chili is prepared with tiny chunks of beef instead of ground beef. A rich and spicy tomato sauce cooks with the meat until it is tender and the flavors are developed. If any chili is leftover, it freezes well if tightly covered.

1½ pounds	boneless chuck roast, cut in ½-inch cubes
2 tablespoons	salad oil
1 can (10¾ ounces)	condensed tomato soup
½ soup can	water
1 can (about 15 ounces)	pinto beans, undrained
1 cup	chopped onion
2 large	bay leaves, crushed
1 large	clove garlic, minced
2 tablespoons	tomato and Jalapeño peppers
1 tablespoon	ground cumin seed
1 tablespoon	oregano leaves, crushed
1 tablespoon	paprika
¼ teaspoon	salt
⅛ teaspoon	crushed red pepper

In large saucepan, brown beef in oil. Stir in remaining ingredients. Cover; cook over low heat 1 hour 30 minutes or until done. Stir occasionally. Serve over rice. Makes 5 cups.

Menu:
*Chile con Carne
Cornbread Squares
Red and Green Pepper Salad
Banana Ice Cream

Pollo con Naranjas

This delicately-scented chicken dish is a classic from east-central Mexico. It is colorful with oranges, nuts and raisins; and it tastes as good as it looks.

2 pounds	chicken parts
2 tablespoons	salad oil
1 can (10¾ ounces)	condensed cream of chicken soup
¾ cup	orange juice
1 cup	sliced onion
2 tablespoons	slivered almonds
2 tablespoons	raisins
2 medium	cloves garlic, minced
⅛ teaspoon	ground cinnamon
⅛ teaspoon	ground cloves
Generous dash	crushed saffron or ground turmeric

In skillet, brown chicken in oil; pour off fat. Stir in remaining ingredients. Cover; cook over low heat 45 minutes or until done. Stir occasionally. Garnish with orange slices. Makes 4 servings.

Menu:
Guacamole Dip
*Pollo con Naranjas
Kidney Bean Salad
Fried Sweet Puffs

Ensalada de Camarón

This typical seafood salad has a variety of interesting textures—chopped shrimp, celery, cucumber and eggs. The creamy salad dressing has just a hint of chili. The longer the ingredients marinate, the better the flavor.

1 can (10¾ ounces)	condensed cream of potato soup
⅓ cup	sour cream
½ teaspoon	chili powder
¼ teaspoon	salt
⅛ teaspoon	cayenne pepper
3 cups	cut-up cooked shrimp
1 cup	chopped celery
1 cup	diced cucumber
3	hard-cooked eggs, coarsely chopped

In bowl, combine soup, sour cream, chili powder, salt and cayenne. Add remaining ingredients; chill. Serve on salad greens. Makes about 5 cups.

Menu:
*Ensalada de Camarón
*Garbanzos con Pimientos
Steamed White Rice
Papaya with Lime Wedges

Tacos de Carne Picada

Browned ground meat with chili powder and other seasonings makes a spicy filling for tacos as well as enchiladas or tostadas. Set filling and condiments in bowls and let everyone assemble their own taco.

1 pound	ground beef
½ cup	chopped onion
2 teaspoons	chili powder
1 teaspoon	oregano leaves, crushed
1 large	clove garlic, minced
1 can (11¼ ounces)	condensed chili beef soup
¼ cup	water
Generous dash	cayenne pepper
12	taco shells
Garnishes:	Shredded Cheddar cheese, shredded lettuce, chopped onion and diced tomato

In saucepan, brown beef and cook onion with chili powder, oregano and garlic until tender. Add soup, water and cayenne. Cook over low heat 5 minutes; stir occasionally. Fill each taco shell with about ¼ cup meat mixture; top with remaining ingredients. Makes 12 tacos.

Picadillo

Picadillo is a Mexican version of hash except there are some surprise ingredients—apples, raisins and almonds. This makes a pleasant filling for enchiladas or tacos.

1 pound	ground beef
½ cup	chopped onion
1 large	clove garlic, minced
1 can (10¾ ounces)	condensed tomato soup
⅓ cup	water
1 cup	chopped apple
½ cup	raisins
¼ cup	toasted sliced almonds
1 tablespoon	vinegar
¼ teaspoon	ground cinnamon
¼ teaspoon	ground cumin seed

In skillet, brown beef and cook onion with garlic until tender. Stir to separate meat; pour off fat. Add soup and remaining ingredients. Cover; cook over low heat 25 minutes or until done. Stir occasionally. Serve over rice. Makes about 4 cups.

Menu:
Corn Chowder
*Picadillo over Rice
Zucchini Salad
Fried Bananas

Seviche

Seviche is made from chunks of mild-flavored fish which are "cooked" by marinating them in lemon or lime juice. Then it is chilled in a piquant dressing. The fish looks as though it had been poached.

1 pound	fillets of white fish, cut in 1-inch pieces
½ cup	fresh lemon juice
1 can (10¾ ounces)	condensed chicken broth
1 cup	cherry tomatoes cut in half
1 can (4 ounces)	whole roasted green chilies, drained and cut in strips
¼ cup	salad oil
1 tablespoon	Chablis or other dry white wine
1 teaspoon	ground coriander seed
1 teaspoon	oregano leaves, crushed
½ teaspoon	basil leaves, crushed
¼ teaspoon	salt
⅛ teaspoon	pepper

In shallow dish, arrange fish; pour lemon juice over all. Chill 2 hours; stir occasionally. Add broth, tomatoes, chilies, oil, wine and seasonings. Chill 4 hours or more; stir occasionally. Serve with sliced avocado. Makes about 3½ cups.

Menu:
*Seviche
*Arroz con Pollo
Olive and Orange Salad
Guava Shells and Cheese Squares

Estofado de Res

Not all Mexican food is tacos or enchiladas, but most is done on top of the stove. This stew can be partially prepared the night before. Add green peppers and tomatoes when ready to serve following the method given.

1½ pounds	beef cubes (1 inch)
2 tablespoons	salad oil
1 can (10¾ ounces)	condensed beefy mushroom soup*
1 can (10½ ounces)	condensed beef broth
1 cup	water
1 cup	chopped onion
½ teaspoon	marjoram leaves, crushed
½ teaspoon	oregano leaves, crushed
½ teaspoon	thyme leaves, crushed
¼ teaspoon	pepper
5 small	potatoes (about 1 pound), cut in half
2 large	green peppers, cut in strips
2 tablespoons	water
1 tablespoon	cornstarch
2 medium	tomatoes, cut in quarters

In large heavy pan, brown beef in oil. Add soup, broth, 1 cup water, onion and seasonings. Cover; cook over low heat 30 minutes. Add potatoes; cook 20 minutes. Add green peppers; cook 10 minutes more until done. Stir occasionally. Combine 2 tablespoons water and cornstarch; stir into sauce. Add tomatoes. Cook, stirring until thickened. Makes about 8 cups.

*1 can (10¾ ounces) condensed golden mushroom soup may be substituted for beefy mushroom soup.

Capirotada

Apples, cheese and raisins combine to make an unusual dessert. The thrifty Mexican housewife makes good use of her leftover breads. Serve warm and top with whipped cream or ice cream.

1 can (11 ounces)	condensed Cheddar cheese soup
1 cup	milk
½ cup	packed brown sugar
½ teaspoon	ground cinnamon
2 tablespoons	butter or margarine
6 cups	toasted bread cubes (about 9 slices)
½ cup	chopped almonds
½ cup	raisins
2 cups	sliced peeled apple
½ cup	shredded Monterey Jack or Cheddar cheese

In saucepan, combine soup, milk, brown sugar and cinnamon. Bring to boil; reduce heat. Simmer 2 minutes to blend flavors. Add butter, toast, almonds and raisins. Spoon half of soup mixture in bottom of 1½-quart casserole; top with apples and remaining toast mixture. Cover; bake at 350°F. for 25 minutes or until hot. Uncover; sprinkle with cheese. Bake 5 minutes more. Serve with whipped cream. Makes 6 servings.

Tamale Pie

Tamales are traditionally made with a zesty meat filling and a coating of masa dough. This recipe is less time-consuming than the original, but the flavor is much the same.

1 pound	ground beef
¼ pound	ground pork sausage
½ cup	chopped onion
1 can (10¾ ounces)	condensed tomato soup
½ cup	water
1 can (about 8 ounces)	whole kernel golden corn, undrained
⅓ cup	sliced pitted ripe olives
1 to 2 tablespoons	chili powder
1 tablespoon	chopped Jalapeño peppers
Generous dash	crushed red pepper
4 cups	water
1 cup	cornmeal
1 teaspoon	salt
1 cup	shredded sharp Cheddar cheese

In skillet, brown beef and cook sausage and onion until done. Stir to separate meat; pour off fat. Add soup, ½ cup water, corn, olives, chili powder, Jalapeño peppers and red pepper. Heat; stir occasionally. Meanwhile, bring 3 cups water to boil. Combine cornmeal, salt and 1 cup *cold* water; pour into boiling water, stirring constantly. Cook 5 minutes; stir often. Pour hot soup mixture into 2-quart shallow baking dish (12×8×2″); spread with cornmeal mixture. Bake at 350°F. for 15 minutes; sprinkle with cheese. Bake 15 minutes more. Spoon off fat before serving. Makes 6 servings.

Chalupas

Chalupas are made in Mexico from masa dough. This is an easier version made with regular pie crust. Turning up the edges form little boats, which is what chalupas means.

1 package (10 ounces)	pie crust mix
2 to 3 tablespoons	cornmeal
1½ pounds	ground beef
½ cup	chopped onion
2 cans (11¼ ounces each)	condensed chili beef soup
¼ cup	water
1½ cups	shredded lettuce
1 cup	shredded Cheddar cheese

Prepare pie crust mix as directed on package. Divide into 8 round patties; coat with cornmeal. Roll each into 6-inch circle, adding more cornmeal as needed. Place each circle on 6-inch square sheet of aluminum foil (double thickness or heavy duty). With aid of foil, turn up pastry to form a shell with a 1-inch stand-up rim. Prick pastry with fork. Bake on cookie sheet at 425°F. for 12 minutes or until done; remove foil. Meanwhile, in skillet, brown meat and cook onion until tender; stir to separate meat (use shortening if necessary). Pour off fat. Add soup and water. Heat; stir occasionally. Line each pastry shell with ¼ cup lettuce; top with meat mixture. Sprinkle with cheese. Makes 4 servings.

Menu:
*Chalupas
Hot Refried Beans
Sliced Tomatoes and Onions
Caramel Custard

Middle East

Shish Kebob

The cuisine of the Middle East is as exotic and colorful as the people themselves. It is indeed a traditional and deeply-rooted way of eating with recipes handed down from mother to daughter or daughter-in-law.

Some of the ingredients in this peasant cuisine date from civilizations that go back to earliest known history. The simple foods of the desert and oasis—lamb, milk turned into yogurt and dates—merge with what is available in the maze of food stalls or *souks* in the markets of towns and cities. Here are olives of brown, green, red and black, rice, dried beans of all colors and varieties, wheat, peppers, onions and garlic.

The results of this merging are creations that are as appealing to the eye as to the palate. Beautiful vegetables are hollowed out and filled with seasoned combinations of meat, rice, nuts and spices or leaves such as from the grapevine wrap around these tasty mixtures.

Generous hospitality is the most important phenomenon in the Near East and no one is ever turned away. Whether you stop for a visit in the morning or afternoon, a long-handled brass pot of fragrant coffee, a platter of sweets and a bowl of fruits such as quinces or pomegranates would appear.

An invitation for dinner is almost an embarrassment of one rich dish after another. These appear on a low round table after you partake of an elaborate hand-washing ceremony with water sometimes perfumed with rose or orange blossoms. Everyone then serves himself from cooking pots that double as serving platters and eats with the first three fingers of the right hand. Because forks and plates are not offered, flat rounds of *khoubz* or *pita* bread become important for grasping meat or vegetables or even sopping up some sauce.

But where did this custom of foods such as *shish kebob* or *couscous* or *moussaka* get their start? No one really knows. There are legends about ancient tribesmen from Turkey skewering their catch of game on their swords and grilling it over a fire. The word "shish" means sword or skewer; "kebob" means meat or more specifically, lamb.

Much of the food of this area comes from a culinary pool of foods common to the people from Athens to Teheran to Tangiers. These lands have been the crossroads of civilizations. The ancient Phoenicians and Greeks were responsible for providing a source of food and oil from the olive trees they planted in their colonies around the Mediterranean.

Later, the Arabs became traders, dealing in exotic spices from caravan trips to further eastern lands. Cardamom, cinnamon, cumin, coriander, ginger, anise, turmeric and saffron became an integral part of seasoning Middle Eastern foods. The Persians provided rice and luscious fruits such as melons, peaches and apricots to their diet.

In the 7th century, the Arabs in the name of Allah swept through the Near East and North Africa and introduced local specialties such as *burghul* or cracked wheat from Turkey and *couscous* from Morocco to other neighboring lands. They also brought citrus fruits with them along with their new religion.

Later during the 16th century, when this area was under Ottoman domination, the thin-flaky pastry known as *phyllo* as well as a new way of brewing coffee—sweetened and aromatic—that the Turks favored became popular. Today throughout the Middle East, this coffee is still called Turkish coffee, except in Greece. There it is called Greek coffee.

Each country, of course, has developed its own specialties from the range of products it has available. In some cases, the names are simply changed a little—such as the clarified butter from rich sheep or goat's milk. This is used to flavor the wheat and other grain dishes and is called *samneh* throughout the Middle East. It becomes *smen* in Morocco.

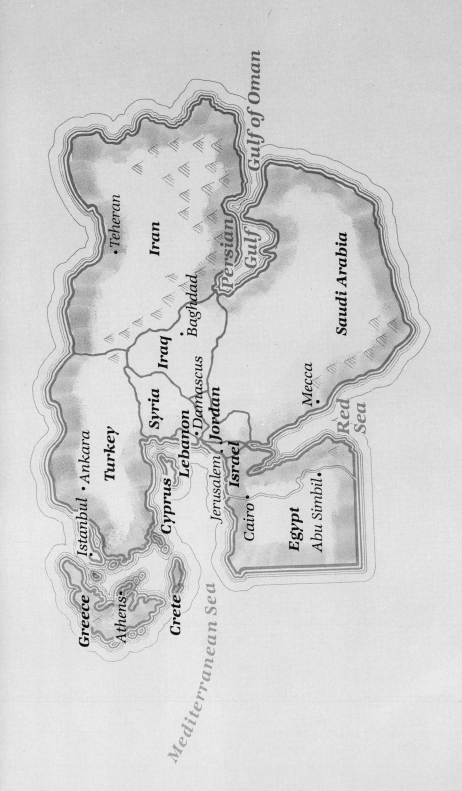

Greece
Athens·

Crete

Istanbul ·Ankara
Turkey

Cyprus

Lebanon
Jerusalem·Damascus
Israel· Jordan

Cairo·

Egypt
Abu Simbil·

Syria

Iraq
Baghdad
·

·Teheran

Iran

Persian Gulf

Gulf of Oman

Saudi Arabia

Mecca
·

Red Sea

Mediterranean Sea

Let's begin our cook's tour in Greece, which is part of Europe but has strong culinary strings to the Near East. The rugged mountainous terrain makes it an ideal place for raising sheep, which is quite naturally a favorite meat. Lemons, rice and eggplant were all borrowed from invaders, but what the Greeks do with them is all their own.

Here is the land of *moussaka,* that marvelous layered dish of eggplant, ground lamb seasoned with onions, oregano and cinnamon and then topped with an eggy white sauce and cheese. Slow-cooking stews known as *stefados* are a frequent menu item made from lamb or beef with tomatoes, onions and just a hint of cinnamon. The Greeks are also famous for their *avgolemono* sauce, an egg and lemon concoction used to flavor soups, chicken, fish or vegetables.

The real way to sample Greek food is to sit in a *taverna* or cafe where you would sip *ouzo* or a heady Greek wine and nibble on *mezedakia* (which translates loosely to mean "something to whet the appetite"). *Mezedakia* is called *meze* in the rest of the Near Eastern world. Munch on freshly roasted nuts, *feta* cheese, olives or miniature *phyllo*-covered savories filled with *feta* cheese, egg and dill *(tyropitta)* or spinach and *feta* cheese *(spanakopitta).*

The Greeks are said to have acquired *phyllo* dough from the Persians and it covers not only savory items such as those mentioned above but also sweet ones. *Galactoboureko,* a *phyllo* pastry filled with vanilla or orange-scented custard or *baklava,* layers of buttered *phyllo,* cinnamon, nuts and honey are irresistible to the Greek sweet tooth.

The Fertile Crescent, otherwise known as Lebanon, Syria and Iraq, is the ancient land of the prophets and patriarchs. Coffeehouses are the scene of *mezes.* Here you might find toasted pumpkin seeds, grilled bits of lamb liver, *sfeena* (tiny ground-meat pies) and *baba ghannouj,* a delicious eggplant dip flavored with *tahini,* garlic and lemon juice. This is served with *khoubz* or *pita* bread.

Soups in this land of "milk and honey" are really meals in themselves. *Kishik* soup is made from *leban* or yogurt, cracked wheat and spices; it's a cooling summer dish. A hearty winter warmer is *shouraba lubee,* created from dried beans, tomatoes, onion, garlic, rosemary and caraway seeds.

Salads are a popular way of serving vegetables and no meal is complete without them. *Salata kuthra* is a combination of tomatoes, peppers, radishes and onions with olives and yogurt, cheese or *lebanee*, tossed with lemon, olive oil and mint. No picnic in the Fertile Crescent would be complete without *tabooleh*, a summer salad of cracked wheat, mint, parsley, green onions and tomatoes. *Burghul* as bulgur or cracked wheat is known there, adds a crunchy texture and a nutty flavor to this salad.

The local favorite meat dish is *kibbi*, also known as the hamburger of the Middle East. Finely ground lamb is mixed with *burghul*, onions and spices; it is then served raw or baked in *samneh* butter.

Dried fruits play an important part in Near Eastern cooking. Near Damascus is an area called Goota where *qamardeen*, which is dried apricots pressed into thin cakes like a fruit jerky comes from. Another sweet treat is *halwa* or *halva* as it is known in Israel.

Nearby Israel is really a melting pot of cuisines. The country itself is a little over 20 years old so its food styles are still evolving from the mixture of primarily Eastern European and Middle Eastern immigrants.

Among the new foods introduced to Israel are avocados, which are enjoyed in a dip with Middle Eastern overtones of onions, garlic and lemon. A more purely native dish is *falafel*, a seasoned ground chick pea and *burghul* mixture that is deep-fried and served between pieces of split *khoubz* or *pita* bread.

The dietary regulations of the Orthodox Jews forbid the consumption of pork and shellfish as well as the mixing of meat and milk dishes. Jews are also prohibited from cooking on the Sabbath, so they created a dish which could be slowly simmered from the

night before. *Cholent* is a savory stew of dried beans or chick peas, barley or *burghul* with potatoes and beef. The addition of *burghul* and chick peas add a native Israeli taste.

Another traditional Jewish dish which has been retranslated is *tzimmes*. It's a sweet-sour stew made from beef, potatoes, turnips, carrots, dried prunes and apricots with honey and lemon juice. Desserts appear in a more familiar European form—such as honey cake or *ugah duvshan* but may have a hint of the Near East with rose-water flavoring.

Egypt is another country of the Bible. Its lentil soup, *shouraba il addis*, is probably not terribly different from the lentil potage for which Biblical Esau sold his birthright. Chick peas or *hummus* are supposedly a gift of the Phoenicians; they are a prime ingredient in a popular *mezes* called *hummus bi tahini*, a dip of garlic, lemon, onions and *tahini*.

Milookhiyya is the name of a green vegetable-herb and also the name of a soup. The leaf tastes much like spinach but has the thickening properties of okra, another popular vegetable. Egyptians enjoy *djeena*, a slow-cooking stew of beef, potatoes, onions, chick peas, garlic, spices and eggs hard-cooked in the shell.

Eggs are served hard-cooked as a snack, but a tasty Arab way to eat eggs is *eggah* (or *kuku* in Iran). It's a thick flat omelet cooked with vegetables, meat, chicken or noodles. It is cut into slices and served hot or cold.

Beans also play an important part in the Egyptian as well as Middle Eastern diet. *Fool misdammis* is a traditional brown bean dish which is frequently served with eggs hard-cooked in the bean liquid. Another interesting recipe is *famiya* or *fava* beans masked with garlic, onions, parsley, coriander and cayenne.

Iran, situated in a strategic position between the Fertile Crescent, Russia and Pakistan, has developed a piquant but not hot style of seasoning. Try for example, *eshkeneh Shirazi*, a refreshing combination of cold yogurt, cucumbers, raisins, dill and hard-cooked eggs. In a dish they call *fesenjan*, roast duck or chicken is simmered in a sauce with walnuts, pomegranate and cardamom; the result is a balance between sweet and sour.

Cooking rice is a fine art in Iran. It is served as *chelo*, a buttered and then steamed rice cooked separately from its stewy sauce, *khoresht*. Or as *polo*, which is buttered rice slowly cooked with other ingredients, which may range from meat to chicken, fruits to vegetables, nuts, herbs and spices. Carrots, nuts and raisins may appear in *polo*, or it may include spinach, cumin, coriander and garlic. The Iranians also combine meat and vegetables in stews, which they call *abgusht*.

On the other side of the Middle East, lies Morocco, where fruit and lamb also appear in *tagines*. They are prepared in *tagine slaoul*, an earthenware pot with a high conical top; this doubles as a serving platter. The Moroccans have invented some delicious soups; one of these is *harira*, a tasty combination of chick peas, vegetables, lemons, eggs and turmeric.

Spices play a crucial role in Moroccan cooking. *Mechoui*, the Berber version of roast lamb is rubbed with garlic and cumin. *Harissa*, a condiment-sauce, is made from crushed chili peppers,

garlic, caraway, coriander, cumin and oil. It is served with salads, mixed with cheese or thinned with more oil and served with kebobs or *couscous.*

Couscous has a double meaning; it is tiny pasta-like pellets made from the inner part of the wheat which is steamed. It is also the national dish of Morocco, which is a heady stew of chicken, vegetables and lamb. Another not-to-be missed specialty is *bisteeya,* a flaky pie filled with chicken, eggs and lemon in an onion sauce with toasted, sweetened almonds. The pastry is like *phyllo* but is called *warka.*

The foods of the Middle East are rich and varied, but the meal pattern follows a similar path. Following the Muslim tradition, breakfast, *fatour,* starts early at dawn. In many countries, it consists of coffee, olives, eggs scrambled with ground cumin, cheese and *khoubz* bread.

Lunch is the main meal of the day and is called *ghada.* It might include a few *meze* and then a hearty dish of *kibbi* or *shish kebob* or *tagine* with a vegetable salad and *khoubz* bread. Dessert may be fresh dates or sliced melon with cookies or a pastry and mint tea or turkish-style coffee. In the late afternoon, it is time to go to the coffeehouse and nibble on more pastries such as *baklava* between nips of strong coffee.

The third meal of the day is served at sundown, although Moroccans and Iranians like to eat later. This again would be a repeat of the lunchtime meal but simpler—perhaps a bowl of *harira* or *avgolemono* soup plus some bread and a salad of tomatoes and onions. When guests appear, however, the meal becomes a banquet with course after course served, until the guest finally waves his coffee cup from side to side, indicating that he cannot eat another thing.

Glossary

Abgusht (AHB-goosht)—an Iranian-style stew of meat and vegetables.

Arak (AH-rahk)—powerful anise-flavored aperitif; in Syria and Lebanon, it is made from grapes; in Egypt and Iraq, it is made often from dates. In Greece, it is called *ouzo* and is made from grain; in Turkey, it is known as *raki* and can be made from plums, grapes or grain.

Baba ghannouj (bah-bah gah-NOODGE)—an eggplant dip flavored with *tahini*, garlic and lemon juice.

Baklava (BAHK-lah-vah)—Greek sweet pastry made with layers of tissue-thin *phyllo* dough, sugar, cinnamon, chopped nuts and soaked in honey; also known as *baklawa* in Arabic.

Bisteeya (biss-TEE-yah)—pie filled with chicken, eggs and lemon in an onion sauce with toasted, sweetened almonds.

Borek (BOH-reck)—Turkish flaky pastry dish filled with seasoned meat or cheese.

Burghul (BOHR-goll)—cereal made from whole grains of wheat; known as bulgur in U.S. or cracked wheat.

Chelo (CHELL-oh)—Iranian buttered steamed rice, cooked separately from *Khoresht*, with which it is topped. Frequently served with raw egg yolk and *sumak*, which is mixed in before sauce is added.

Cholent (CHOH-lent)—a savory Israeli stew of dried beans or chick peas, barley or *burghul* with potatoes and beef.

Couscous (KUSH-kush)—pasta-like grains made from the inner part of the wheat; also, the national dish of Morocco, a stew of chicken, vegetables and lamb.

Djeena (d'JEE-nah)—an Egyptian stew of beef, potatoes, onions, chick peas, garlic, spices and hard-cooked eggs.

Dolma (DOHL-mah)—"to stuff"; highly seasoned filling of rice, grains and meats or vegetables in hollowed-out vegetables such as eggplant or tomatoes or wrapped in vine or cabbage leaves. Also known as *dolmeh* in Iran.

Eggah (EGG-ah)—thick Arab omelet, almost cake-like, with a variety of vegetables, meats, noodles or chicken. It is served flat and cut into slices. It is known in Iran as *kuku*.

Eshkeneh shirazi (ESH-keh-neh SHEE-rah-zee)—a combination of cold yogurt, cucumbers, raisins, dill and hard-cooked eggs.

Falafel (fah-la-FELL)—small deep-fried fritters of chick peas crushed with *burghul*; served on *pita* or *khoubz* bread.

Famiya (fah-MY-ah)—a type of bean similar to *fava*.

Fatour (fah-TOOR)—breakfast in Arabic countries.

Fesenjan (FESS-en-jahn)—Iranian roast duck or chicken in a sauce with walnuts, pomegranate and cardamom.

Feta (FAY-tah)—Greek firm white cheese made from goat or sheep's milk; has a pickled, salty taste.

Fool (FOOL)—*fava* or broad beans.

Fool misdammis (FOOL mees-DAH-miss)—traditional brown bean dish, often served with eggs hard-cooked in the bean liquid.

Galactoboureko (gah-lahk-toh-BOO-reh-koh)—a *phyllo* pastry filled with a vanilla or orange-scented custard.

Ghada (GAY-day)—lunch or main meal of the day in Arabic countries.

Halva (hahl-VAH)—candy-like dessert made from semolina, rice flour or farina; flavored with nuts, fruits, spices or flower petals. Also known as *halwa* in Arabic.

Harira (hah-REE-rah)—a Moroccan soup of chick peas, vegetables, lemons, eggs and turmeric.

Harissa (hah-REE-sah)—a condiment sauce made from crushed chili peppers, garlic, caraway, coriander, cumin and oil.

Hummus (HAWM-us)—chick peas.

Jezve (JEZ-veh)—long-handled brass coffee pot with narrow neck, used for making Turkish coffee.

Kefta (KEFF-tay)—finely ground and liberally spiced lamb or beef that is skewered and grilled; served with *pita* or *khoubz* bread.

Khoresht (KOH-resht)—stew-like sauce of meat and poultry with vegetables, fruits, nuts, herbs and spices served over *chelo* in Iran.

Kibbi (KEE-bih)—ground lamb and *burghul* with onion and spices; national dish of Syria and Lebanon; served raw or baked in butter.

Leban (LAY-bahn)—yogurt.

Lebanee (LAYB-nay)—a fresh-curd cheese, usually sprinkled with olive oil.

Matzoh (MAHT-so)—Israeli, crisp, flat unleavened bread.

Mechoui (me-KOO-ih)—Berber version of roast lamb rubbed with garlic and cumin.

Meshwi (MAYSH-wee)—grilled.

Meze (MAY-zay)—hors d'oeuvres or foods eaten as snack or with *arak*; also known as *mezedakia* in Greece.

Milookhiyya (mih-lowk-HEE-yah)—green-leaved vegetable used in soup; similar in taste to spinach with thickening powers of okra.

Moussaka (MOO-sah-kah)—Greek casserole with ground lamb, eggplant and onions baked in a sauce. A number of variations exist.

Orzo (OR-zoh)—Greek pasta that resembles grains of rice.

Ouzo (OO-zoh)—see *arak*.

Panir (pah-NEER)—hard, white goat's cheese of Iran.

Phyllo (FEE-loh)—tissue-thin sheets of flaky pastry, used for sweet desserts and as covering for meats, cheese and vegetable mixtures.

Pita (PEE-tah)—round, flat, slightly leavened bread with hollow pocket for a filling for beans, meats, cheese or salads. Also known as *khoubz* in Arabic countries.

Polo (POH-loh)—Iranian rice slowly cooked with fruits, meats, chicken and vegetables.

Qamardeen (kah-mahr-DEEN)—dried apricots pressed into thin cakes; also called *mishmish*.

Rose water—flavoring made from crushed rose petals; used to flavor desserts.

Salata kuthra (sah-LAH-tah kooth-RAH)—combination of tomatoes, peppers, radishes and onions with olives and yogurt, cheese or *lebanee*, tossed with lemon, olive oil and mint.

Samneh (SAHM-neh)—clarified butter made from sheep or goat's milk, similar to the Indian *ghee*. Known as *smen* in Morocco.

Sfeena (SFEE-nah)—small ground meat pies.

Shish kebob (SHEESH keh-bahb)—chunks of meat, usually lamb, broiled on skewers.

Shouraba lubee (SHOO-rah-bah LOOB-yay)—winter soup made from dried beans, tomatoes, onion, garlic, rosemary and caraway seeds.

Shouraba il addis (SHOOR-ah-bah ill AHD-iss)—lentil soup.

Souk (SOOK)—shop, store or stall where things are bought or sold in Middle Eastern bazaars.

Spanakopitta (SPAH-nah-koh-pee-tah)—*phyllo*-covered savories filled with spinach and *feta* cheese.

Stefado (steh-FAH-doh)—a Greek stew made from lamb or beef with tomatoes, onions and a bit of cinnamon.

Sumak (SOO-mahk)—sharp, sour red berry from the sumac tree, used as flavoring; pronounced "soo-MAHGH" in Iran.

Tabooleh (tah-BOO-lay)—summer salad of cracked wheat, mint, parsley, green onions and tomatoes.

Tagine (tah-JEE-neh)—slow-simmered stew from Morocco.

Tagine slaoul (tah-JEE-neh slah-OOL)—earthenware pot with high conical top in which *tagine* is cooked and served.

Tarama (tah-RAH-mah)—light, colored carp or grey mullet roe preserved in salt and oil; used in Greece and in Middle East to make *taramasalata*, a dip with the consistency of pinkish mayonnaise.

Taratoor (tah-rah-TOOR)—Arabic sauce made from garlic, *tahini* and lemon.

Tyropitta (TEE-roh-pee-tah)—*phyllo*-covered savories filled with *feta* cheese, egg and dill.

Tzimmes (tsim-MESH)—a sweet-sour Israeli stew made from beef, potatoes, turnips, carrots, dried prunes and apricots with honey and lemon juice.

Ugah duvshan (uh-GAH doov-SHAHN)—honey cake sometimes flavored with rose water; an Israeli dessert.

Warka (WAHR-kah)—fine pastry leaves used in Morocco for making *bisteeya*, similar to *phyllo* but more like egg roll skins.

Zaatar (zah-TAHR)—seasoning mixture of thyme and sumak.

Tzimmes

Dolmas

Challah

Tagine Qamama

Harira

Harira is really more than a Moroccan soup. It's a rich and delicately spiced soup-stew of beef, vegetables and chick peas. It makes a meal in a bowl or is perfect with a light main dish.

1 pound	beef cubes (½ inch)
1 cup	diced carrot
1 cup	diced celery
1 cup	chopped onion
½ teaspoon	ground cinnamon
¼ teaspoon	crushed saffron or ground turmeric
2 tablespoons	butter or margarine
1 can (10½ ounces)	condensed beef broth
1 can (10½ ounces)	condensed tomato bisque soup
2 soup cans	water
¼ cup	barley
1 can (about 16 ounces)	chick peas, drained
1 cup	diced tomatoes
½ cup	chopped parsley
2 tablespoons	lemon juice

In large heavy pan, brown beef and cook carrots, celery and onion with seasonings in butter until *just* tender. Add broth, soup, water and barley. Cover; cook over low heat 1 hour 15 minutes. Add chick peas, tomatoes, parsley and lemon juice. Cook 15 minutes more or until done; stir occasionally. Makes about 9 cups.

Menu:
*Harira
Stuffed Eggplant with Rice, Dates and Almonds
Radish and Orange Salad
Konafa

Avgolemono

The liquid must be bubbly hot before carefully blending the egg-lemon mixture into this tasty soup. Then serve at once. The soup should not be reheated for best results.

1 can (10½ ounces)	condensed chicken with rice soup
1 soup can	water
1	egg
2 tablespoons	lemon juice

In saucepan or double boiler, combine soup and water. Bring to boil; remove from heat. Beat egg until light and frothy; gradually add lemon juice and 1 cup hot broth. Gradually stir egg mixture into soup. *Do not boil.* Cook a few minutes over *very low heat*, stirring until egg is thoroughly blended with soup. Garnish with lemon. Serve immediately. (Overheating will cause curdling.) Makes about 2½ cups.

Menu:
*Avgolemono
*Moussaka
Marinated Artichoke Hearts
Baklava

Stefado

This spiced beef and onion dish is braised slowly to develop a rich taste. Feta cheese should be added at last minute to allow to soften.

1 teaspoon	pickling spice
1½ pounds	beef cubes (1½ inch)
1 large	clove garlic, minced
2 tablespoons	butter or margarine
1 can (10¾ ounces)	condensed tomato soup
⅓ cup	water
1 can (about 16 ounces)	tomatoes, cut up
2 tablespoons	wine vinegar
⅛ teaspoon	pepper
1 pound	small whole white onions (about 16)

Tie pickling spice in cheesecloth. In large heavy pan, brown beef with garlic in butter. Add soup, water, tomatoes, vinegar, pickling spice bag and pepper. Cover; cook over low heat 1 hour 30 minutes. Add onions; cook 30 minutes or until done. Stir occasionally. Uncover; cook to desired consistency. Remove pickling spice. Serve over rice; garnish with feta cheese. Makes 5 cups.

Menu:
*Dolmas
*Stefado
Mixed Green Salad with Tomatoes and Greek Olives
Walnut Butter Cookies

Burghul Pilav

Bulgar can be used as a substitute for rice. This savory recipe combines bulgar with spices we associate with desserts. Add carrots, tomato and broth and the flavor becomes anything but sweet. It's the perfect base for broiled meat or poultry.

¾ **cup**	bulgar (cracked wheat)
⅓ **cup**	chopped onion
1 large	clove garlic, minced
½ **teaspoon**	ground cinnamon
¼ **teaspoon**	ground ginger
¼ **teaspoon**	ground cardamom seed
⅛ **teaspoon**	ground cloves
¼ **cup**	butter or margarine
1 can (10½ ounces)	condensed consomme
1 tablespoon	lemon juice
½ **cup**	finely chopped carrots
⅓ **cup**	golden raisins
½ **cup**	chopped fresh mint leaves or 1 tablespoon dried mint leaves, crushed
½ **cup**	chopped tomato

In saucepan, brown bulgar and cook onion with garlic and seasonings in butter until tender. Add consomme, lemon juice, carrots, raisins and mint. Bring to boil; reduce heat. Cover; simmer 20 minutes or until done. Stir occasionally; stir in tomatoes. Makes about 3 cups.

Bisteeya

Bisteeya requires some time to prepare but the results are worth the effort. Keep the phyllo leaves covered with dampened towel to prevent drying out. Filling can be made ahead and held until you are ready to assemble the flaky turnover.

1 can (10¾ ounces)	condensed chicken broth
½ cup	water
1	cinnamon stick (1 inch)
¼ teaspoon	ground ginger
⅛ teaspoon	ground turmeric
½ cup	chopped onion
⅓ cup	chopped parsley
1 large	clove garlic, minced
4 whole	chicken breasts, split, skinned, boned and cut in strips (2 pounds boneless)
½ cup	chopped toasted slivered almonds
2 tablespoons	confectioners' sugar
¼ teaspoon	ground cinnamon
2 tablespoons	lemon juice
5	eggs, slightly beaten
16	phyllo leaves (about ½ pound)
¾ cup	melted butter or margarine

In large heavy pan, combine broth, water, cinnamon stick, ginger, turmeric, onion, parsley and garlic; add chicken. Bring to boil; reduce heat. Cover; simmer 10 minutes or until done. Meanwhile, combine almonds, confectioners' sugar and ground cinnamon; set aside. Remove chicken from broth. Reduce broth to 1½ cups; add lemon juice. Remove cinnamon stick. Gradually pour eggs into simmering broth, stirring

gently until eggs are set; chill. In buttered 12″ round baking pan, arrange 4 phyllo leaves; brush each with butter. Top with 4 more phyllo leaves, allowing ½ of each leaf to extend beyond edge of pan; brush each with butter. Arrange chicken over phyllo leaves; spoon egg mixture over chicken. Sprinkle with almond mixture. Cover with 4 more phyllo leaves; brush each with butter. Fold extended leaves over top; brush ends with butter. Arrange remaining 4 leaves over top; brush each with butter. Tuck in ends; brush with butter. Bake at 425°F. for 10 minutes; invert on large buttered baking sheet. Bake 15 minutes more or until done. Invert on serving platter; dust with additional confectioners' sugar and cinnamon. Serve immediately. Makes 8 servings.

Menu:
Falafel
Pita Bread
*Bisteeya
Pickled Vegetable Salad
Dried Fruit Compote

Bamia

This dish gives an authentic taste of Egypt. It's perfect for busy-day cooking. It can be prepared ahead, covered and then baked later.

1 pound	ground beef
½ cup	finely chopped onion
1 large	clove garlic, minced
1 can (10¾ ounces)	condensed tomato soup
⅛ teaspoon	pepper
1	egg, slightly beaten
2 tablespoons	fine dry bread crumbs
1 package (10 ounces)	frozen whole okra, cooked and drained

In skillet, brown beef and cook onion with garlic until tender (use shortening if necessary); stir to separate meat. Pour off fat. Add soup, pepper, egg and bread crumbs. Bring to boil; reduce heat. Simmer 5 minutes; stir occasionally. In buttered 1-quart casserole, arrange okra around casserole with tips toward center and ends along the outside. Spoon soup mixture over okra. Bake at 375°F. for 30 minutes or until set. Let stand 10 minutes. Invert on serving platter; garnish with lemon slices. Makes 4 servings.

Menu:
*Bamia
Bean Croquettes or Fritters
Sliced Tomatoes and Onion with Mint
Wedges of Fresh Melon with Lime

Morg Polo

"Polo" is often called pilaf in the United States. It means rice mixed with other ingredients in the cooking. The apricots, raisins and cinnamon add an exotic flavor to this chicken dish.

4 pounds	chicken parts
2 tablespoons	butter or margarine
⅓ cup	chopped dried apricots
1 can (10¾ ounces)	condensed chicken broth
1 can (10¾ ounces)	condensed cream of chicken soup
1 cup	chopped celery
¼ cup	raisins
1 teaspoon	ground cinnamon
½ cup	dried apricot halves

In large heavy pan, brown chicken in butter. Add chopped apricots and remaining ingredients except apricot halves. Cover; cook over low heat 30 minutes. Add apricot halves. Uncover; cook 15 minutes more or until done. Stir occasionally. Serve over rice. Garnish with parsley. Makes 8 servings.

Menu:
*Morg Polo
Saffron-Flavored Rice
Fresh Spinach and Onion Salad with Yogurt Dressing
Halva or Other Sweets

Tagine Qamama

Tagine is eaten in North Africa with couscous, rice or bulgar. The traditional Moroccan way is to eat the hearty lamb stew with pieces of bread to soak up the sauce.

2 pounds	lamb cubes (1½ inch)
½ teaspoon	ground ginger
¼ teaspoon	ground cinnamon
Generous dash	crushed saffron or ground turmeric
3 tablespoons	butter or margarine
1 can (10½ ounces)	condensed beef broth
½ soup can	water
4 tablespoons	honey
½ pound	small whole white onions (about 8)
¼ cup	water
3 tablespoons	cornstarch
2 medium	cooking apples, cut in wedges

In skillet, brown lamb with seasonings in 2 tablespoons butter. Add broth, ½ soup can water and 3 tablespoons honey. Cover; cook over low heat 1 hour. Add onions; cook 30 minutes more or until done. Stir occasionally. Mix ¼ cup water and cornstarch; gradually blend into broth. Cook, stirring until thickened. Meanwhile, in skillet, cook apples with remaining honey, butter and dash cinnamon until glazed; stir often. Arrange lamb mixture on platter; garnish with apples, sprinkle with toasted sesame seed. Makes 6 to 8 servings.

Menu:
Pickled Green Peppers
*Tagine Qamama
Warmed Pita Bread
Cucumber and Yogurt Salad
Saffron Rice Pudding

Shish Kebob

*Grilled and skewered meats are a favorite way of preparing
meat in the Middle East. For extra flavor, marinate overnight.
Cook vegetables and meat on different skewers. This prevents
vegetables from overcooking before meat cubes are done.*

2 pounds	lamb cubes (1 inch)
3 medium	onions, cut in half and partially cooked
1 medium	green pepper, cut in 12 squares
12	cherry tomatoes
1 can (10¾ ounces)	condensed chicken broth
½ cup	Chablis or other dry white wine
2 tablespoons	olive oil
1 tablespoon	dried mint leaves, crushed
1 large	clove garlic, minced

Arrange lamb, onions, green peppers and tomatoes in shallow
dish. To make marinade, in saucepan, combine broth, wine,
oil, mint and garlic; bring to boil. Pour over lamb and
vegetables. Marinate 6 hours or overnight; stir occasionally.
Remove lamb and vegetables from marinade. To make
vegetable kebobs, on 2 long skewers, arrange alternately
tomatoes, onions and green peppers. To make lamb kebobs,
on 2 long separate skewers, arrange lamb; place on broiler
pan. Broil 4 inches from heat 10 minutes, turning and
brushing with marinade. Add vegetable kebobs; broil 10
minutes more or until desired doneness, turning and brushing
with marinade. Serve with bulgar. Makes 6 servings.

Menu:
*Shish Kebob
*Burghul Pilav
Deep-Fried Zucchini Slices
Apricots in Yogurt

Challah

A traditional braided bread with origins in Europe, Challah is enjoyed in Israel. It is rich in eggs and very moist. It makes a marvelous base for French toast.

1 can (10¾ ounces)	condensed chicken broth
1¼ cups	water
2 envelopes	active dry yeast
3	eggs, well beaten
¼ cup	salad oil
1 tablespoon	salt
1 tablespoon	sugar
9 cups	all-purpose flour
1	egg, well beaten

In saucepan, combine broth and water; heat to lukewarm (110°F.). Pour over yeast. Stir to dissolve; add 3 eggs, oil, salt and sugar. Stir in enough flour to make a stiff dough. On floured board, knead dough until smooth (about 5 minutes), adding more flour as needed. Place in greased bowl, turning once. Cover; let rise in warm place until doubled (about 1 hour 30 minutes). Punch down; on floured board, knead until smooth (about 5 minutes). To make loaves, divide into 8 equal pieces. Roll each piece into a 10-inch long rope. Arrange 4 ropes with ends touching in the shape of an X; press ends together in center. To braid, lift the ends of two opposite ropes and twist them over the other two to reverse their positions and to maintain the X. Then lift and reverse the remaining two, continuing to maintain the X. Repeat, lifting and reversing one pair at a time until a compact braid is formed.

Place on greased baking sheet. Repeat with remaining 4 ropes. Brush with remaining egg. Cover; let rise in warm place until doubled (about 1 hour). Bake at 350°F. for 30 minutes or until done. Cool. Makes 2 loaves.

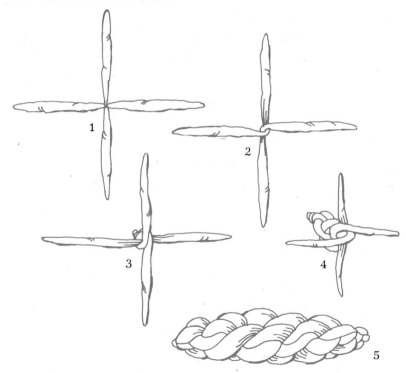

Moussaka

*This is practically a meal in a dish. If you prepare it ahead and
let it sit, the better the flavor. Be sure to cover and refrigerate
while letting sit.*

1 medium	eggplant (about 1½ pounds), cut in ¼-inch slices
½ cup	salad oil
1½ pounds	ground lamb or beef
3 cups	sliced fresh mushrooms (about ½ pound)
1 can (11 ounces)	condensed tomato bisque soup
¼ cup	Burgundy or other dry red wine
1 large	clove garlic, minced
1 teaspoon	basil leaves, crushed
Generous dash	pepper
1 can (10¾ ounces)	condensed cream of onion soup
2	egg yolks, well beaten
½ cup	buttered bread crumbs
½ cup	freshly grated Parmesan cheese
¼ cup	chopped parsley

In skillet, brown eggplant in oil; drain on absorbent towels. In
same skillet, brown lamb and mushrooms (use additional oil
if necessary); stir to separate meat. Pour off fat. Stir in tomato
bisque soup, wine, garlic, basil and pepper; cook 5 minutes to
blend flavors. In 2-quart shallow baking dish (12×8×2″),
arrange 2 alternate layers of eggplant and meat mixture,
beginning and ending with eggplant. Blend onion soup and
egg yolks; pour over eggplant. Combine bread crumbs,
Parmesan cheese and parsley; sprinkle over soup mixture.
Bake at 325°F. for 45 minutes. Let stand 10 minutes before
serving. Makes 6 servings.

Kibbi

Kibbi is the national dish of Lebanon. The mixture of finely cracked wheat and lamb is traditionally ground together, so mix well. Don't forget to soak the bulgar first.

1 can (10½ ounces)	condensed beef broth
½ soup can	water
1 cup	bulgar (cracked wheat)
2 pounds	ground lamb
1 cup	finely chopped onion
⅛ teaspoon	salt
Dash	pepper
⅓ cup	pine nuts
¼ teaspoon	ground allspice

In saucepan, bring broth and water to boil; stir in bulgar. Let stand 1 hour. Drain *thoroughly*, reserving liquid. Mix *thoroughly* soaked bulgar, 1 pound lamb, ½ cup onion, salt and pepper. Meanwhile, in skillet, brown remaining lamb and cook onion and nuts with allspice in reserved liquid until onion is tender. Stir to separate meat. In 2-quart shallow baking dish (12×8×2″), spread one half of uncooked lamb mixture; top with cooked lamb mixture. Gently spread remaining uncooked lamb mixture over cooked lamb. Cut diagonal slashes on top; brush with melted butter. Bake at 375°F. for 45 minutes or until done. Let stand 10 minutes; cut into squares. Serve with plain yogurt. Makes 8 servings.

Menu:
* Kibbi with Yogurt
Eggplant, Tomato and Peppers Fried in Olive Oil
Buttered Rice with Almonds
Orange Sherbert

Tzimmes

Tzimmes is enjoyed all year round in Israel, but particularly during Passover. It is another example of how meat can be combined with vegetables and fruit. In this case, the fruit is prunes.

2-pound	boneless beef brisket
2 tablespoons	shortening
1 can (10½ ounces)	condensed consomme
1 soup can	water
2 tablespoons	honey
2 tablespoons	lemon juice
⅛ teaspoon	ground allspice
3 medium	potatoes (about 1 pound), cut in half
3 medium	carrots (about 1 pound), cut in half crosswise and lengthwise
2 medium	onions, quartered
1 cup	pitted cooked prunes
½ cup	water
¼ cup	flour

In large heavy pan, brown beef in shortening; pour off fat. Add consomme, 1 soup can water, honey, lemon juice and allspice. Cover; cook over low heat 1 hour. Add potatoes, carrots and onions. Cook 30 minutes; add prunes. Cook 10 minutes more or until done; stir occasionally. Remove meat and vegetables to platter; keep warm. Gradually blend ½ cup water into flour until smooth; slowly stir into sauce. Cook, stirring until thickened. Serve with meat and vegetables; garnish with parsley. Makes 6 servings.

Dolmas

This is a favorite appetizer in Greece and throughout the Middle East. It can be easily made ahead and served either hot or cold.

2 cans (10½ ounces each)	condensed consomme
1 pound	ground beef
½ pound	ground lamb
¾ cup	raw regular rice
½ cup	finely chopped onion
½ cup	pine nuts
⅓ cup	chopped parsley
1 large	clove garlic, minced
1 teaspoon	dried mint leaves, crushed
1 jar (about 8 ounces)	grapevine leaves, drained
¼ cup	lemon juice

Mix *thoroughly*, ½ cup consomme, beef, lamb, rice, onion, pine nuts, parsley, garlic and mint. Meanwhile, gently rinse grape leaves; pat dry with absorbent towels. Arrange leaf shiny-side down; place about 1 tablespoon meat mixture in center. Tuck in ends, roll tightly toward point of leaf. In large heavy pan, arrange stuffed leaves seam-side down in layers; add remaining consomme and lemon juice. Cover with a heavy plate to prevent leaves from opening. Cook over low heat 45 minutes. Serve with plain yogurt. Garnish with lemon slices. Makes about 40 stuffed grapevine leaves.

Scandinavia

Fiskepudding

To appreciate the richness and abundance of good food that comes from the Scandinavian countries, it is essential to understand the importance that food plays in this area of long wintery evenings and equally long summery days.

Denmark, Finland, Norway and Sweden are connected not only by the harsh climate and rugged geography but also by their mutual enjoyment of food. Many of their dishes are the same or similar. This fact reflects a long history of trading as well as shifting borders.

Norway, for example, was part of Denmark for almost 400 years and yet the two could not be more dissimilar. Denmark is like one huge garden with fairly flat terrain. Norway is almost all mountains and magnificent *fjords*, so farming is quite difficult. Finland to the extreme east, next to Russia, is a combination of forests and lakes. Its taste in food is somewhat related to its proximity to Russia. Sweden in the middle seems to be a composite of the three others— farms, mountains, woods and lakes.

Nowhere can the richness and abundance of food be better seen than in the incredible display of buffet dishes called *smörgåsbord*. Literally translated, it means "bread and butter table" in Swedish, but that scarcely describes the selection of mouth-watering foods.

The whole idea of this buffet is said to have originated in the isolated country homes. Parties given for weddings and christenings were the occasions to which each guest brought a different dish. These dishes were then gathered on a long table. Today, this tradition can be seen in Scandinavian homes as well as restaurants, in the country and in the city. *Smörgåsbord* may be as simple as herring, cheeses, bread and butter or as elaborate as a mixture of meat, fish, vegetable and egg salads and other dishes. There is an order to eating all these foods.

The first plate begins with salty foods—herring and other marinated or preserved fishes such as mussels, mackerel or eels plus bread and butter. Picking up the second plate, you would then select a variety of cold egg and vegetable salads and perhaps some sliced meat or *pâtés*. Save room for more because the third plate features hot foods. *Köttbullar* (Swedish meatballs) or *kroppkakor* (potato dumplings stuffed with pork) might be featured.

A final plate would include a fruit salad and some local cheeses such as Jarlsberg or Creme Dania on crisp flat rye bread. It's all overwhelming. Don't think, however, that this is the way Scandinavians eat every day, but it is a good way to get acquainted with their cuisine. Actually many times, *smörgåsbord* or *kaldt bord* (in Norwegian) or *voileipäpöytä* (in Finnish) is a simple appetizer or hors d'oeuvres for lunch.

Atlantic Ocean

Sweden

Finland

Norway

Bergen

Oslo

Helsinki

Stockholm

North Sea

Gulf of Finland

Denmark

Helsinger

Copenhagen

Baltic Sea

The foods from Scandinavia are satisfying but simple. One look at the map of the area will show how important the ocean, seas and lakes are as a source of food. The Baltic Sea, which is common to all the Scandinavian countries, provides herring. From the Atlantic and North Sea come cod, haddock and mackerel. The rivers and lakes are a source for pike, perch, trout, salmon and eels. The list goes on and on.

Scandinavians do not exist on fish alone. Grazing land is scarce, so aged beef is in short supply. Chicken, lamb and veal are popular menu items. Because of the short growing season, fresh vegetables are scarce in the winter months; the hearty root vegetables such as potatoes, carrots, turnips and beets or those that will store well like cabbage supply the color, crunch and vitamins through those long dark days.

Thrifty and ingenious are good words to describe the Scandinavian homemaker. Not a scrap of food or a bone goes to waste. What appears as a roast one day, for example, may reappear the next day sauced with horseradish, dill or mustard, three favorite flavorings or get recycled into a Swedish hash such as *pyttipanna*, a combination of diced cooked meat, onions and potatoes with gravy. The food might also be featured again cold with a fruit relish or in a salad form.

To explore the variety of the Scandinavian diet, let's take a quick tour of the area. Each country features a delicious assortment of foods to which it adds its own unique flavor.

In Denmark, for instance, there is great pride in the dairy industry. Butter, cream and cheese are all integral to its cooking. A luscious pastry or coffeecake is a part of their cuisine for which the Danes have become famous. The word "Danish" is really synonymous with those delicious, buttery creations that are called *wienerbrød*.

Soups are served in a variety of ways and include interesting ingredients. Fruit soups appear on the table in the summer. *Aeblesuppe* is a refreshing combination of apples, wine and sugar, slightly thickened with cornstarch. It is usually served at the end of a meal or can be a tangy meal in itself. Another typical Danish soup is

øllebrød, a beer and bread soup flavored with cinnamon, sugar and lemon.

Anytime is a good time for *frikadeller*, tasty veal and pork patties, traditionally served with boiled potatoes, pickled beets and cucumbers or red cabbage. The Danes do amazing things with pork, such as stuffing a loin of pork with prunes and apples, which they call *mørbrad med svesker og aebler*. The Christmas goose, *gåsesteg*, is also stuffed with a similar fruity mixture. It is served with *brunedekartofler*, tiny new potatoes coated with a thin caramel sauce, which cuts the heaviness of the goose.

In Sweden, smoked pork flavors their national dish, *ärter med fläsk*, a rich yellow split pea soup, which is traditionally served on Thursdays with *plättar*, sweet thin pancakes and jam. White cabbage soup or *vitkålssoppa* is usually served with veal meatballs or *köttbullar*. Another delicious concoction from Swedish soup kettles is *tisdagssoppa* or "Tuesday soup" of barley, carrots, parsnips, turnips and potatoes in a creamy base. This might be served alone or with *stekt fläsk med äppleringer och bruna bönor*, fried pork slabs (like bacon) with apple rings and brown beans.

Sailor's beef or *sjömansbiff* is a Swedish favorite combination of slow-stewed beef, onions and potatoes. Another popular recipe is *Janssons frestelse* (which means Jansson's temptation), a scalloped potato and onion dish with special Swedish anchovies.

During the short summer season, the Swedes preserve as many fruits and berries as possible so that during the cold winter they can enjoy such delicacies as *äpplekaka med vanilijsås*, applecake with vanilla sauce. The preserves and jams are not only ingredients in cakes and puddings but also are often whipped with cream or used as a filling for their many-layered tortes.

Norwegians also share a love of fruit. *Blåbaersuppe*, a blueberry-based soup is a summertime dessert. Another soup served, however, at the beginning of the meal is *Dagmarsuppe* or Princess soup, a royal combination of bouillon, peas and cream thickened with tapioca. *Fiskepudding*, Norwegian fish pudding and *torsk med eggesaus*, poached cod with a chopped egg sauce, are two favorites. Leftover fish might reappear on Norwegian plates as *fiskesalat med pepperrotsaus*, a fish salad with horseradish dressing.

The Norwegians depend on sheep and goats for meat, milk and cheese; these animals are perfectly suited to their mountainous terrain. *Får i kål* is a popular mutton and cabbage stew. *Gjetost*, a flavorful goat cheese, is eaten with bread and butter for breakfast, lunch or dinner. Almonds, cardamom and citron are ingredients in many Norwegian desserts. *Julekake*, Christmas cake, includes a heady combination of all three.

The Finns have an amazing assortment of berries for their desserts. Raspberries, cranberries, lingonberries and blueberries are served throughout the year in *kiisseli*, a porridge-like dish. Like their western neighbors, the Swedes, they also enjoy a hot and hearty pea soup on Thursday called *hernekeitto*. Summer soup or *kesäkeitto* is a creamy soup with potatoes and summer vegetables such as peas and spinach. Most of their soups are so filling that they really could be a main course. Another specialty is *patakukko*, which roughly translates to "pot-cock." It's a delicious combination of fish and meat (usually pork) baked as a pot pie with a crunchy crust of rye bread dough. *Dillilammas* is another Finnish stew combination of lamb and dill. Karelian hot pot or *karjalanpaisti* is a slow-simmered stew of meat, potatoes and turnips.

Many similar dishes originated when energy-conscious Finnish women wanted to make the best use of the heat from their baking ovens. The most famous product of these ovens is a sour rye bread. In eastern Finland, the bread is thick and slightly rounded; in western Finland, the loaf is flattened with a hole in the center.

Despite the diversity among the Scandinavian countries, there is a similarity in the meal pattern. Breakfast or *frukost* in Sweden is served early and usually consists of coffee or tea plus a piece of pastry or coffeecake. In the winter, especially in the country, hearty appetites demand a creamy, buttery porridge of oats or rye. Sometimes an open-faced sandwich, called *smørrebrød* in Denmark might be another alternative.

Lunch is served at midday. Again it might be a combination of open-faced sandwiches which are eaten with a knife and fork or a selection of *smörgåsbord* dishes. If eaten at a restaurant, there would be a choice of *smörgåsbord* appetizer or soup, then a fish or meat course with vegetables such as *kåldolmar* (Swedish stuffed cabbage) or *silakkalaatikko* (Finnish baked herring and potatoes in cream). Coffee and dessert follow.

In the evening, the pattern is much the same as lunch with hot dishes but much lighter. A one-dish recipe such as *kalops med rårakor* (Swedish beef stew with paper-thin potato pancakes) might be the whole meal with the usual assortment of whole-grain breads, butter and cheese or a sweet pudding. It's a hearty and satisfying way of eating.

~~Glossary~~ *

Aamiainen (AH-mee-eye-nen)—breakfast in Finland.

Aebleskiver (EP-leh-shiv-ehr)—rounded Danish doughnuts, usually filled with fruit, that are prepared in a special pan.

Aeblesuppe (EPP-leh-suh-peh)—a Danish combination of apples, wine and sugar, slightly thickened with cornstarch.

Akvavit (AH-kvah-vit)—Danish and Swedish for "water of life," a liquor made by distilling potatoes, similar to gin.

Äpplekaka med vanilijsås (EPP-leh-kaw-kah med vah-NILL-ee-sohss)—Swedish apple cake served with vanilla sauce.

Ärter med fläsk (AIR-tehr med FLESK)—national dish of Sweden, a rich yellow split-pea soup flavored with smoked pork and served on Thursdays with *plättar*.

Blåbaersuppe (BLOW-behr-suh-peh)—a blueberry-based soup served as dessert in Norway.

Brännvin (BREN-veen)—Swedish for "burned wine," another name for *akvavit* or brandy.

Brunedekartofler (BROO-neh-deh-kahr-TOFF-lehr)—tiny new potatoes coated with a thin caramel sauce, served in Denmark to accompany the *gåsesteg*.

Dagmarsuppe (DAHK-mahr-suh-peh)—Princess soup, a royal Norwegian combination of bouillon, peas and cream thickened with tapioca.

Dillilammas (DILL-ee-LAH-mahss)—a Finnish stew combining lamb and dill.

Fågelbo (FOHG-el-boo)—Swedish for "bird's nest," i.e., chopped parsley, beets, capers, onions and anchovies arranged in rings around a raw egg yolk.

Får i kål (FOHR ih KOHL)—a mutton and cabbage stew popular in Norway.

Fenelår (FEN-eh-lore)—Norwegian dried, salted and smoked mutton.

Fiskepudding (FISS-keh-PUH-ding)—Norwegian fish pudding.

Fiskesalat med pepperrotsaus (FISS-keh-sah-LAHT med PEP-ehr-roht-sowss)—a Norwegian fish salad with horseradish sauce.

Frikadeller (FRICK-ah-DELL-ehr)—Danish term for veal and pork patties.

Frokost or **Frukost** (FROH-kohst, FRUH-kohst)—Norwegian and Swedish for breakfast.

Gåsesteg (GOH-seh-stayk)—the Christmas goose in Denmark, usually stuffed with a fruit mixture.

Gjetost (YAY-tohst)—a Norwegian goat cheese eaten for breakfast, lunch or dinner.

Glögg (GLEGG)—hot spiced wine punch served throughout Scandinavia, usually at Christmas.

Gravlax (GRAHV-lahks)—Swedish salmon cured in salt, sugar, dill and pepper, sliced thinly and served with mustard-dill sauce.

Hernekeitto (HAIR-neh-KAY-toh)—a hearty Finnish pea soup, traditionally served on Thursdays.

Hiukasu (HEE-uh-kah-soo)—"salt-hunger," Finnish word for the need for salty foods.

Husmankost (HOOS-mahn-kohst)—home cooking in Swedish.

Janssons frestelse (YAHN-sohns FREH-stell-seh)—"Jansson's temptation," a Swedish dish consisting of scalloped potatoes and onions with special Swedish anchovies.

Julekaka (YOO-leh-kah-kah)—Norwegian Christmas cake, made with almonds, cardamom and citron.

Kåldolmar (KOHL-dohl-mahr)—Swedish stuffed cabbage.

Kalops med rärakor (KAH-lawps med REH-rah-kohr)—Swedish beef stew with paper-thin potato pancakes.

Karjalanpaisti (KAHR-yah-lahn-PICE-tee)—a slow-simmered Finnish stew of meat, potatoes and turnips.

Kesäkeitto (KESS-a-KEY-toh)—"summer soup," a Finnish cream soup with potatoes and summer vegetables such as peas and spinach.

Kiisseli (KEE-sel-lee)—a thick Finnish pudding.

Knäckebröd (KNECK-eh-bred)—"break bread," Swedish flat bread.

Kolde bord (KOHL-deh BOORD)—"cold table," similar to Swedish *smörgåsbord*; term used in Denmark; in Norway, it is written *kaldt bord*.

Köttbullar (KETT-buhl-lahr)—Swedish meatballs.

Kroppkakor (KRAWP-kah-kohr)—Swedish potato dumplings stuffed with pork.

Krumkaker (KRUHM-kahk-ehr)—"rolled cookies," Norwegian Christmas cookies.

Lutefisk or **Lutfisk** (LUH-teh-fisk, LUHT-fisk)—Norwegian or Swedish word for a dish made from dried cod, which is soaked in lye before cooking.

Middag (MID-dawk)—noon or main meal in Denmark, Sweden and Norway.

Mørbrad med svesker og aebler (MEHR-braht med SVEH-skehr ohk EPP-lehr)—in Denmark, a loin of pork stuffed with prunes and apples.

Nattmat (NAHT-maht)—"night food," usually offered just before a party ends in Sweden so guests go home full.

Øllebrød (ELL-eh-bred)—a Danish beer and bread soup flavored with cinnamon, sugar and lemon.

Päivällinen (PA-EE-val-lee-nen)—the main meal in Finland, eaten during the day.

Patakukko (PAH-tah-KOO-koh)—"pot cock" in Finnish, a combination of fish and meat (usually pork) baked as a pot pie with a crunchy crust of rye bread dough.

Plättar (PLET-tahr)—Swedish pancakes.

Plättar panna (PLET-tahr PAHN-ah)—special cast-iron skillet with small round indentations used for making Swedish pancakes.

Pyttipanna (PEET-ih-PAHN-ah)—"tidbits in the pan," Swedish hash.

Rårakor (REH-rah-kohr)—Swedish potato pancakes.

Ryyppy (REE-pee)—a shot of vodka in Finland.

Silakkalaatikko (SEE-lahk-kah-LAH-tee-koh)—Finnish baked herring and potatoes in cream.

Sill (SILL)—Swedish for herring from other than the Baltic Sea.

Sjömansbiff (SHEH-mahnss-biff)—a Swedish combination of slow-stewed beef, onions and potatoes.

Skål (SKOHL)—"toast" or "health"—in Danish and Swedish, usually said when drinking *akvavit*.

Smörgåsbord (smehr-GOHSS-boord)—"bread and butter table," a long buffet table laden with an assortment of cold and hot dishes in Sweden, eaten as hors d'oeuvres or as a whole meal.

Smørrebrød (SMER-eh-bred)—"buttered bread," open-faced sandwiches in Denmark.

Stekt fläsk med äppleringer och bruna bönor (STEKT FLESK med EPP-leh-ring-ehr ohk BROO-nah BAY-nohr)—a Swedish dish consisting of fried pork slabs (like bacon) with apple rings and brown beans.

Strömming (STREM-ing)—Swedish for herring from the Baltic Sea.

Suomalaissleipä (SOO-OH-mah-lice-LAY-ee-pa̱)—Finnish rye bread.

Tisdagssoppa (TEESS-dawks-saw-peh)—Swedish for "Tuesday's soup" of barley, carrots, parsnips, turnips and potatoes in a creamy base.

Torsk med eggesaus (TOHRSK med EGG-eh-sowss)—Norwegian poached cod with a chopped egg sauce.

Vitkålssoppa (VEET-kohl-saw-peh)—Swedish white cabbage soup.

Voileipäpöytä (VOY-lay-ee-pa̱-POY-ta̱)—Finnish equivalent of *smörgåsbord,* called *seisovapöytä,* "standing table."

Vörtbröd (VERT-bred)—Swedish rye bread flavored with orange and sometimes beer.

Wienerbrød (VEE-nehr-bred)—Danish pastries.

* The line under an "a" in a Finnish word indicates the sound of "a" in English hat.

Kesäkeitto

Brunbröd

Lindstromin Pihoi

Skinkrulader

Karrysalat

Karrysalat

This creamy salad makes a perfect addition to a soup-and-salad meal so enjoyed by the Danes. The menu below is like a mini-smörgåsbord.

3 cups	cooked elbow macaroni
1 can (10¾ ounces)	condensed cream of mushroom soup
1 cup	diced cucumber
1 cup	sliced pickled herring
½ cup	sliced radishes
⅓ cup	sour cream
¼ cup	lemon juice
2 tablespoons	salad oil
2 teaspoons	curry powder
⅛ teaspoon	pepper

In bowl, combine all ingredients. Chill; stir occasionally. Makes about 5 cups.

Menu:
Dried Green Pea Soup
*Karrysalat
Apple Cole Slaw
Pickled Beets
Fresh Fruit and Butter Cookies

Brunbrød

The combination of rye and wheat flours plus cornmeal make a firm, heavy bread. It should be sliced thin and buttered; it makes a good base for open-faced sandwiches.

1¼ cups	cornmeal
1¼ cups	rye flour
1¼ cups	whole wheat flour
2½ teaspoons	baking powder
1 teaspoon	baking soda
1 can (10½ ounces)	condensed beef broth
1¼ cups	sour cream
1 cup	molasses

In large bowl, sift together cornmeal, flours, baking powder and baking soda. In small bowl, combine broth, sour cream and molasses. Add to dry ingredients; stir until well blended. Pour into 2 well-greased 1-pound coffee cans; cover securely with foil. Place on trivet in large pan. Add boiling water to ½ height of cans. Cover; steam 3 hours. Remove from water; uncover and loosen edges of bread with knife. Unmold while hot; cool. Makes 2 loaves.

Kesäkeitto

This soup is traditionally served in Finland in the early summer when vegetables are very young and tender. You can enjoy it anytime with frozen vegetables.

2 cans (10¾ ounces each)	condensed cream of chicken soup
1 soup can	water
½ soup can	milk
1 cup	frozen cut green beans
1 cup	diced carrots
1 cup	cauliflowerets
1 cup	frozen peas
¾ cup	diced potato
½ teaspoon	dried dill weed, crushed
¼ teaspoon	salt
Generous dash	pepper
1½ cups	chopped fresh spinach
½ cup	quartered radishes

In large saucepan, combine all ingredients except spinach and radishes. Bring to boil; reduce heat. Simmer 5 minutes. Add spinach; simmer 5 minutes more. Stir occasionally. Add radishes. Makes about 7½ cups.

Menu:
*Kesäkeitto
*Lihamurekepiiras
Cucumbers in Sour Cream
Summer Fruit Cup

Janssons Frestelse

No one is quite sure who Jansson was, but these creamy scalloped potatoes are a tempting dish to add to any menu.

4 cups	sliced onions
2 tablespoons	butter or margarine
1 can (10¾ ounces)	condensed creamy chicken mushroom soup
½ cup	light cream
⅛ teaspoon	pepper
4 cups	sliced potatoes
1 can (2 ounces)	anchovy fillets, drained

In skillet, cook onions in butter until tender. To make sauce, in bowl, combine soup, cream and pepper. In buttered 2-quart casserole, arrange alternate layers of potatoes, onions, anchovies and sauce. Cover; bake at 375°F. for 1 hour. Uncover; bake 15 minutes more or until done. Makes about 5 cups.

Menu:
Mustard-Glazed Pork Chops
*Janssons Frestelse
Red Cabbage
Blueberries with Sour Cream and Brown Sugar

Skinkrulader

This is an easy idea for buffet entertaining. The ham rolls can be made ahead, covered and refrigerated until serving time. Diced apples add a unique texture to filling.

1 can (10¾ ounces)	condensed cream of celery soup
1 package (8 ounces)	cream cheese, softened
1½ cups	diced apples
1 cup	cooked peas
2	hard-cooked eggs, coarsely chopped
¼ cup	diced pimiento
2 teaspoons	capers
1 package (10 ounces)	frozen asparagus spears, cooked and drained
16 thin slices	boiled ham (about 1 pound)

In bowl, gradually blend soup into cream cheese until smooth. Add remaining ingredients except asparagus and ham. Cover; chill. To make each ham roll-up, place about ¼ cup soup mixture and asparagus spear on narrow end of each ham slice. Roll up; place seam-side down on serving platter. Garnish with pimiento strips if desired. Makes 6 to 8 servings.

Menu:
Cold Potato Soup with Chives
*Skinkrulader
Sliced Tomatoes and Onions
Mixed Green Salad
Creamy Mocha Pudding

Fiskepudding

The preparation of this dish is easily done in a few minutes in the blender or food processor. You can substitute any white-fleshed local fish for the cod. The finished pudding has a smooth texture; it's delicious served with Hollandaise sauce.

1½ pounds	fresh fillets of cod, cut in small pieces
1 can (10¾ ounces)	condensed cream of chicken soup
¾ cup	heavy cream
1 tablespoon	cornstarch
⅛ teaspoon	ground nutmeg
⅛ teaspoon	pepper

In electric blender or food processor, blend fish, a few pieces at a time, with small amounts of soup and cream; blend until smooth. Remove; repeat until all fish is puréed. In large bowl, combine fish and remaining ingredients. Butter 5-cup fish mold; sprinkle with fine dry bread crumbs, tilting pan to coat bottom and sides evenly. Pour fish mixture into mold; cover tightly with buttered aluminum foil. Place in large baking pan; add boiling water to ½ height of mold. Bake at 350°F. for 30 minutes or until knife inserted comes out clean. Let stand 5 minutes; unmold on serving platter. Makes 6 servings.

Menu:
*Fiskepudding
Buttered Boiled Potatoes
Shredded Carrot Salad
Cranberry Pudding

$\mathcal{L}$indstromin $\mathcal{P}$ihoi

This Finnish meatloaf is made from beef, potato soup and beets. The flavor is delicious and the color slightly red. When cool, slice thickly; it is a good sandwich filling.

2 pounds	well-done cooked beef
1 can (10¾ ounces)	condensed cream of potato soup
1 cup	sliced cooked beets
4	eggs, slightly beaten
½ cup	fine dry bread crumbs
2 tablespoons	finely chopped onion
1 tablespoon	chopped capers
½ teaspoon	pepper
¼ teaspoon	salt
2 cups	sliced onions
2 tablespoons	butter or margarine
1 can (about 16 ounces)	stewed tomatoes
1 tablespoon	chopped parsley
1 teaspoon	cornstarch
1 teaspoon	prepared mustard

Put meat, soup and beets through food grinder or processor. In large bowl, mix *thoroughly* meat mixture, eggs, bread crumbs, onions, capers, pepper and salt. Press *firmly* into well-greased loaf pan (9×5×3″). Bake at 350°F. for 1 hour. Let stand 10 minutes; invert on serving platter. Meanwhile, to make sauce, in skillet, cook onions in butter until tender; remove. Add remaining ingredients. Cook, stirring until thickened. Arrange onions on loaf; serve with sauce. Makes 10 to 12 servings.

Menu:
*Lindstromin Pihoi
*Pinaattiohukaist
Buttered Squash
Plums in Port Wine

Frikadeller

Tender and juicy meatballs are as popular in Denmark as hamburgers are in the United States. Rye bread crumbs hold meat juices in.

¾ pound	ground beef
¾ pound	ground pork
¾ cup	fresh rye bread crumbs
½ cup	chopped onion
¼ cup	milk
1	egg, slightly beaten
½ teaspoon	salt
⅛ teaspoon	pepper
2 tablespoons	shortening
1 can (10¾ ounces)	condensed creamy chicken mushroom soup
½ cup	sour cream
¼ cup	water

In large bowl, combine meats, bread crumbs, onion, milk, egg, salt and pepper. Shape into 32 meatballs. In large skillet, brown meatballs in shortening; pour off fat. Add remaining ingredients. Cover; cook over low heat 15 minutes or until done. Stir occasionally. Serve over noodles. Makes about 4½ cups.

Menu:
*Brunbrød with Tilsit or Muenster Cheese
*Frikadeller
Buttered Noodles
Green Bean Salad
Cherry Coffee Cake

Pinaattiohukaist

The Finns love pancakes of any kind and this recipe is no
exception. Nutmeg adds a nutty taste to the spinach but
remember to drain spinach well before adding to batter.

1 can (10¾ ounces)	condensed chicken broth
¾ cup	flour
2	eggs, slightly beaten
2 tablespoons	melted butter or margarine
⅛ teaspoon	ground nutmeg
1 package (9 ounces)	frozen chopped spinach, thawed, well drained and finely chopped

In bowl, combine all ingredients except spinach. With rotary
beater, beat until smooth; stir in spinach. To make each
pancake, in hot, lightly buttered 6-inch skillet, pour about 2
tablespoons batter, tilting pan slightly to quickly spread batter
thinly and evenly. Lightly brown first side; turn and cook
second side a few seconds. Serve as a vegetable. Garnish with
sour cream. Makes about 20 pancakes.

Ärter med Fläsk

Thursday is pea soup day in Sweden. The Swedes use yellow split peas, but green split peas can be substituted. This is traditionally accompanied by tiny Swedish pancakes for dessert.

1 pound	dried split peas (about 2 cups)
2 cans (10¾ ounces each)	condensed chicken broth
2 soup cans	water
3 cups	ham cut in ½-inch strips (about 1 pound)
1½ cups	thinly sliced onion
1 teaspoon	marjoram leaves, crushed
¼ teaspoon	ground ginger
¼ teaspoon	pepper

Sort peas; wash and drain. In large saucepan, combine all ingredients. Bring to boil; reduce heat. Cover; simmer 1 hour 30 minutes or until done. Stir occasionally. Serve with spicy brown mustard. Makes about 8 cups.

Bergen Fiskesuppe

This simple soup is a tasty way to begin a cold weather meal. And it only takes ten minutes to prepare—but the flavor tastes like you have been simmering it all day.

1 can (10¾ ounces)	condensed cream of potato soup
1 can (10½ ounces)	condensed vegetable soup
2 soup cans	water
1 pound	fillets of cod, cut in 2-inch pieces
½ cup	diagonally sliced celery
½ cup	diagonally sliced green onions
⅛ teaspoon	pepper
1 medium	bay leaf
¼ cup	chopped parsley

In large saucepan, combine all ingredients except parsley. Bring to boil; reduce heat. Simmer 10 minutes or until done; stir gently now and then. Remove bay leaf. Add parsley. Serve with sour cream. Makes about 7 cups.

Menu:
*Bergen Fiskesuppe
Stuffed Cabbage Rolls
Mushroom Salad
Cranberry Pudding

Grønne Bønner

Green beans and mushrooms are mixed with a light creamy chicken-flavored sauce. Almonds add a special crunch. Best of all, it takes almost no time to prepare.

1 pound	fresh whole green beans, cut diagonally in half
3 cups	sliced fresh mushrooms (about ½ pound)
2 tablespoons	butter or margarine
1 can (10¾ ounces)	condensed cream of chicken soup
⅔ cup	light cream
1 tablespoon	lemon juice
½ cup	sliced almonds

Cook beans in boiling water 15 minutes or until tender; drain. In saucepan, brown mushrooms in butter. Add soup, cream, lemon juice and beans. Heat; stir occasionally. Garnish with almonds. Makes about 4 cups.

Menu:
Herbed Roast Chicken
Rye Bread Stuffing
*Grønne Bønner
Prune Danish Pastry

Dillkött på Lamm

Prepare the lamb ahead, if you wish and then at the last minute make the easy-to-do sauce. The creamy, smooth sauce is enriched with egg and lemon. It adds a piquant taste to the tender lamb cubes.

2 pounds	lamb cubes (about 1½ inch)
1 can (10¾ ounces)	condensed cream of mushroom soup
¼ cup	water
1½ teaspoons	dried dill weed, crushed
2 tablespoons	chopped parsley
⅛ teaspoon	pepper
1 medium	bay leaf
1 cup	thinly sliced carrot
1 cup	frozen peas
1	egg yolk, slightly beaten
1 tablespoon	lemon juice

In large saucepan, combine lamb, soup, water, dill, parsley, pepper and bay leaf. Cover; cook over low heat 1 hour 20 minutes. Stir occasionally. Add carrots and peas; cook 10 minutes more or until done. Pour about 1 cup hot liquid into beaten egg yolk and lemon juice, stirring constantly. Stir egg mixture into soup mixture. Cook over low heat, stirring until thickened. Remove bay leaf. Serve with rice. Garnish with lemon. Makes about 4½ cups.

Menu:
*Dillkött på Lamm
Buttered Parslied Rice
Buttered Green Beans
Rhubarb and Strawberry Tarts

Lihamurekepiiras

The combination of ground pork, cheese and creamy mushroom sauce makes a delicious filling for this Finnish pot pie. Top with additional sauce when serving.

2 tablespoons	butter or margarine
1 package (about 10 ounces)	pie crust mix
1 cup	sour cream
2	eggs, slightly beaten
2 pounds	ground pork
1 can (10¾ ounces)	condensed cream of mushroom soup
1 cup	shredded Swiss cheese
¼ cup	chopped onion
¼ cup	chopped parsley
¼ teaspoon	salt
⅛ teaspoon	pepper
2 to 4 tablespoons	milk

To make crust, in bowl, cut butter into pie crust mix until mixture resembles coarse cornmeal. Add ½ cup sour cream and 1 egg; divide mixture in half. Cover; chill overnight. On lightly floured board, roll each half into 11-inch circle. Line 9″ pie plate with one circle; trim to fit pie plate. To make filling, in large skillet, brown pork; stir to separate meat. Pour off fat. Add ½ can soup, cheese, onion, parsley, salt and pepper. Spoon into pie shell; top with remaining pastry. Seal and trim edges. Prick top with fork; brush with remaining egg. Garnish with additional pastry if desired. Bake at 375°F. for 45 minutes or until brown. Meanwhile, in saucepan, heat remaining soup, sour cream and milk. Serve with pie. Makes 8 servings.

South America

Matambre

The food of South America is a colorful and spicy eating adventure.
The ingredients are as diverse as the tropical rain forests, grassy
plains, snow-capped mountains and fertile valleys from which they
come. The cuisines of Peru, Argentina, Brazil, Colombia and
Venezuela are much affected by this geography as well as by a
tradition of cooking developed by their earliest inhabitants. These
countries were singled out from the rest of the South American
nations because of the culinary ingenuity of their local cooks. They
created the most varied dishes and foods as a result of blending of
Indian, African and European influences.

The early Indians who inhabited these lands lived by hunting,
fishing and the gathering of wild foods. Agriculture was in a
primitive stage. They grew maize or Indian corn, which was the
mainstay of their diet and which was supplemented with nourishing
dried beans of a wide variety of shapes and sizes.

In the Andes, where beans and corn do not grow well, the natives
cultivated potatoes. Because they had no natural source of fat, foods
were either stewed, roasted or toasted over open fires.

In the 16th century, the Spanish and later the Portugese came in
search of gold. They found great Indian civilizations flourishing and
they also discovered many of the same ingredients that predomir.ate
in the local markets of South America today.

A wide variety of squashes and pumpkins were used for their
flesh as well as their seeds; the large ones with hard shells became
containers for serving food. Tropical root vegetables were all new to
the Spanish. Tomatoes and peppers, sweet and hot, were viewed as
oddities by the Conquistadores. They were also totally unprepared
for the wealth of tropical fruit they found.

The Spanish and Portugese did not come to the bottom half of the
New World empty-handed. They brought with them onions, olives,
almonds, raisins, pigs, chickens and cows—as well as the know-how
for turning pork fat into lard and cow's milk into cheese, butter and
creamy desserts. The combination of all these foods, Indian as well

as European, eventually created a style of cooking known today as *cocina criolla*, Creole cooking.

The Portugese were a sea-faring people, and dried salt cod accompanied their adventurers on the long and hazardous ocean voyage to the New World. *Bacalhau* and dried shrimp are still popular ingredients in such Brazilian specialties as *caruni*, a shrimp stew with peppers, tomatoes, coconut milk and *farofa*, toasted *cassava* meal.

The Spanish and Portugese also introduced sugar, cinnamon and almonds to the Indians. The Iberian—meaning Spanish and Portugese (from Iberian Penninsula)—concept of dessert runs to custards, puddings, sweet cakes and cookies. *Flan*, a traditional caramel custard, takes on a South American flavor with the addition of coconut, pineapple or even ground nuts native to this area of the world, such as cashews or Brazil nuts.

Because the South American food heritage is an exciting blend of Indian and Spanish or Portugese, the countries of Peru, Argentina, Brazil, Colombia and Venezuela all share a common cooking style. However each has created its own very different cuisine.

Peru is a mountainous country cut off from all but its most immediate neighbors by the Andes Mountains. Here, for hundreds of years there thrived a very advanced Indian civilization which had been developed by the Incas. They had no written language, but their culinary heritage was passed down through the generations by word of mouth.

For example, the Peruvians eat a tremendous amount of potatoes, which grow well in place of the more common corn and beans found throughout the rest of South America. Potatoes commonly appear as *papas a la huancaina*, boiled potatoes with chili-cheese sauce or *causa a la limeña*, potatoes mashed with onion, lemon juice and oil and garnished with shrimp, olives and hard-cooked eggs.

Peruvians also enjoy *ceviche*, which is small pieces of raw fish that are "cooked" in a salted lemon-lime juice marinade and flavored with garlic, onion and *ají*. This dish is a common appetizer all over South America. *Chupe de camarones* is a typical Peruvian soup/stew of shrimp, tomatoes, peppers, potatoes and chunks of corn.

Corn is also found in *humitas*, local *tamales* made with fresh corn dough and filled with pork, chicken or beef plus eggs, raisins and olives; this is wrapped in corn husks and steamed.

Colombia in the northwestern part of South America has two seacoasts, one on the Pacific and another on the Caribbean, as well as a lot of mountains. Colombian cooking is as varied as its

Caribbean Sea

Venezuela

Guyana

Surinam

French Guiana

Colombia

Ecuador

Peru

Brazil

Bolivia

Paraguay

• Rio de Janeiro

Chile

Argentina

Uruguay

• Montevideo

Pacific Ocean

Atlantic Ocean

geography. But no matter where they are located, all Colombians enjoy their own kind of *tamale*, called *hallacas*. It's made of cornmeal dough stuffed with spiced chicken, pork or beef and wrapped in banana leaves before steaming. Colombians have also created many interesting ways to use potatoes. Two favorite potato dishes are *papas chorreadas*, boiled potatoes with a chili, tomato, cheese and scallion sauce and *ajiaco bogotana*, a creamy chicken and potato soup with avocados, capers and *chilies*.

Like many other South Americans, the Colombians enjoy beef. One of the more unusual creations is *sobrebarriga*, which is a steak that is stewed, then breaded and broiled. It is served with a heady sauce made from the vegetables in the stewing liquid.

Nearby Venezuela is another country with sandy beaches and snow-capped mountains. The dishes of this country make good use of the abundant seafood along its coastline as well as the local vegetables and fruits. And like their Colombian neighbors, the Venezuelans have a taste for beef. Two of their typical dishes are *asado antiguo*, larded pot roast with a sweet-sour gravy and *pabellón caraqueño*, a steak dish that is served with rice, *plátanos*, or plantains, fried as chips and black beans. The Venezuelans call mashed black beans *caviar criollo*, which roughly translates as "native caviar." *Tostones* are fried and refried slices of plantains; *tortas de plátano* are fried cakes of plantains and cheese which are sweetened and served with cinnamon.

The Venezuelans make interesting use of corn in *arepa*, a grilled cornbread which dates back to the ancient Indians. *Arepa* resembles a thick *tortilla* and it was traditionally grilled rather than fried because the Indians at that time did not have fat or oil. The Venezuelan contribution to *arepa* was to create *bollos pelones*. *Arepa* dough is wrapped around seasoned ground meat and then simmered in a sauce or soup like dumplings or deep-fried.

The Venezuelans also rely on local fish for cooking. *Corbullón mantuano* is striped bass in a sweet pepper and tomato sauce. *Sancocho* is another favorite, made with any type of local fish, pumpkin, tomatoes and lemons.

Brazil has a long coastline, so fish is also important there. The Portugese brought *bacalhau* or dried salted cod, with them. And it is still enjoyed today in a typical dish known as *bacalhau à baiana*, which is served with a creamy sauce of tomatoes, peppers, scallions and coconut milk.

Much of Brazilian cooking is still influenced by the West Africans who were brought over as slaves in colonial days. *Dendê*, the nutty palm oil, is a major contribution. *Quibebe*, a squash soup with tomatoes, hot peppers and beef broth makes use of the coloring benefits of *dendê*.

Beans and rice are the base for most Brazilian culinary creations. The most famous of these is *feijoada completa*, a hearty dish of dried and fresh beef, sausage and smoked meats in *feijão*, or black beans, to which coconut milk is sometimes added. This dish is always served with *arroz brasileiro*, rice cooked with tomatoes and onions, orange slices, cooked, chopped collard greens and *farofa*, or toasted *cassava* meal, fried in butter, eggs and seasonings. Although *farofa* is served plain in *feijoada*, this toasted meal can also be served with cheese, bacon, raisins and chopped meats, or used as a stuffing. *Cassava* meal is called *farinha de mandioca* in Brazil and is used in soups, stews and on the table in a shaker, the same way Parmesan cheese is used in Italy; the meal, in fact, looks like coarsely grated Parmesan cheese. It is also served as a porridge-like starch, known as *pirão*, when cooked with coconut milk and rice flour or cornmeal and cheese.

Chicken is a popular menu item in Brazil. *Coxinhas*, chicken legs covered with a creamy spice paste and breaded and fried, and *canja*, a hearty chicken soup with ham, are two examples of their specialties.

Hearts of palm or *palmitos*, are usually prepared as salads in the United States. In Brazil, however, they become a cream soup, *sopa de creme de palmito* or are served with rice, as in *arroz com palmito*, which is rice cooked with hearts of palm, sausage and tomatoes.

To the south of Brazil is Argentina, land of the pampas, those rich grasslands where lush fields of wheat are cultivated and fat beef cattle are raised.

Beef is a way of life for the Argentines. One of the more famous beef recipes is *matambre*, which translates as "kill hunger." It's a flank steak which is marinated and then stuffed with spinach, carrots, onions and hard-cooked eggs before rolling and cooking; *matambre* can be eaten hot or cold with a spicy parsley sauce. *Carbonada criolla*, a beef and vegetable stew with corn and potatoes, is served in a large pumpkin or squash shell. The Argentines also combine corned and fresh beef with corn, other vegetables, garbanzo beans and rice to make *puchero*; the results are similar to a New England boiled dinner.

One of the most popular ways of serving beef is *churrasco*—huge slabs of beef are spit-roasted over an open fire. This is also called *asado criollo* and is said to have originated with the guachos— Argentine cowboys.

Like the fish of Peru *(ceviche)* that is marinated in a peppery pickling sauce, there is the Argentine cold pickled chicken with lemons and onions or *escabeche de gallina*. This is a favorite appetizer. Another popular appetizer or snack is *empanadas*, flaky pastry turnovers filled with chopped meat, raisins, olives and onions.

Besides sharing a common food heritage, South Americans also share similar meal patterns. Breakfast is a very simple meal—coffee, rolls with butter and *carne de membrillo* (quince jelly) or *guayaba* (guava jelly).

The main meal of the day is served in the middle of the day. It may include a soup course, a fish or shrimp course, then meat or chicken course with rice and beans or *cassava* meal and a simple dessert, such as guava paste with a slab of mild cheese. Tea is served in the late afternoon with pastries or tea sandwiches. However, should a guest be included, tea becomes a more substantial meal. Following the Spanish custom, dinner is usually eaten very late, beginning no sooner than 10:00 p.m. If it is eaten at home, it would be a simpler version of lunch, including a cold appetizer, such as *ceviche* or *humitas* or soup and a meat and vegetable stew with a fruit dessert. If eaten out, dinner can become a meal of many courses.

Glossary

Acarajé (ah-kah-rah-ZHEH)—a dried bean and onion fritter served with a shrimp and hot pepper sauce.

Achiote (ah-CHYOH-teh)—dried seed of the annatto tree which is used as a flavoring and coloring for South American cooking.

Aguacate (ah-gwah-KAH-teh)—avocado.

Ají (ah-HEE)—Peruvian chili pepper or hot pepper sauce.

Ají de gallina (ah-HEE deh gah-YEE-nah)—fricassée of chicken in an *ají*-nut sauce.

Ajiaco bogotana (ah-HYAH-koh boh-goh-TAH-nah)—a chicken and potato soup with avocados, capers and *chilies*.

Anticuchos (ahn-tee-KOO-chohss)—strips of grilled marinated beef heart (or liver or kidneys).

Arepa (ah-REH-pah)—the corn bread of Venezuela, cooked on a griddle like *tortillas* but slightly thicker. The dough is also used as an outer covering for seasoned meat.

Arroz brasileiro (ah-RROHSS brah-zee-LAY-ruh)—rice cooked with tomatoes and onions, orange slices, collard greens and *farofa*.

Arroz com palmito (ah-RROHSS cohm-pahl-MEE-tuh)—rice cooked with palm hearts, sausage and tomatoes.

Asado (ah-SAH-thoh)—roasted meat; barbecued.

Asado antiguo (ah-SAH-thoh ahn-TEE-gwoh)—larded pot roast with a sweet-sour gravy.

Bacalhau (bah-kah-LYOW)—dried salted codfish, eaten primarily in Brazil.

Bacalhau à baiana (bah-kah-LYOW ah bah-YAH-nah)—dried salted cod served with a sauce of tomatoes, peppers, scallions and coconut milk.

Bollos pelones (BOH-yohss peh-LOH-nehss)—*arepa* dough wrapped around seasoned ground meat and simmered in sauce or soup like dumplings or deep-fried.

Calabaza (kah-lah-VAH-sah)—large round or oval winter squash or pumpkin; shell is sometimes used as a container for soups or stews.

Camarón (kah-mah-ROHN)—type of shrimp.

Canja (KAHN-zhah)—chicken soup with ham.

Cara pulcra (KAH-rah POOL-krah)—combination of pork, chicken, potatoes, garlic, onion and *ají*, garnished with hard-cooked eggs.

Carbonada criolla (kahr-voh-NAH-thah kree-OH-yah)—beef and vegetable stew with corn and potatoes.

Carne de membrillo (KAHR-neh deh mehm-BREE-yoh)—quince jelly.

Carne seca (KAHR-neh SEH-kah)—sun-dried salted beef; beef jerky.

Caruni (kah-ROO-nee)—a Brazilian shrimp stew with peppers, tomatoes, coconut milk and *farofa*.

Cassava (kah-SAH-vah)—brown-skinned tropical root vegetable used as a potato substitute, boiled or fried. It is also grated and toasted in meal form to be used in soups and stews. Also called manioc.

Causa a la limeña (KOW-sah ah lah lee-MEH-nyah)—potatoes mashed with onion, lemon juice and oil and garnished with shrimp, olives and hard-cooked eggs.

Caviar criollo (kah-VYAHR kree-OH-yoh)—Venezuelan term for mashed black beans.

Ceviche (seh-VEE-cheh)—pieces of raw fish marinated in lemon or lime juice; a popular appetizer.

Chuños (CHOO-nyohss)—a sort of freeze-dried potatoes eaten by peoples of the Andes.

Chupe de camarones (CHOO-peh deh kah-mah-ROH-nehss)—Peruvian soup/stew of shrimp, tomatoes, peppers, potatoes, cheese and chunks of corn.

Churrasco (choo-RRAHSS-koh)—meat barbecued over an open fire in Brazil or Argentina.

Cocina criolla (koh-SEE-nah kree-OH-yah)—Creole-style cooking; dishes made of native ingredients but cooked in the Spanish or Portuguese style.

Conchita (kohn-CHEE-tah)—type of scallop.

Corbullón mantuano (kohr-voo-YOHN mahn-TWAH-noh)—striped bass in a sweet pepper and tomato sauce.

Corvina (kohr-VEE-nah)—corbina; a type of fish.

Coxinhas (koh-SHEE-nyahss)—chicken legs covered with a creamy spice paste and breaded and fried.

Cuscuz paulista (kooss-KOOSS pow-LEE-stah)—Brazilian variation of North African *couscous*; made with cornmeal instead of wheat, plus vegetables, shredded beef, collard greens, hard-cooked eggs and tomatoes.

Cuy (KWEE)—guinea pig.

Dendê (den-DEH)—Brazilian palm oil which gives food an orangey-yellow color and has a nutty flavor.

Empanadas (ehm-pah-NAH-thahss)—small pastry turnovers filled with meat, raisins, olives and onions.

Ensalada de aguacate (ehn-sah-LAH-thah deh ah-gwah-KAH-teh)—chunks of avocado tossed with olive oil and white wine vinegar.

Escabeche de gallina (ehss-kah-VEH-cheh deh gah-YEE-nah)—pickled chicken with lemons and onions.

Farinha de mandioca (fah-REE-nyah dih mahn-DYAW-kah)—Brazilian name for *cassava* meal.

Farofa (fah-RAW-fah)—toasted *cassava* meal; looks like coarsely grated Parmesan cheese.

Feijão (fay-ZHOW)—Brazilian dried beans.

Feijoada (fay-zhoh-AH-dah)—Brazilian national dish of rice, beans and fresh and cured meats.

Flan (FLAHN)—caramel custard.

Frijoles (free-HOH-lehss)—dried beans in Spanish-speaking South America, used as a base for many dishes.

Guayaba (gwahee-YAH-vah)—guava jelly.

Hallacas (ah-YAH-kahss)—similar to the Mexican *tamales*; Colombian cornmeal dough stuffed with spiced chicken, beef or pork and wrapped in banana leaves before steaming.

Humitas (oo-MEE-tahss)—similar to the Mexican *tamales*; Peruvian fresh corn dough stuffed with pork, chicken or beef plus eggs, raisins and olives and wrapped in corn husks before steaming.

Matambre (mah-TAHM-breh)—"kill hunger"; Argentine flank steak which is marinated and then stuffed with vegetables and hard-cooked eggs before rolling and cooking.

Pabellón caraqueño (pah-veh-YOHN kah-rah-KAY-nyoh)—a Venezuelan steak dish served with rice, plantains and black beans.

Palillo (pah-LEE-yoh)—a Peruvian herb which is dried and ground. It gives yellow color to food; turmeric can be substituted.

Palmito (pahl-MEE-tuh)—palm heart; creamy inside of young palm shoots.

Papas a la huancaina (PAH-pahss ah lah wahn-KAH-ee-nah)—boiled potatoes with chili-cheese sauce.

Papas chorreadas (PAH-pahss choh-rreh-AH-thass)—boiled potatoes with a chili, tomato, cheese and scallion sauce.

Pirão (pee-ROW)—*cassava* meal mush.

Plátanos (PLAH-tah-nohss)—plantains or cooking bananas—a tropical starchy vegetable that must be cooked before eating; usually fried or boiled. Served as a starch substitute or as an appetizer in chip form.

Pollo al espeto (POH-yoh ahl ehss-PEH-toh)—marinated chicken barbecued on a spit.

Puchero (poo-CHEH-roh)—an Argentine version of the New England boiled dinner, with fresh and corned beef, vegetables, garbanzo beans and rice.

Quibebe (kee-BEH-bih)—a squash soup with tomatoes, hot peppers and beef broth.

Rellenos (rreh-YEH-nohss)—stuffed or filled.

Salsa criolla (SAHL-sah kree-OH-yah)—a fiery barbecue sauce.

Sancocho (sahn-KOH-choh)—a vegetable-based stew; ingredients vary from area to area.

Sobrebarriga (soh-vreh-vah-RREE-gah)—steak that is stewed, then breaded and broiled.

Sopa de creme de palmito (SOH-pah dih KREH-mih dih pahl-MEE-tuh)—cream of palm heart soup.

Taro (TAH-roh)—a tropical root vegetable with a brown skin and whitish flesh which is cooked like a potato.

Tortas de plátano (TOHR-tahss deh PLAH-tah-noh)—fried cakes of plantains and cheese, sweetened and served with cinnamon.

Tostones (tohss-TOH-nehss)—fried and refried plantain slices.

Vatapá (vah-tah-PAH)—Afro-Brazilian dish of shrimp, fish or chicken, seasoned with coconut milk and palm oil.

Torta de Pasa

Tallarines con Salsa de Hongos

Puchero Criollo

Quibebe

Quibebe

Squash and pumpkin are popular vegetables throughout South America, especially in Brazil. Any winter squash can be substituted including crookneck squash.

2 cans (10½ ounces each)	condensed beef broth
1½ soup cans	water
4 cups	cubed butternut squash (about 2 pounds)
1 cup	chopped tomato
½ cup	chopped onion
⅛ teaspoon	crushed red pepper

In saucepan, combine all ingredients. Bring to boil; reduce heat. Cover; simmer 20 minutes or until done. Stir occasionally. Serve with grated Parmesan cheese. Makes about 7½ cups.

Menu:
*Quibebe
Pot Roast Garnished with Orange Slices
Hearts of Palm Salad
Brazil Nut Brownies

Potato-Cheese Soup
=====

Potatoes are enjoyed in many ways. In Ecuador, they are often the base for a potato-cheese soup. Toss avocado slices with lemon juice to prevent darkening while preparing soup.

½ cup	chopped onion
1 teaspoon	paprika
2 tablespoons	butter or margarine
2 cans (10¾ ounces each)	condensed cream of potato soup
2 soup cans	milk
1 cup	shredded Monterey Jack cheese

In saucepan, cook onion with paprika in butter until tender. Add remaining ingredients. Heat; stir occasionally. Garnish with avocado. Makes about 6 cups.

Menu:
*Locro
Shrimp Fritters
Lima Bean and Pepper Salad
Fresh Fruit

Matambre

In Argentina, this dish means "kill hunger" and it is a very hearty way to serve flank steak. The meat and vegetable juice make the base for the satisfying sauce.

2 pounds	flank steak
⅓ cup	wine vinegar
1 teaspoon	thyme leaves, crushed
2 medium	cloves garlic, minced
2 cups	fresh spinach
½ cup	soft bread crumbs
½ cup	frozen peas
4 slices	bacon, cooked and crumbled
2 tablespoons	milk
⅛ teaspoon	pepper
2 medium	carrots, cut in long strips and cooked
2	hard-cooked eggs, quartered
1 can (10¾ ounces)	condensed beefy mushroom soup*
1 cup	water
2 to 4 tablespoons	flour

To butterfly steak, with a long, very sharp knife slit the steak horizontally from one long side to within ½ inch of other side. Open steak, place between 2 sheets of waxed paper; pound with flat side of knife. To make marinade, combine vinegar, thyme and garlic. In shallow dish, arrange steak; pour marinade over steak. Cover; marinate 6 hours or overnight. Remove steak from marinade; arrange spinach on steak to within 1-inch of edges. In bowl, combine bread crumbs, peas, bacon, milk and pepper; sprinkle over spinach. Arrange carrots and eggs with the grain of the meat on spinach mixture. Roll up; tuck in ends. Tie with string. In 2-quart shallow baking dish (12×8×2″), arrange roll-up. Combine soup and ½ cup water; pour over roll-up. Cover; bake at 375°F. for 1 hour or until done. Remove roll-up to heated platter; let stand 10 minutes before slicing. Meanwhile, blend remaining ½ cup water into flour until smooth; slowly stir into sauce. Cook, stirring until thickened. Makes 6 to 8 servings.

*1 can (10½ ounces) condensed beef broth may be substituted for beefy mushroom soup.

Menu:
*Matambre
Fried Potato Chips
Sliced Tomato Salad
Tropical Fruits in Rum

Escabeche de Gallina

Escabeche is a cold, pickled dish which frequently features fish and shellfish. This delicious dish from Bolivia is made instead with chicken and is always garnished with lemons.

1 can (10¾ ounces)	condensed chicken broth
2 pounds	chicken parts
2 cups	sliced onions
1 cup	white vinegar
3 medium	carrots, diagonally sliced
2 medium	bay leaves
1 envelope	unflavored gelatine
1	lemon, sliced

In large saucepan, combine all ingredients except gelatine and lemon. Cover; cook over low heat 45 minutes or until done. Cool. Remove chicken from broth, reserving broth. Remove chicken from bone; chop. In saucepan, sprinkle gelatine over ½ cup reserved broth to soften. Place over low heat, stirring until gelatine is dissolved. Add to remaining broth mixture. In loaf pan (9 × 5 × 3″), arrange lemon slices; cover with about ¼-inch thick layer of gelatine mixture. Chill until slightly firm. Chill remaining gelatine mixture; fold in chicken. Pour chicken mixture onto bottom layer. Chill until firm. Makes 6 servings.

Menu:
Corn Soup
*Escabeche de Gallina
Avocado and Tomato Salad
Pineapple Custard

Hallacas

Traditionally hallacas are cornmeal dough/filled patties with a highly seasoned meat mixture which is steamed in banana leaves. This less complicated version is made in a cornmeal lined casserole.

¾ cup	cornmeal
1¼ cups	water
2 tablespoons	butter or margarine
1	egg, slightly beaten
½ pound	diced lean round steak
½ pound	diced lean pork loin
2 tablespoons	olive oil
1 can (10¾ ounces)	condensed tomato bisque soup
1 cup	chopped onion
1 large	green pepper, chopped
1 tablespoon	wine vinegar
1 large	clove garlic, minced
½ cup	raisins
⅓ cup	sliced pimiento-stuffed olives
2 teaspoons	capers

In saucepan, combine cornmeal and water. Bring to boil, stirring constantly. Add butter; simmer 15 minutes. Stir occasionally. Remove from heat; add egg. Line bottom and sides of well-greased 1½-quart casserole with cornmeal mixture. Meanwhile, in saucepan, brown beef and pork in olive oil; add soup, onion, green pepper, wine vinegar and garlic. Cook over low heat 15 minutes or until done; stir occasionally. Add remaining ingredients; pour into lined casserole. Cover; bake at 350°F. for 30 minutes. Makes 4 servings.

Chupe de Camarones

In Peru, the traditional garnish for this soup is finely chopped hard-cooked egg. Serve in a tureen and let everyone help themselves.

1 cup	chopped onion
2 large	cloves garlic, minced
½ teaspoon	basil leaves, crushed
⅛ to ¼ teaspoon	cayenne pepper
2 tablespoons	olive oil
2 cans (10¾ ounces each)	condensed cream of potato soup
1 soup can	milk
1 soup can	water
1 pound	medium shrimp, (31-35/pound) cleaned and deveined
1 cup	frozen peas
1 cup	chopped tomato
½ cup	cooked whole kernel golden corn

In large saucepan, cook onion with garlic, basil and cayenne in oil until tender. Add remaining ingredients. Bring to boil; reduce heat. Simmer 5 minutes or until done. Stir occasionally. Makes about 9 cups.

Menu:
*Chupe de Camarones
Avocados Stuffed with Chicken Salad
Crusty Rolls
*Torta de Pasa

264

Torta de Pasa

This sweet is a tasty combination of raisins, walnuts and brown sugar. Serve it at room temperature. It's the perfect way to end a South American meal.

1 can (10¾ ounces)	condensed chicken broth
1 cup	sugar
2 tablespoons	cornstarch
2 cups	raisins
1 cup	chopped walnuts
3½ cups	sifted cake flour
1 tablespoon	baking powder
1 cup	butter or margarine
1½ cups	packed brown sugar
1 teaspoon	vanilla extract
4	eggs
1 cup	milk

Preheat oven to 350°F. To make filling, in saucepan, combine broth, sugar, cornstarch, raisins and nuts. Cook, stirring until thickened; cool. To make batter, sift flour and baking powder. In large bowl of electric mixer, beat butter, brown sugar and vanilla on medium speed, scraping sides and bottom of bowl constantly. Add eggs, one at a time, beating after each addition. Add dry ingredients alternately with milk. Pour half of batter into well-greased 3-quart shallow baking dish (13 × 9 × 2″). Spread filling evenly over batter. Top with remaining batter, covering filling. Bake 40 minutes or until done. Cool. Makes 24 squares (2 inch).

Carbonada Criolla

The Argentinians have a marvelous way of combining meat and fruit. The peaches add a special flavor to this delicious stew.

1½ pounds	beef cubes (1 inch)
2 tablespoons	olive oil
1 can (10½ ounces)	condensed beef broth
1½ soup cans	water
1 cup	chopped onion
1 large	clove garlic, minced
1 can (10¾ ounces)	condensed cream of potato soup
2 small	zucchini squash, cut in strips
2 cups	sliced sweet potatoes
1½ cups	chopped tomatoes
1 can (about 16 ounces)	peach halves, drained
½ cup	diced green pepper

In large heavy pan, brown beef in oil; pour off fat. Add broth, water, onion and garlic. Cover; cook over low heat 1 hour 45 minutes. Add remaining ingredients. Cook 15 minutes more or until done. Stir occasionally. Makes about 11½ cups.

Menu:
*Carbonada Criolla
Corn Pancakes
Tossed Green Salad
Caramel Custard

Moqueca de Peixe

From the northern region of Bahia comes this Brazilian specialty. The fish is cooked in a spicy tomato sauce to bring out the flavor.

½ cup	chopped onion
2 tablespoons	salad oil
1 can (10¾ ounces)	condensed tomato bisque soup
1 pound	fillets of sole or other white fish, cut in 2-inch pieces
1 tablespoon	ground coriander seed
1 tablespoon	lemon juice
1 medium	clove garlic, minced
⅛ teaspoon	crushed red pepper

In skillet, cook onion in oil until tender. Add remaining ingredients. Cook over low heat 10 minutes or until done; stir gently now and then. Serve over rice. Makes about 3 cups.

Menu:
*Moqueca de Peixe
Black Beans
Buttered Rice
Coconut Cake

Puchero Criollo

Puchero is a famous Argentine boiled dinner, much like our own New England variety, except the ingredients and flavor are quite different. It's ancestor is the Spanish cocido.

2 cans (10¾ ounces each)	condensed tomato bisque soup
2 soup cans	water
2 pounds	well-trimmed boneless chuck roast (about 1½-inches thick)
8	chicken wings (about 1½ pounds)
3 medium	carrots (about ½ pound), cut in 2-inch pieces
8 small	whole white onions (about ½ pound)
2 small	purple-top turnips, quartered (about ¼ pound)
1 can (about 16 ounces)	chick peas, drained
½ pound	pepperoni, sliced ½-inch thick
½ small	head cabbage, cut in wedges

In large heavy pan, combine soup, water and beef. Cover; simmer 1 hour. Add chicken wings, carrots, onions and turnips; simmer 10 minutes. Add remaining ingredients; simmer 15 minutes more or until done. Stir occasionally. Spoon off fat. Arrange meat and vegetables on heated platter; serve broth as soup. Makes 6 to 8 servings.

Tallarines con Salsa de Hongos

This is a busy day dish from Paraguay that takes only 15 minutes to prepare from start to finish. Top with crumbled bacon; drippings are used to flavor the sauce.

4 slices	bacon
½ cup	chopped onion
1 can (10¾ ounces)	condensed tomato soup
3 cups	sliced fresh mushrooms (about ½ pound)
1 cup	thinly sliced pepperoni (about ¼ pound)
½ cup	water
2 cups	cooked wide noodles

In large skillet, cook bacon until crisp; remove and crumble. Cook onion in drippings until tender. Add remaining ingredients except noodles. Cook over low heat 10 minutes; stir occasionally. Add noodles; heat. Garnish with bacon. Makes about 4 cups.

Menu:
Zucchini Soup
*Tallarines con Salsa de Hongos
Cornbread
Fried Bananas Rolled in Sugar

Chupe de Marisco

Chupe is practically Peru's national chowder. It can be made with cubes of white-fleshed fish or even shrimp. Garnish with chopped parsley, if you wish.

½ cup	sliced green onions
⅛ teaspoon	cayenne pepper
⅛ teaspoon	ground nutmeg
¼ cup	butter or margarine
2 tablespoons	flour
½ cup	Chablis or other dry white wine
1 can (10¾ ounces)	condensed cream of shrimp soup
1½ pounds	scallops, cut in half or white fish, cut in 2-inch pieces
¼ cup	heavy cream

In saucepan, cook onions with cayenne and nutmeg in butter until tender; stir in flour. Cook a few minutes, stirring constantly. Remove from heat. Add wine, a little at a time, stirring until smooth after each addition. Add soup. Cook, stirring until thickened. Add scallops; cook over low heat 10 minutes or until done. Stir occasionally. Add cream; heat. Serve over rice. Makes about 3 cups.

Menu:
*Chupe de Marisco
Seasoned Rice
Spinach with Tomatoes
Brown Sugar Pudding

Guianas

The combination of tomatoes and orange juice make this sauce an interesting flavor combination but quite typical of many South American recipes.

2 pounds	chicken parts
2 tablespoons	butter or margarine
1 cup	chopped onion
⅓ cup	sliced celery
1½ teaspoons	ground nutmeg
1 can (10¾ ounces)	condensed tomato soup
4 cups	shredded potatoes
¼ cup	orange juice
½ teaspoon	salt
⅛ teaspoon	pepper

In skillet, brown chicken in butter; remove. Add onion, celery and nutmeg; cook until tender. Add soup; reserve ½ cup soup mixture. Combine remaining soup mixture, potatoes, orange juice, salt and pepper. In greased 2-quart shallow baking dish (12×8×2″), spoon potato mixture; arrange chicken on potatoes. Pour reserved soup mixture over chicken. Bake at 400°F. for 45 minutes or until done. Makes 4 servings.

Menu:
*Guianas
Braised Squash
Sponge Cake Filled with Cream Filling

Spain

Cocido

The food of Spain is hearty and uncomplicated—born in the harsh, arid land of the Iberian Peninsula where peasant women use what is available. Nothing about the Spanish cuisine is hot or spicy, unlike the cooking of their former colony, Mexico. It is a simple but subtle fare made from recipes handed down through the generations. Most food is simmered or roasted and then colorfully sauced.

Tradition plays an important role in the Spanish kitchen. Perhaps the blender makes the preparation of *gazpacho*, that refreshing salad-in-a-soup-bowl, easier, but the ingredients remain the same.

Geography has a lot to do with the development of Spanish cooking. Spain and its next-door neighbor, Portugal, are somewhat isolated in the southwestern corner of Europe—just a little off the mainstream. The dry, sun-drenched land is surrounded on three sides by water, so fish plays an important part in the diet of most Spaniards. Before the age of refrigeration and rapid transportation, the Spanish preserved some of their fish by salting and drying it into *bacalao*, so the people of the interior plains could enjoy fish also. Salt cod is still enjoyed today, even though everyone has access to fresh fish.

Spain is the land of olive oil, garlic and tomatoes. These three ingredients flavor most of the dishes but do not overwhelm them.

Olive oil is their cooking fat. It also adds a rich taste to everything from soups to salads to stews. Garlic, too, appears in many dishes. Its use is like a perfume—never overpowering. It is frequently cooked whole and unpeeled or added to hot olive oil and discarded before the cooking of the main ingredients. Tomatoes add a lively color to so many Spanish foods; it acts as a *béchamel* or white sauce does for French food. Tomatoes, onions, garlic and peppers cooked in olive oil until they become a sauce is *sofrito* ("lightly fried"). This is the seasoning base for many sauces.

These three ingredients which are such an integral part of the Iberian cuisine—olive oil, garlic and tomatoes—were actually legacies from other cultures. The Romans occupied Spain more than two thousand years ago. They brought with them olive trees, grapevines

274

and an innocent white bulb-like plant we know today as garlic.

The Moors, Arabic tribes from North Africa, swept over Spain next and stayed for over seven hundred years. They left behind a collection of beautiful buildings and castles, but more importantly a taste for rice, fruits (such as melons, peaches and citrus fruits), nuts (especially pine nuts, or *piñones* and almonds) and spices (saffron, cinnamon, cumin and pepper), to name a few. These were absorbed into the Spanish diet.

In 1479, Spain was united under Isabella and Ferdinand. Once things at home were under control, the country turned its attention to the New World. During the 17th and 18th centuries, the Indian cultures of Latin America sent in tribute to the Motherland culinary gold in the form of tomatoes, peppers, potatoes and chocolate. These products enriched the cooking pots of Spain even further.

Like so many other nations in Europe, Spain was once a series of small kingdoms—some isolated by mountains, others removed by language and customs. A traveller in Spain might find *gazpacho* or *paella* on many menus, but these two dishes have fascinating regional variations, so the results may be quite different.

To understand these differences, let's take a quick tour around Spain. Beginning in the northwest, in the mountainous area between France and Spain, are the Basque provinces. Cooking is a serious occupation here. *Bacalao*, or salt cod, is simmered with garlic and parsley in a traditional earthenware casserole; the delicious results are called *bacalao al pil-pil*. The Basques have a complicated language, quite different from Spanish. *Pil-pil* means "simmered" in Basque. Their sauces are deceptively simple—either green or red. *Patatas a la vasca*, or potatoes in green sauce, are a Spanish version of home-fried potatoes cooked with garlic and lots of parsley. This is a good example of Basque inventiveness.

In the northeast is Catalonia, a long fertile strip along the Mediterranean Sea toward Valencia. The Catalans have their own language and customs. On their tables, you will find such delicacies as baby eel or baby octopus in garlic sauce. If these sound a little exotic, try *tallinas a la catalana*, a stew of tiny clams prepared much like the steamed mussels of the French, or *xáto*, a peppery salad of curly endive, vinegar, oil and hot peppers.

Also from this area come two famous condiment-sauces: *all-i-oli*, a white thickened mixture of garlic, oil and lemon juice, to which egg is sometimes added to make a garlic mayonnaise, and *romesco*, a zippy sauce of tomatoes, hot peppers, garlic and oil. These condiments are frequently mixed and served with grilled fish or broiled meats. Another local specialty is *escudella a la catalana*, a hearty soup/stew of beans, sausages and vegetables.

In the northwestern part of Spain, north of Portugal, are the provinces of Galicia and Asturias. The climate is cold and wet, but the land is rich agriculturally. In Galicia, you'll sample a favorite dish, *lacón con grelos*, a specially-cured ham shoulder stewed with turnip greens. The same ham is also part of *caldo gallego*, a hearty meat and vegetable soup/stew. *Empanada gallega* is a double-crust turnover filled with anything from fried fish, onions and peppers to leftover meat and onions. It makes a hearty one-dish meal and can be served hot or cold.

In nearby Asturias, the emphasis is also on hearty dishes. *Fabada asturias*, a bean, blood sausage and beef stew is one good example. Asturias produces a sweet-sour cider, which makes a good accompaniment to tasty *caldereta asturiana*, a Spanish variation of *bouillabaisse* flavored with sherry, nutmeg and peppercorns.

Aragon and Castile are located in the high central plain of Spain. Aragon is known for two very special dishes. *Pollo al chilindrón* is a piquant combination of chicken, ham, peppers, tomatoes and garlic. Lamb, pork or rabbit may be substituted for the chicken. *Cordero cochifrito* is an Aragonese recipe for lamb sautéed in garlic, lemon and paprika. It is also frequently used with other meats or fowl.

Nearby Castile covers an enormous area and is the land of baby lamb, suckling pig and garbanzos or chick peas. *Cordero asado*, or roast lamb, is often served with a side dish of chick peas. The full-bodied Rioja wines, the most famous of Spain, are produced in this area.

A little further south of the Rioja Valley is La Mancha, legendary home of Don Quixote and real home of *sopa de ajo*, a fascinating soup of garlic, bread, broth and egg. Cervantes mentions a local specialty in

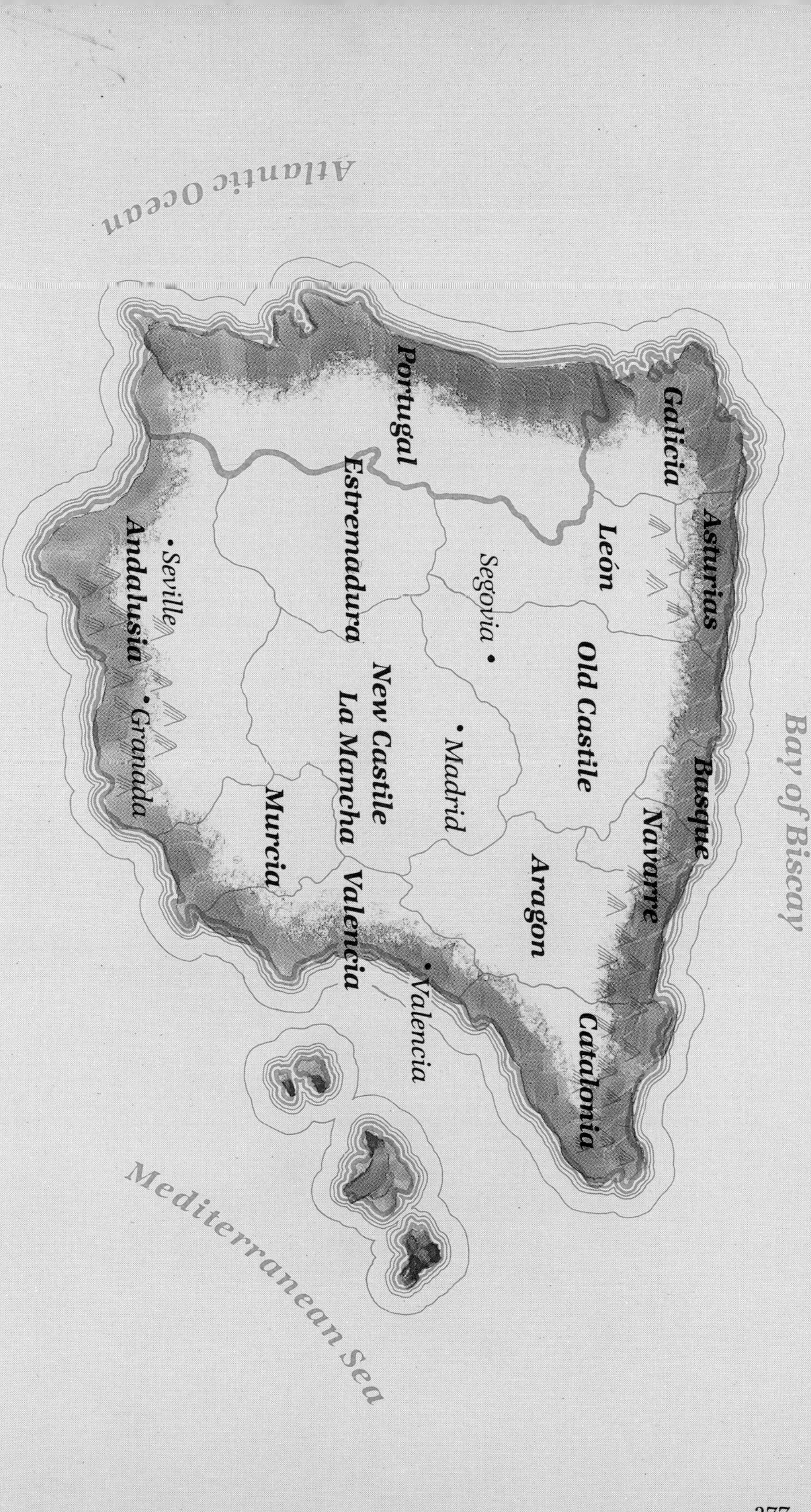

Atlantic Ocean

Galicia

Asturias

Basque

Navarre

León

Old Castile

Portugal

Estremadura

Segovia •

Andalusia

• Seville

• Granada

New Castile

La Mancha

Valencia

Murcia

• Madrid

Aragon

Catalonia

• Valencia

Bay of Biscay

Mediterranean Sea

his book about the adventures of Don Quixote—*olla podrida* (which literally means "rotten pot"); it is one of Spain's oldest dishes. It's a boiled dinner prepared in an *"olla"*, or earthenware pot and is served in two courses: first the broth, and then the meat and vegetables. In Madrid, this dish is called *cocido madrileño*.

Along the eastern coastline is an area known as the Levante, where saffron, rice and bitter oranges are grown. The latter are the basis for the sweet-sour English marmalades. It was here that *paella a la valenciana* was devised. It's a sensational blend of chicken, assorted seafood, peas and peppers in a nest of saffron-flavored rice. The individual ingredients may vary from town to town in this area.

The Moors, who influenced the Levante architecturally as well as gastronomically, left behind *turrón*, a half-candy, half-dessert of almonds and honey. No one is quite sure if they were also responsible for the creation of *tortillas*, which are not the large bready corn pancake of Mexican fame, but a flat omelet. *Tortilla murciana* has tomatoes, peppers and onions as a flavoring. *Tortilla española* is one made of potatoes and onions. These are often served cold as the filling for a sandwich, or *bocadillo*.

The last province to explore in our culinary tour is Andalusia in the deep south. The warmer climate is a perfect foil for the famous *gazpacho*, which is said to be a variation of a Moorish dish. *Huevos a la flamenca* is another regional delight from Seville. To make it, eggs

with asparagus, peas, peppers, *serrano* ham and *chorizo* sausages are baked over a layer of *sofrito*.

Andalusia is a sea of olive groves, and with the plentiful supply of fresh olive oil, frying is a favorite cooking technique. *Gambas al ajillo*, or shrimp with garlic, is a simple but effective dish using fresh olive oil. Sherry comes from an area south of Seville known as Jerez. Some people think that sherry is really a mispronunciation of the word *jerez*.

From Andalusia to Galicia, one thing is quite similar—the Spanish love of eating. *Desayuno*, or breakfast, consists of a cup of coffee or chocolate plus some crusty bread and jam or a sweet roll. By mid-morning, it's time for some serious eating—*almuerzo* is a second breakfast. A *tortilla española* with bread or wine might be eaten. An open sandwich of grilled sausage, tomatoes and oil, or a hot meal of baked beans and *chorizo* sausages are other alternatives.

Around 2:00 p.m. it's time for *comida*, the main meal of the day. It usually begins with *entreméses*, appetizers or a soup. Salad is served as a separate course at the beginning of the meal, rather than with the main course. Vinegar is used sparingly and most salads are arranged, not tossed. A course of fish, meat or game follows, with vegetables either served as a side dish or incorporated in with the meat. Fruit is a likely choice for dessert, or there might be a light dessert such as *natillas*, a soft custard with lemon or cinnamon, or *flan*, the famous caramel custard.

Throughout the meal, wine is served. Coffee usually signals the end of the meal and is accompanied by a small glass of Spanish brandy. At 6:00 p.m. everything stops for *merienda*, a mid-evening snack of coffee and pastries, cookies, fruit tarts or honey desserts. It's the Spanish version of the British high tea. *Churros*, tiny fried strips of puff pastry, are a possible nibble. If guests are invited, the menu becomes much more elaborate.

At around 10:00 p.m. *cena*, or supper, is served. At that hour, it may be as simple as soup and an omelet, or fish, salad and fruit, if eaten at home. However, those Spaniards who prefer to eat late in the evening will consume a full-course meal if *cena* is eaten out. Before supper—usually from 8:00 to 10:00 p.m.—it is time to sip a glass or two of sherry or wine and to nibble on *tapas*, an array of tempting snacks. They may be as simple as freshly roasted almonds or olives or as complicated as a cold seafood *escabeche* or *empanadas*. *Migas* are always a popular *tapas* component; they are fried bread in oil and garlic, much like croutons but more irregular in shape.

Glossary*

A la andaluza (ah lah ahn-dah-LOO-thah)—simmered in a sauce of tomatoes and pimientos.

All-i-oli (ah-lyee-OH-lee)—"garlic oil"; thick white mixture of garlic, lemon juice and olive oil, used as a condiment for meats or fish.

Almuerzo (ahl-MWEHR-thoh)—second breakfast or mid-morning meal; the first substantial meal of the day.

Asado (ah-SAH-thoh)—roast.

Aves (AH-vehss)—fowl; poultry.

Bacalao (bah-kah-LAH-oh)—cod; salt cod.

Bocadillo (boh-kah-THEE-lyoh)—"little mouthful"; sandwich.

Bodega (boh-THEH-gah)—wine cellar.

Caldo (KAHL-doh)—broth; stock; sauce; or wine.

Caldo gallego (KAHL-doh gah-LYEH-goh)—meat and vegetable soup/stew.

Carne (KAHR-neh)—meat.

Cena (THEH-nah)—late supper, usually served at around 10:00 p.m.

Chorizo (choh-REE-thoh)—bright red pork sausage made with garlic and paprika.

Churros (CHOO-rrohss)—tiny fried strips of puff pastry.

Cocido (koh-THEE-thoh)—boiled; cooked; meat and vegetable soup.

Cocido madrileño (koh-THEE-thoh mah-THREE-LEH-nyoh)—name for *olla podrida* in Madrid.

Cordero asado (kohr-THEH-roh ah-SAH-thoh)—roast lamb.

Cordero cochifrito (kohr-THEH-roh koh-chee-FREE-toh)—lamb sautéed in garlic, lemon and paprika.

Dulces (DOOL-thehss)—sweets; candy.

Ensalada (ehn-sah-LAH-thah)—salad.

Entremés (ehn-treh-MEHSS)—hors d'oeuvres; can also be a salad or snack.

Escabeche (ehss-kah-VEH-cheh)—marinate.

Estafado (ehss-tah-FAH-thoh)—stew.

Flan (FLAHN)—caramel custard.

Huevos a la flamenca (WEH-vohss ah lah flah-MEHN-kah)—eggs with asparagus, peas, peppers, *serrano* ham and *chorizo* sausages, baked over a layer of *sofrito*.

Jerez (kheh-REHTH)—sherry; also, the city in Spain after which this drink is named.

Lacón con grelos (lah-KOHN kohn GREH-lohss)—specially-cured ham shoulder stewed with turnip greens.

Mahonesa (mah-oh-NEH-sah)—mayonnaise made of olive oil.

Olla (OH-lyah)—jar, pot; term for meat and vegetable soup in Basque and Catalonia provinces.

Olla podrida (OH-lyah poh-THREE-thah)—literally, "rotten pot"; a boiled dinner prepared in an *olla*.

Paella (pah-EH-lyah)—a saffron-flavored stew of chicken, seafood, various vegetables and rice.

Paella a la valenciana (pah-EH-lyah ah lah vah-lehn-THYAH-nah)—mixture of chicken, assorted seafood, peas and peppers in a bed of saffron-flavored rice.

Paellera (pah-eh-LYEH-rah)—broad, flat, round metal pan with 2-inch slanted sides, used for making *paella* and other rice dishes.

Pescado (pehss-KAH-thoh)—fish.

Picada (pee-KAH-thah)—minced; mortar-mashed food added for flavor or as a thickening agent.

Pisto (PEESS-toh)—fresh vegetables stewed in olive oil, cooked almost to a purée; served with roast meats.

Postres (POHSS-trehss)—desserts.

Serrano ham (seh-RRAH-noh)—a specially-cured sweet-salty ham, similar to the Italian prosciutto.

Sopa (SOH-pah)—soup.

Sopa de ajo (SOH-pah deh AH-khoh)—garlic soup.

Tapa (TAH-pah)—appetizer.

Tortilla (tohr-TEE-lyah)—a flat omelet.

Tortilla española (tohr-TEE-lyah ehss-pah-NYOH-lah)—*tortilla* made with potatoes and onions.

Tortilla murciana (tohr-TEE-lyah moor-THYAH-nah)—*tortilla* made with tomatoes, peppers and onions.

Turrón (too-RROHN)—sweet, candy-like almond dessert.

Zarzuela (thar-THWEH-lah)—Spanish musical comedy; a northern Spanish seafood stew in a peppery sauce.

*The pronunciations given here are those characteristic of central Spain, rather than the Latin American variants.

Arroz con Leche

Chuletas de Cordero a la Navarra

Empanadas Gallega

Habas a la Catalana

Ensalada de Arroz

This is a tasty way to use leftover rice. Salads in Spain are served as a first course. Prepare this recipe ahead for a better flavor.

6 cups	cooked rice
1½ cups	diced tomatoes
1 cup	diced green pepper
¼ cup	finely chopped onion
¼ cup	chopped parsley
1 can (10¾ ounces)	condensed creamy chicken mushroom soup
¼ cup	wine vinegar
2 tablespoons	olive oil
1 medium	clove garlic, minced

In bowl, combine rice, tomatoes, green pepper, onion and parsley. Meanwhile, in blender, combine remaining ingredients; blend until smooth. Toss with rice mixture; chill 4 hours or more. Serve on salad greens. Makes about 8 cups.

Sopa al Cuarto de Hora

It literally takes 15 minutes to simmer this soup and the flavor is very Spanish—tomatoes, onions and garlic used in moderation.

¾ cup	diced cooked ham
½ teaspoon	paprika
Generous dash	crushed saffron or ground turmeric
1 tablespoon	olive oil
1 can (10½ ounces)	condensed onion soup
1 can (11 ounces)	condensed tomato rice soup
1½ soup cans	water
1 pound	frozen cleaned raw shrimp
1 cup	frozen peas
2 tablespoons	lemon juice
1	hard-cooked egg, chopped

In saucepan, brown ham with paprika and saffron in oil. Add remaining ingredients except egg. Bring to boil; reduce heat. Simmer 15 minutes or until done. Stir occasionally. Garnish with egg. Makes about 6½ cups.

Arroz con Leche

Rice appears at any course during a Spanish meal. Nowhere is it more enjoyed than as a sweet rice pudding.

1 can (10¾ ounces)	condensed Cheddar cheese soup
4 cups	milk
½ cup	sugar
1 tablespoon	vanilla extract
1	cinnamon stick (3 inch)
½ teaspoon	grated orange rind
⅓ cup	raw regular rice

In large saucepan, blend soup, milk, sugar, vanilla, cinnamon and orange rind. Bring to boil; add rice. Cook over low heat 1 hour or until done; stir often. Remove cinnamon stick. Pour into individual dessert dishes (5-ounce size); chill. Garnish with toasted coconut. Makes about 4 cups.

Pollo al Chilindrón

This method of preparation is popular in the Province of Aragon. Lamb or veal could also be substituted for the chicken in this delicious dish.

1 can (about 8 ounces)	tomatoes
2 pounds	chicken parts
2 tablespoons	olive oil
½ cup	finely chopped ham
1 cup	sliced onion
2 large	cloves garlic, minced
1 can (10¾ ounces)	condensed tomato bisque soup
1 small	green pepper, cut in ¼-inch strips
1 small	red pepper, cut in ¼-inch strips
¼ cup	sliced pitted ripe olives

Drain tomatoes, reserving juice. Cut up tomatoes. In skillet, brown chicken in oil. Add ham, onion and garlic; cook until onion is tender. Blend in soup and reserved tomato juice. Cover; cook over low heat 30 minutes. Uncover; add peppers, tomatoes and olives. Cook 15 minutes more; stir occasionally. Thicken if desired. Serve over rice. Makes 4 servings.

Menu:
*Pollo al Chilindrón
Fried Eggplant
Marinated Asparagus Salad
*Bizcocho con Crema

Bizcocho con Crema

A moist and tender cake is filled with a heady rum filling. Both the cake and the creamy filling can be made ahead and then assembled before serving.

5	eggs, separated
⅓ cup	sugar
⅛ teaspoon	salt
¼ teaspoon	grated lemon rind
2 teaspoons	lemon juice
¼ teaspoon	lemon extract
½ cup	all-purpose flour
1 can (11 ounces)	condensed Cheddar cheese soup
1 cup	milk
½ cup	sugar
⅓ cup	cornstarch
3 tablespoons	dark rum
½ teaspoon	vanilla extract
3	egg yolks, slightly beaten

To make cake, grease two 8″ cake pans; line with waxed paper. Grease and flour bottom and sides of lined pans, removing excess flour. In bowl, beat egg yolks, sugar, salt, lemon rind, juice and lemon extract until thick and lemon-colored. Stir in flour. In another bowl, beat egg whites until soft peaks form. Gently fold egg whites into flour mixture. Pour into pans. Bake at 400°F. for 15 minutes. Remove from pans. Remove waxed paper; cool. To make filling, in saucepan, blend soup, milk, sugar, cornstarch, rum and vanilla until smooth. Cook over low heat, stirring until thickened. Remove from heat; pour about 1 cup of hot liquid into beaten egg yolks, stirring constantly. Stir egg mixture into soup mixture. Cook over low heat, stirring until thickened. Cover with waxed paper. Cool to room temperature. Cut each layer horizontally in half. Spread ⅓ filling between each layer. Stack layers. Sprinkle top with confectioners' sugar; garnish with lemon slices. Makes 8 to 10 servings.

Pollo en Pepitoria

Chicken is an economical dish in Spain as it is in the U.S. The addition of sherry and saffron make this recipe one that you'll want to save for your most favorite guests.

2 pounds	chicken parts
¼ cup	seasoned flour
2 tablespoons	olive oil
1 can (10½ ounces)	condensed onion soup
¼ cup	dry sherry
1 medium	bay leaf
2 tablespoons	chopped parsley
2	hard-cooked egg yolks
3 tablespoons	ground almonds
2 large	cloves garlic, minced
Generous dash	crushed saffron or turmeric

Dust chicken with flour. In skillet, brown chicken in oil. Add soup, sherry, bay leaf and parsley. Cover; cook over low heat 45 minutes or until done. Stir occasionally. Combine egg yolks, almonds, garlic and saffron. Stir into sauce. Heat; stir occasionally. Remove bay leaf. Makes 4 servings.

Menu:
*Ensalada de Arroz
*Pollo en Pepitoria
Spinach with Ham
Fresh Oranges

Sopa de Primavera

*The secret in making this soup is not to overcook the vegetables
and also the addition at the last minute of sofrito, a sautéed
onion and tomato flavoring base.*

2 cans (10¾ ounces each)	condensed tomato soup
1½ soup cans	water
4 cups	cabbage cut in long thin shreds (about ½ pound)
1 large	potato, cut lengthwise in 1½-inch long strips (about 1½ cups)
1 small	bay leaf
¼ cup	chopped green onions
1 large	clove garlic, minced
2 tablespoons	olive oil
1 cup	chopped tomatoes
2 tablespoons	chopped parsley
1 cup	frozen cut asparagus
1 large	carrot, cut in 3-inch long strips (about 1 cup)
½ cup	frozen peas

In large saucepan, combine soup, water, cabbage, potato and
bay leaf. Bring to boil; reduce heat. Cover; cook over low heat
20 minutes. Meanwhile, to make *sofrito*, in small skillet, cook
onions with garlic in oil until tender. Add tomatoes and
parsley; simmer 5 minutes. Add *sofrito* and remaining
ingredients to soup mixture; cook 5 minutes more or until
vegetables are done. Stir occasionally. Remove bay leaf. Makes
about 8 cups.

Chuletas de Cordero a la Navarra

Lamb is a very popular meat in Spain. Pour the creamy onion and tomato sauce over the chops before baking. The peppery sausage is then added at the end. The results are tender and juicy.

8	rib lamb chops (about 1½ pounds)
1 tablespoon	olive oil
1 can (10¾ ounces)	condensed cream of onion soup
1 cup	chopped canned tomatoes
2 large	cloves garlic, minced
1 small	bay leaf
⅛ teaspoon	paprika
⅛ teaspoon	thyme leaves, crushed
¼ pound	pepperoni, sliced (about 1 cup)

In oven-proof skillet, brown lamb chops in oil; pour off fat. Blend in soup, tomatoes, garlic, bay leaf, paprika and thyme. Cover; bake at 350°F. for 25 minutes. Add pepperoni; bake 10 minutes more or until done. Remove bay leaf. Garnish with lemon slices. Makes 4 servings.

Menu:
*Chuletas de Cordero a la Navarra
Fried Potatoes
Cauliflower in Hot Vinegar Sauce
Plums in Dry Sherry

Habas a la Catalana

Beans of all types are an important part of the Spanish diet. They are often used to stretch a small piece of meat and contribute protein to the meal.

1 pound	garlic-flavored sausage, cut in 2-inch pieces
¼ cup	chopped green onions
2 large	cloves garlic, minced
2 tablespoons	butter or margarine
1 can (10¾ ounces)	condensed cream of celery soup
¼ cup	water
1 small	bay leaf
Generous dash	cayenne pepper
1 package (9 ounces)	frozen baby lima beans
1 cup	chopped tomatoes

In large saucepan, brown sausage and cook green onions with garlic in butter until tender. Blend in soup, water, bay leaf, cayenne and lima beans. Bring to boil; reduce heat. Cover; cook over low heat 15 minutes. Add tomatoes; cook 5 minutes more or until done. Stir occasionally. Remove bay leaf. Garnish with lemon slices. Makes about 4½ cups.

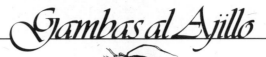

Gambas al Ajillo

Traditionally, gambas are served in small individual earthenware casseroles as a first course or with spaghetti as a main dish. Either way, be careful not to overcook the shrimp.

1 can (10¾ ounces)	condensed chicken broth
8 large	cloves garlic, minced
¼ cup	chopped parsley
¼ teaspoon	cayenne pepper
1 small	bay leaf
2 tablespoons	olive oil
1½ pounds	medium shrimp (31-35/pound), shelled and deveined
2 tablespoons	sauterne or other dry white wine
2 teaspoons	lemon juice
2 teaspoons	cornstarch
4 cups	cooked thin spaghetti

Reserve ¼ cup broth. In skillet, cook garlic, parsley, cayenne and bay leaf in oil a few minutes. Add remaining broth, shrimp, wine and lemon juice. Bring to boil; reduce heat. Cover; simmer 5 minutes or until done. Stir occasionally. Meanwhile, mix reserved broth and cornstarch; gradually blend into shrimp mixture. Cook, stirring until thickened. Remove bay leaf; toss with spaghetti. Makes about 6 cups.

Menu:
*Gambas al Ajillo
*Habas a la Catalana
Roasted Pepper Salad
Seasonal Fresh Fruit

Empanadas Gallega

*Large and small pastries filled with meat, fish or vegetables
make a tasty light meal, especially when combined with a soup.
The Spanish serve empanadas cold as well as hot.*

¼ cup	finely chopped onion
¼ cup	green pepper squares
2 medium	cloves garlic, minced
2 tablespoons	olive oil
1 can (10¾ ounces)	condensed tomato soup
½ cup	chopped prosciutto (Italian ham)
2 cups	diced cooked chicken
2 cans (10 ounces each)	refrigerated buttermilk biscuits
1	egg, slightly beaten
¼ cup	water

To make sauce, in saucepan, cook onion and green pepper
with garlic in oil until tender. Add soup and prosciutto. To
make filling, in bowl, combine ½ cup sauce and chicken.
Meanwhile, roll each biscuit into 3½-inch circles. To make
empanadas, spoon about 2 tablespoons filling on 10 circles;
top with remaining circles. Seal edges. Arrange on cookie
sheet; brush with egg. Bake at 375°F. for 15 minutes or until
brown. Meanwhile, blend water into remaining sauce. Heat;
stir occasionally. Serve with empanadas. Makes 10 empanadas.

Menu:
Mixed Fish Soup
*Empanadas Gallega
Potatoes with Peas and Parsley
Lemon Crullers

Pisto a la Riojana

Pisto is similar to a vegetable combination of the French Basques called piperade. This is often served with egg dishes and you can vary the vegetables to your family's taste.

½ cup	finely chopped ham
½ cup	finely chopped onion
2 medium	cloves garlic, minced
2 tablespoons	olive oil
1 can (10¾ ounces)	condensed tomato bisque soup
⅓ cup	water
2 tablespoons	vinegar
8 cups	cubed eggplant (about 1½ pounds)
1 package (9 ounces)	frozen Italian green beans
1 medium	green pepper, cut in strips

In large heavy pan, brown ham and cook onion with garlic in oil until tender. Blend in soup, water and vinegar. Add eggplant and green beans. Cover; cook over low heat 10 minutes. Add green peppper; cook 5 minutes more or until done. Stir occasionally. Serve with rice. Makes about 7 cups.

Menu:
Potato and Onion Omelet
*Pisto a la Riojana
Boiled Rice
Dried Figs and Cheese

Tortilla Murciana

A tortilla is a flat (not folded) omelet to the Spanish and it is served with a rich and flavorful sauce, such as this one. Be sure the butter and pan are hot before adding the egg mixture for a perfect "tortilla."

1 cup	sliced fresh mushrooms (about ¼ pound)
⅓ cup	chopped onion
¼ cup	chopped green pepper
1 medium	clove garlic, minced
6 tablespoons	butter or margarine
1 can (10¾ ounces)	condensed tomato soup
¼ cup	water
1 large	bay leaf
⅛ teaspoon	cayenne pepper
12	eggs
6 tablespoons	milk

To make sauce, in saucepan, brown mushrooms and cook onion and green pepper with garlic in 2 tablespoons butter until tender. Blend in soup, water, bay leaf and cayenne. Bring to boil; reduce heat. Simmer 30 minutes; stir occasionally. Remove bay leaf. To make omelets, beat eggs, milk, salt and pepper to taste. In skillet, melt 2 tablespoons butter. Pour in half of egg mixture. Cook slowly; as undersurface becomes set, lift slightly to allow uncooked egg to flow underneath and cook. Keep warm. Repeat, making 1 more omelet. Serve with sauce. Makes 6 servings.

Menu:
*Tortilla Murciana
Grilled Sausage
White Bean Salad
Melon of the Season

Cocido

Cocido (which means "boiled") is the Spanish version of a boiled dinner. It can be eaten in one dish or as two courses: the soup with meat and vegetables served later.

2 pounds	veal shank cross cuts (about 2 shanks)
2 tablespoons	shortening
2 cans (10½ ounces each)	condensed beef broth
1½ soup cans	water
½ cup	sliced onion
2 medium	cloves garlic, minced
Generous dash	crushed red pepper
3 medium	carrots, sliced (about ½ pound)
1 large	zucchini, sliced (about ½ pound)
1 can (about 16 ounces)	baby ears of corn, drained

In large saucepan, brown veal shanks in shortening; pour off fat. Add broth, water, onion, garlic and red pepper. Cover; cook over low heat 1 hour 25 minutes. Stir occasionally. Add vegetables; cook 5 minutes more or until done. Makes about 8 cups.

Menu:
*Cocido
Grilled Tomatoes
Garbanzo or Chick Pea Salad
*Arroz con Leche

Recipe Index

ENGLISH TITLES

Numerals in bold italics indicate a photograph of the recipe.

PASTA, RICE AND CORNMEAL

POULTRY